CLASSICS IN PSYCHOLOGY

CLASSICS IN PSYCHOLOGY

LECTURES

ON THE

ELEMENTARY PSYCHOLOGY · OF
FEELING AND ATTENTION

BY

EDWARD BRADFORD TITCHENER

ARNO PRESS
A New York Times Company
New York ★ 1973

Reprint Edition 1973 by Arno Press Inc.

Reprinted from a copy in
The University of Illinois Library

Classics in Psychology
ISBN for complete set: 0-405-05130-1
See last pages of this volume for titles.

Manufactured in the United States of America

————◆————

Library of Congress Cataloging in Publication Data

Titchener, Edward Bradford, 1867-1927.
    Lectures on the elementary psychology of
feeling and attention.

    (Classics in psychology)
    Reprint of the ed. published by Macmillan, New York.
    1. Senses and sensation. 2. Attention.
I. Title. II. Series. ₍DNLM: BF T618L 1908F₎
BF233.T57 1973   153.7'33   73-2994
ISBN 0-405-05166-2

Arn+ 1900 |ı|u|74

A NOTE ABOUT THE AUTHOR

EDWARD BRADFORD TITCHENER was born in England in 1867. He graduated from Oxford and then spent two years in Wundt's laboratory, receiving a Ph. D. from Leipzig in 1892. Titchener immediately emigrated to America and accepted a position at Cornell. He became full Professor in 1895 and remained at the Ithaca institution until his death in 1927.

Despite his Anglo-American ties, Titchener devoted his academic life to the clarification and dissemination of the structural psychology he had learned from Wundt. He believed that psychologists should study the normal adult mind, and that the point of departure for such a study must be the experience of an individual. He viewed feelings as independent elementary states, and attention was related to specific aspects of sensory experience. In a number of major textbooks and outlines, Titchener contrasted his point of view with the American psychology which was gaining in prominence during his time. He inveighed against functionalism, claiming that the uses to which mental processes were put were not of major concern for the psychologist; and he could not accept the behaviorist rejection of introspective and conscious phenomena. Titchener's point of view did not lead to the formation of a structuralist school in America, but his scholarship, grasp of the field of psychology, brilliant pedagogy, and personal integrity inspired the many students and colleagues with whom he came into contact.

FEELING AND ATTENTION

LECTURES

ON THE

ELEMENTARY PSYCHOLOGY OF FEELING AND ATTENTION

BY

EDWARD BRADFORD TITCHENER

New York

THE MACMILLAN COMPANY

1908

Norwood Press
J. S. Cushing Co. — Berwick & Smith Co.
Norwood, Mass., U.S.A.

To

EDMUND CLARK SANFORD

PREFACE

THE eight lectures which make up this little book were read during my tenure of a non-resident lectureship in psychology at Columbia University, February, 1908. I have printed them as they were written for delivery, except that quotations from the French and German have, for accuracy's sake, been restored from English translation to their original form.[1]

I have not been able, either in the lectures themselves or in the appended notes, to take account of all that is important in the current psychology of feeling and attention. Indeed, my sins of omission are obvious. I can only say that they weigh heavily upon my scientific conscience, and that, were it not for other and imperative claims upon my time, I should have delayed publication until I had done what I could to correct them.

My thanks are due to my wife; to my colleague, Professor I. M. Bentley, who has read

[1] Professor Pillsbury's English work on Attention reached me too late for reference in the text, though I have cited it in the notes.

the manuscript of the book and during its preparation gave me unsparingly of his time and
counsel; to Professor J. McK. Cattell, of Columbia University, whose invitation prompted
the writing of the lectures; and to many kindly
critics among my hearers. I have dedicated
the volume to Professor E. C. Sanford, of Clark
University, my close friend and trusted mentor
of the past sixteen years. Would that it were
worthier of his acceptance!

Cornell Heights, Ithaca, N.Y.,
          March, 1908.

CONTENTS

I

SENSATION AND ITS ATTRIBUTES

LECTURE I

SENSATION AND ITS ATTRIBUTES

THE system of psychology rests upon a three-fold foundation: the doctrine of sensation and image,[1] the elementary doctrine of feeling, and the doctrine of attention. Our views of sensation, of feeling, and of attention determine, if we are logical, the whole further course of our psychological thought and exposition. Where systems differ by anything more than relative emphasis and fulness of treatment, their differences invariably lead us back to the consideration of these fundamental doctrines. It is, therefore, more than important — it is necessary — that the student of psychology have a firm grasp of the issues involved and a comprehensive knowledge of the relevant facts.

These requirements are, however, by no means easy of fulfilment. Look, first of all, at sensation. We know a great deal about sensation itself, as an elementary process; we know a great deal about the simpler syntheses; and we have working theories in most of the sense-departments. On all these points we owe a debt,

3

which we must gratefully acknowledge, to physiological interest and physiological equipment.
Methods and results, together with apparatus
that embodied methods and assured results, were
at our disposal as soon as we had the skill to
use and the funds to acquire. We have bor-
rowed freely from physiology, and we have turned
the loan to such good account that physiology is
not ashamed, on occasion, to borrow again from
us. Nevertheless, with all the advantage that
comes of an experimental tradition, and with all
the facilities for work afforded by the local differentiation of the sense-organs, we are still far
removed, in this sphere of sensation, from finality
or general agreement. A mental element can
be defined only by the enumeration of its attributes. Turn, now, to the table of contents of
the *Physiologische Psychologie*, and you find but
two attributes of sensation : intensity and quality.
Turn to Ebbinghaus' *Grundzüge*, and you find
that sensations have both special and general
attributes, and that the latter include such apparently heterogeneous things as extension and
duration, movement and change, likeness and
difference, unity and multiplicity.[2]

But if there is difference of opinion as regards sensation, what shall we say of feeling
and attention ? The unsettled state of the psy-

chology of feeling is notorious. Here are problems on which, as it would almost seem, the
trained and the untrained, the professional and
the amateur psychologist exchange ideas on equal
terms; here is a field in which one man's casual
opinion is as valuable as another man's reasoned
conclusion, in which a general impression is
worth as much as an experimental result.
And, what is worse, the path of inference is so
precarious, and the experimental results are as
yet so few, that psychologists *von Fach* are themselves tempted to overhasty generalisation, and
become dogmatic before criticism has done its
work. Does not Wundt base the psychology of
language on his theory of affective pluralism? [3]
Nor is attention in much better case: the first
sentence of the preface to Pillsbury's recent book
refers to the 'chaotic state of current theories of
attention.' [4] It is, perhaps, true that the problems of attention are less widely discussed, have
attracted less general notice, than the problems
of feeling. If, however, this is the fact, the problems are none the less insistent; and their neglect by the educated public means simply that
popular psychology long ago worked out a theory
of attention for its own use, and so far has not
felt the need of reconsideration.

It follows, plainly enough, that I cannot in

these Lectures give you any complete or finished account of the psychology of affection and attention; if time allowed, the nature of the case would forbid. It follows also that my account, such as it is, will of necessity take on an individual colouring. It would be absurd to make the claim of impartiality when all one's efforts, whether of criticism or of construction, are determined by training and temperament. Besides, the attitude of impartiality is irrelevant, so long as every set of observations is coupled with the name of the observer, and every observer has his private interpretation. I shall, however, keep as closely as possible to documents and to experimental results; and where I venture a personal opinion, I shall offer it as an opinion and as nothing more.

So much may be said by way of general introduction. But now, before we come to close quarters with affection and attention, we must give a little time to sensation. This special introduction is necessary for the reason that, throughout the following discussions, sensation will be our standard of reference. When we ask whether the affective processes show distinctive features, we are in search of features that distinguish affection from sensation; when we speak of the laws of attention, we have always in mind a distribution or redistribution of the sense-processes that make up the consciousness of the moment. Hence it is important that we understand clearly what sensation is : or at any rate, that we frame a working definition of sensation, adequate to our present purpose and free of ambiguity.

It will help to clear the ground if we distinguish, at the outset, between the sensation or sensory element of psychology and the sensory element of psychophysics. The sensation of psychology is any sense-process that cannot be further analysed by introspection : every one of the forty thousand lights and colours that we can see, every one of the eleven thousand tones that we can hear, is a psychological sensation. The sensations of psychophysics, on the other hand, are the sense-correlates of the elementary excitatory processes posited by a theory of vision or audition or what not. Thus the six *Urfarben* of Hering's theory of vision — black and white, blue and yellow, carmine and bluish green — are, if that theory be accepted, the psychophysical elements of vision; they are the sources of the whole series of psychological elements. These latter are, none the less, psychologically elementary : a light unsaturated

yellowish green, while psychophysically compound, is introspectively simple; it cannot
be factored into a white, a yellow, and a green,
as a chord may be factored into a number of
simple tones. Similarly, if we could accept
Mach's notion of dull and bright components
in tonal sensation,[5] we should have only two
psychophysical elements in audition; whereas
the Helmholtz theory gives us parallel series
of psychophysical and of psychological sensations. Here, as elsewhere in experimental psychology, the failure to distinguish between
psychophysics and psychology proper has led
to much confused argument.[6]

We are now concerned with the sensory
element of psychology. And a mental element,
as was said above, must be defined by an enumeration of its attributes. What, then, are the
attributes of sensation?

An attribute of sensation, as commonly defined, is any aspect or moment or dimension
of sensation which fulfils the two conditions of
inseparability and independent variability. The
attributes of any sensation are always given
when the sensation itself is given, and the annihilation of any attribute carries with it the
annihilation, the disappearance, of the sensation itself; this is what is meant by the 'insepara-

bility' of the attribute. A sensation that has
no quality, no intensity, no duration, etc., is
not a sensation; it is nothing. Conversely, if
a sensation is to exist, it must come into being
with all of its attributes; we cannot have an
intensive sensation that is dispossessed of quality. These statements are evidently true, and
so far the definition cannot be questioned. But
we are told, in the second place, that the attributes of sensation are independently variable;
quality may be changed while intensity remains
constant, intensity changed while quality remains constant, and so on throughout the list.
Is this statement true? Relatively, yes: true
for certain cases and under certain conditions.
If it were not true, — true, within limits, for the
attributes of intensity and quality, as originally
recognised, — how could it have been made?
what could have suggested it? It is matter of
observation that the intensity of tone or noise
may be varied while the quality is the same,
that warm and cold may change in degree without change in kind. Absolutely true, however,
the statement is not. In certain cases and beyond certain limits the variation of one attribute
implies the concomitant variation of another;
and in extreme instances the separation of the
two can be effected, if at all, only by a sort of

analogical abstraction, — by neglect, we will
say, of quality, and by direction of attention to
what, in the light of previous experience, we conceive to be intensity. I come to the concrete
in a moment. What I now wish to emphasise
is the fact that there are bound attributes as
well as free, and that the test of independent
variability, useful enough for a preliminary
survey, must be applied with caution when we
demand accuracy of detail.

Having thus amended the definition of 'attribute,' we might proceed at once to enumerate
the distinguishable attributes of the various
classes of sensation. The result would be a
list, longer or shorter according to the sense-
department, in which term followed term in
conventional order, — an empirical list, in which
every term stood apart from every other, and
all terms were on the same level. I think that
we shall do better to cast about for some principle of classification; and I have seemed to
find such a principle in Müller's distinction of
intensive and qualitative change. A sensation
changes intensively, Müller says, when it moves
along the shortest path to or from the zero-
point; it changes qualitatively when it moves in
a direction that neither carries it towards nor
withdraws it from the zero-point.[7] If we gen-

eralise these statements, we may group all the attributes of sensation under the two headings, qualitative and intensive. I should, for instance, rank as intensive attributes, in the broad sense, degree or intensity proper, duration, extension, and clearness. Duration varies between a liminal value and the maximum set by adaptation or fatigue; extension varies between a liminal value and the maximum set by the boundaries of the field of sense; and clearness, too, varies between a liminal value and the maximum set by the limit of attentional concentration. On the other hand, I regard what is ordinarily termed the quality of sensation as, in several cases, a complex of distinguishable qualitative attributes.

We will take the qualitative attributes first, and we will begin with vision. Visual sensations fall, for psychology, into the two great classes of sensations of light and sensations of colour; the whole system finds representation in the double pyramid, which is itself a purely psychological construction. The sensations of light need not detain us. The sensations of colour, however, are interesting in that they have no less than three qualitative attributes. A given colour may be varied in hue or colour tone, in tint or brightness, and in chroma or saturation; and reference to the colour pyramid will show that, within limits, these three

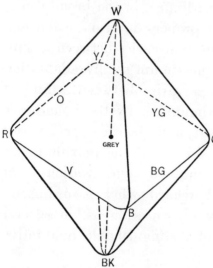

attributes, hue, tint, and chroma, are independent variables, — so that we may change hue while tint and chroma remain the same, change tint without changing hue and chroma, and change chroma with constancy of hue and tint. The limits are set,

FIG. 1. The Colour Pyramid. — H. Ebbinghaus, *Grundzüge der Psychologie*, i., 1905, 199.

of course, by the form of the double pyramid, which, as I have said, is an empirical, psychological construction. But here are three distinguishable attributes under the currently single heading of quality.

When we turn to audition, we are on more debatable ground. I myself believe that tonal sensations show a qualitative duality, — that the quality of tone is a resultant of the two attributes known respectively as pitch and as

voluminousness (Stumpf's *Tongrösse*). I dare
say that, at first thought, it seems far-fetched,
even a little ridiculous, to make volume a qualitative attribute, especially in view of the uses to
which it has been put in systematic psychology.
But I would remind you, in the first place, that
we are inveterately addicted to spatial metaphors, and that the term 'pitch' contains a spatial reference no less obvious, on consideration,
than that of 'volume.' Pitch means height,
elevation; the German equivalent is *Tonhöhe*,
the French *hauteur;* and in characterising
pitch, we speak, in English, of high, low, deep
tones. Yet nobody nowadays would dream
of making pitch an intensive attribute. Nowadays, no! — but listen to Fechner. "Bei den
Tönen," he says, "hat die Höhe, obwohl als
Qualität des Tones fassbar, doch auch eine
quantitative Seite, sofern wir eine grössere und
geringere Höhe unterscheiden können." [8] There
the spatial metaphor was at work. But if this
spatial reference is to be ignored in the case of
pitch, why should we pay regard to it in the case
of volume? May it not be the fact, simply,
that the idea of tonal voluminousness is less
familiar to us than that of tonal pitch, that we
have observed the attribute of volume less frequently or less accurately than we have observed

height and depth, — and so that we are misled by the name? Secondly, I would remind you that, if we are to turn the attribute of volume to account for a theory of space-perception, we must be extremely careful to take it as what it introspectively is, an attribute of tonal sensation, and not to surround it with visual or tactual associates. I may illustrate by a quotation from James, though James is not dealing primarily with tones. "Loud sounds," he says, "have a certain enormousness of feeling. It is impossible to conceive of the explosion of a cannon as filling a small space. In general, sounds seem to occupy all the room between us and their source; and in the case of certain ones, the cricket's song, the whistling of the wind, the roaring of the surf, or of a distant railway train, to have no definite starting-point." [9] These statements are offered as evidence of the general principle that a spatial attribute, extensity, voluminousness, vastness, is inherent in all sensations without exception. But the sensation, as elementary process, knows and says nothing whatever of its stimulus or its organ or its object. An explosive noise, considered as sensation, is not the noise of a cannon or of anything else; a continuative noise, hiss or whistle or roar, considered as sensation, has nothing to do with a starting-point in objective space, definite or indefinite.[10] The evidence must be sought else-where, — sought in sensation proper, under rigid introspective conditions, and sought, more es-pecially, under conditions that rule out the com-plicating attribute of intensity, — for 'loud' sounds may be enormous in one way, and weak sounds in quite a different way.

Make, then, the experiment for yourselves. Take a series of tuning-forks, standing on their resonance boxes, — a series that extends from bass to treble, — and listen to their tones. There can be no manner of doubt that volume is an attribute of tonal sensation. There may, however, I think, be a very considerable doubt whether the volume is in any real sense spatial. Choose your adjectives. The deep tones are bigger, larger, not more massive, perhaps, but more diffuse; the high tones are smaller, thin-ner, sharper. The spatial reference lies very near. Still, when you say more diffuse, thin-ner, sharper, you refer to more than space-form or space-extension; there is a hint in the words of a difference of texture. Try now the terms milder, softer, for the deep tones, and shriller, harder, for the high; do they not fit the facts? Surely, volume is not an in-tensive attribute, a mere bulkiness that ranges between the extremes of pin-point concentration and all-pervading vastness, but a qualitative attribute, moving between the extremes of mild and shrill. Volume and pitch are to the tonal sensation what hue and tint and chroma are to the sensation of colour; and the attributes are independently variable, in the sense that at the two ends of the scale volume changes more quickly than pitch, while over the middle region it changes more slowly.[11]

Little can be said, at present, of the sensations of noise. Both the explosive noise (the pop of a soap-bubble, the sharp drop of a wooden block upon a wooden table) and the continuative noise (the hiss of escaping steam), if heard singly, appear simple to introspection. If, however, we make the observation serial, we can distinguish an attribute of pitch and a concomitant noisiness. The question then arises whether pitch is a constituent of noise quality, or whether it is due to the admixture of tone. Noisiness itself seems to remain constant over fairly wide regions of the scale of pitch; but nothing more definite can be said about it.

The qualitative attribute presents no difficulty in the spheres of taste, smell, and temperature. It is otherwise with cutaneous pressure, cutaneous pain, and many of the organic sensations.

Suppose that a well-defined and responsive pressure spot is stimulated with increasing degrees of intensity. We get at first, with the weakest stimulus, a sensation of tickle. At moderate stimulation, this passes over into pressure; either a quivering, wavery pressure, or a hard, 'cylindrical' pressure. If the intensity of stimulus is still further increased, but not carried to the point at which subcutaneous tissue becomes involved, we have the Goldscheider sensation of 'granular' pressure. I am not now concerned with psychophysical questions, but with psychological; and the peculiarity of these observations, from the psychological side, is that the qualities just mentioned sometimes overlap. I have not noticed, it is true, any overlapping of the granular by the cylindrical pressure. But the ticklishness of weak stimulation is often sensed along with the different quality of quivering pressure, and this again may at times be sensed alongside of the Goldscheider granular pressure. Suppose, again, that a pain spot is similarly stimulated. We get at first, with the weakest stimulus, a sensation of itch. At moderate stimulation, this passes over into prick or sting; and with further increase of the intensity of stimulus, into cutaneous pain. And here, as before, there is over-

c

lapping. A sting may be an itchy sting, and a pain may be a stinging pain.

The same thing holds, apparently, of certain kinæsthetic sensations. The dragging, tired sensation which is probably attributable to the muscle-spindles passes through a sore, achy stage into dull pain : the three stages are introspectively distinguishable; but there is, nevertheless, an overlapping. The strain sensation which seems to be due to stimulation of the Golgi spindles in tendon also passes into dull pain by gradual transition and overlapping of quality.

Finally, I am inclined to think — though I say this with greater reserve — that the same thing holds in the case of alimentary sensations. Isolate hunger and nausea, at fairly low intensities, and you have a dull pressure. The same dull pressure ? It would be overhasty to assert a precise identity; but, at any rate, the likeness revealed by analysis is surprising when we remember the gross difference between the hungry and the nauseated consciousness. It looks as if, with increase of intensity of stimulus, a second qualitative factor — possibly a group of qualitative factors — comes into play in the two cases, differentiating sensations which, at the beginning of the intensive scale, are so nearly alike as to run the risk of identification.[12]

At this point you may very well object that I am confusing two distinct things: the fusion of qualitatively different sensations, and the confluence of different qualitative attributes in one and the same sensation. Tiredness, you may say, does not pass over into pain, but is coloured by, fused with, a pain sensation; the hungry and the nauseated consciousnesses are formations of great complexity, and imply the fusion of a large number of qualitatively different sensations. That may be true. On the other hand, I think that psychology has taken the simplicity of the qualitative attribute in too dogmatic a spirit. There can be no doubt that the sensation of colour is qualitatively compound; there can be no doubt, I believe, about the observations just described in the spheres of pressure and cutaneous pain. And there is no reason *a priori* why the organic sensations should follow the type of taste and smell rather than that of touch. Even, then, if you do not accept the conclusions that I have suggested, you will perhaps be ready to admit that there is a great deal of work still to be done before we can make out a final list of the sense-qualities.

We may now go on to consider the intensive attributes of sensation, and we may start out with intensity proper. Intensity has been so exhaustively discussed, in connection with the methods of quantitative psychology, that it is not necessary to enter into details. Let me remark, however, that the attribute is, in practice, much less free than it is sometimes made in theory. I have already given instances from the cutaneous senses and possible instances from the kinæsthetic. But even in the case of sounds, those who have worked with the Fechner pendulum or with the gravity phonometer know that, beyond narrow limits, independent variation of intensity is exceedingly difficult.

The classical difficulty arises in the sphere of vision. Hering long ago denied the attribute of intensity "im üblichen Sinne des Wortes" to the sensations of the black-white series. Hillebrand, in 1889, declares that intensive differences do not appear anywhere in the domain of visual sensation, though there may be a constant intensity that is never noticed and therefore cannot be empirically demonstrated. Külpe, in 1893, writes that "intensity cannot be ascribed to sensations of sight." Hering repeats, in 1907, that the "Begriff der Intensität auf die Farbe nicht anwendbar ist." Personally, I have never been able to subscribe to this doctrine. It is true, as Müller says, that

"die Empfindung einer und derselben Grau-
nuance kommt in der That in unserer Erfahrung nicht mit merkbar verschiedenen Intensitäten vor," and that "auch eine Farbenempfin-
dung von ganz bestimmter Qualität können
wir . . . nicht in verschiedenen Intensitäten
herstellen." That is matter of observable fact.
But it is surely true, on the other hand, that we
recognise degrees of intensity in visual sensation, and that — by the process of analogical
abstraction of which I spoke earlier in this
Lecture — we are able in some measure to ignore the concomitant change of quality and to
direct our attention to intensity alone. Müller,
in the paper just quoted from, has rescued the
intensity of visual sensation, on the psychophysical side, by his theory of central gray; and
Külpe has now accepted, if not that theory itself,
at any rate the attribute whose behaviour it is
meant to explain. The theory, in brief summary, is this: that we owe the intensive peculiarity of visual sensation to the dual character,
peripheral and central, of the nervous processes
involved. The retinal processes are antagonistic:
two coincident stimuli — black and white, for
instance — are effective for excitation only by
their difference, by excess of the one over the
other. The endogenous, central excitation is

constant. Hence a peripheral stimulation may result in the whitening, lightening, or in the blackening, darkening of the central gray, but there is no way of intensifying that gray without changing its quality, — no way of strengthening its black and white components at the same time and in the same degree.[13]

I have digressed thus briefly into psychophysics, because it is precisely in such cases that that much-abused science shows to its best advantage. Introspection is at fault. Some psychologists will have it that the scale of tints, the black-white series, is a scale of intensities, and will hear nothing of quality; others affirm that it is a scale of qualities, and will hear nothing of intensity; others, again, declare that it is at once qualitative and intensive. Psychophysics not only resolves the difficulty, but shows why the difficulty was there.

Here we may leave intensity, and pass to the consideration of the spatial and temporal attributes, extension and duration. This, as you know, is controversial ground. I cannot help thinking, however, that the psychology of these attributes is simpler than it is ordinarily represented to be. We must, of course, distinguish: we must not identify physical with mental time, or physical with mental space; we must not

confuse processes that in some way mean time,
or mean space, with attributes that in some way
are time and are space; we must not run together time-estimate and durational experience,
or space-estimate and extensional experience.
Granted! But the attributes themselves are
surely obvious enough. What is psychological
extension? It is the aspect of sensation that
we attend to when we are called upon to answer
the questions (perhaps with reference to an after-
image, perhaps with reference to a cutaneous
sensation): How large is it? What shape has
it? Is it regular or irregular? large or small?
continuous or patchy? uniform or broken?
And in the same way, psychological duration
is the attribute that we attend to when we
answer the questions: How long does it last?
When does it disappear? Has it gone out yet?
Is it steady or interrupted?—That is all. The
attributes of sensation are always simultaneously
present,—evidently! since the nullifying of any
attribute annihilates the sensation. But when
we are thus attending to extension or duration
we may have very hazy ideas indeed about intensity and quality; precisely as, when we are
observing intensity, we may have very hazy
ideas about quality and duration. The question what extension and duration are, in direct

experience, is a nonsensical question; we can only reply, tautologically, that duration is a going-on, and extension a spreading-out. But what, then, are quality and intensity 'in direct experience'? Does it help to say that quality is the individualising attribute? That is only saying that quality is quality. Does it help to say that intensity is always a more or a less? What, then, of clearness, or duration, or extension? Or that high intensities make a greater claim upon us, dominate consciousness more exclusively, than low? What, then, of clearness or of the *Eindringlichkeit* that we are to discuss presently? You cannot define the indefinable: at most you get a formal equivalent — 'simplest spatial determination' or the like — that serves you as a paragraph heading. As to the difficulty that duration and extension must find expression in physical units, and that we have no right to equate the psychical and the physical, that is a difficulty which occurs also in the case of intensity, where it has been successfully met. To work over the whole ground again, with simple change of terms, is purely gratuitous labour.[14]

It is more to the point to inquire into the empirical distribution of the two attributes. Duration appears to attach to all sensations. Extension attaches, without any doubt, to all visual sensations. It is also ascribed, in common parlance, to the ' sense of touch.' Touch, however, is an extremely ambiguous term; it may refer to cutaneous pressure, while it may cover all the cutaneous and many of the organic senses. If, now, you ask me which of these component senses has the extensional attribute, I must confess that decision is, in some instances, very difficult, and that my own opinion has differed at different times. Just now, I am inclined to be liberal. I should give the attribute to all four of the cutaneous senses, — pressure, warmth, cold, and pain; I should give it to the organic pains; and I should give it also to the organic sensations, kinæsthetic or other, whose quality suggests the term 'pressure.' It seems to me that in all these sensations we get a true extension, different from the quasi-extensity of tones. Let me repeat, however, that decision is difficult; I have no wish to be dogmatic.[15]

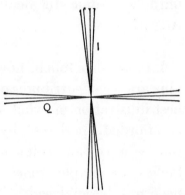

FIG. 2. Schema of a Visual Sensation. The four vertical lines represent the four intensive attributes: intensity, clearness, extension, duration. The three horizontal lines represent the three qualitative attributes: hue, tint, chroma.

Clearness, our fourth intensive attribute, is no more definable than its fellows. It is the attribute which distinguishes the 'focal' from the 'marginal' sensation; it is the attribute whose variation reflects the 'distribution of attention.'[16] We may postpone its discussion until we come to deal with the subject of Attention.

I must also touch, however briefly, upon the appearance of attributes of a higher order. The best illustration of what is meant by the phrase is afforded, perhaps, by tone-colour or tone-tint, — a certain colouring or *timbre* which attaches to simple tones, and which may, but need not, be analysed. We owe the recognition of this compound attribute to Stumpf, who derives it from pitch, intensity (high tones are intrinsically louder than low), and volume. It finds expression in such antitheses as bright and dull, sharp and flat, full and hollow. Other instances are the penetratingness of certain scents, — camphor and naphthaline, *e.g.*, as compared with vanilla and orris-root, — the urgency or importunity of certain pains or of the taste of bitter, the obtrusiveness or self-insistence of certain lights and colours and tones. All these latter attributes involve clearness, in

conjunction with quality, or with intensity, or
with intensity and quality together. Their
investigation in detail cannot but prove fruitful,
whether for psychology or for psychophysics.[17]

I spoke, earlier in this Lecture, of the forty
thousand lights and colours that we can see,
and the eleven thousand tones that we can hear.
The 'forty thousand' was a rough guess at the
number of discriminable qualities included in the
colour pyramid; a modest guess, too, when you
compare it with Ebbinghaus' "many hundred
thousand," or Aubert's "many million"! But
I prefer underestimation to overestimation; and
I think that Ebbinghaus would find it difficult
to bring convincing evidence even of a single
hundred thousand visual qualities. On the
other hand, the eleven thousand tones are distinguished on the basis of pitch alone; and that
number must be increased if investigation proves
— what is *a priori* extremely probable — that
pitch may remain the same while the qualitative attribute of volume undergoes noticeable
change.[18]

Let us, however, raise in conclusion a more
general question. Why do we identify the number of sensations furnished by a particular
sense-department with the number of distin-

guishable sensory qualities? Why is quality
the 'individualising' attribute? Why are not
the different intensities of a given pitch 'different
sensations'?

I suppose that, in strict logic, any noticeable
change in an attribute of sensation gives us a
'different' sensation. As soon as ever introspection turned to the attribute of intensity,
it found differences, not of simple more and less,
but of 'kind.' Lotze, for instance, declares
that a strong sour does not taste the same as
a weak; there are "qualitative Veränderungen
des Empfindungsinhalts, die von jenen [inten-
siven] Differenzen des Reizes abhängen." Now,
to call intensive change a change of 'quality'
is to introduce unnecessary confusion of terms.
We need not do that; but we need not either,
it seems to me, quarrel with those who hold
that sensations of the same quality but of different intensity are, psychologically regarded, different sensations. The innovation would not
lengthen our list of visual sensations; it would,
very considerably, lengthen the list of auditory
sensations.

And what of clearness, duration, extension?
Are we, in their case, dealing again with differences of 'kind,' or merely with differences of
degree? It is really impossible to say; the intro-

spective judgments are lacking. From general impression, I incline to the view that differences of clearness are, like intensive differences, ultimate and distinctive. · On the score of duration and extension I do not like even to hazard a conjecture; though, if I were compelled to take sides, I should fall back on the analogy of intensity.

If, therefore, there is anything to be gained by substituting 'attributive difference' for 'qualitative difference' as a criterion of sensation, I shall be willing to make the change. As things are, I do not see the gain; and I do not see, either, the necessity of logical strictness. Our classification of sensations is a matter of utility, of expediency; the question involved is general, but it is not scientifically important. In science, as in ordinary life, we call things different when their difference is striking and outweighs their likeness, and we call things like when their likeness is striking and outweighs their difference. Red and blue, sour and sweet, are in this sense 'different'; loud and soft, light and heavy, are 'like.' Until it is shown that the new and more elaborate classification brings positive advantage to descriptive psychology, I shall accordingly rest content with the traditional list of sensible qualities.[19]

So this hasty review comes to an end. I do not apologise for its imperfection, its sketchiness; for sensation is not our primary subject, and at the best one cannot say very much about sensation in a single hour. I have tried only to raise such points and to discuss such issues as will put you in tune with me, so to say, for our later study of affection and attention. When I speak of sensation, in the following Lectures, I shall mean by it the kind of process that we have been considering to-day; the fringe of association with which the word is surrounded will be drawn from the circle of ideas within which we have now been moving.

II

SENSATION AND AFFECTION: THE CRITERIA OF
AFFECTION

LECTURE II

SENSATION AND AFFECTION: THE CRITERIA OF AFFECTION

THE psychology of feeling, as I said in the introduction to the preceding Lecture, is in a notoriously unsettled state. We have psychologists of the first rank who posit an elementary affective process alongside of sensation; we have psychologists of the first rank who deny the distinction. Wundt and Lipps stand over against Brentano and Stumpf.[1] I propose, now, in the present hour, to examine the principal arguments that have been urged in favour of an independent feeling element, and the arguments that have been brought forward in reply. I shall use the term 'affection' for the elementary process in question, and for the sake of clearness I shall speak only of the qualities of pleasantness and unpleasantness. These, of course, are recognised by all psychologists alike, — by those who hold a plural as well as by those who hold a dual theory of affective processes at large.

What we may call the gross reason, the obvious reason, for assuming an affective element is,

I suppose, the gross and obvious difference between the intellectual processes of the adult
mind, on the one hand, and the emotive processes,
on the other. As thought differs from emotion,
so must the element of thought, the sensation,
differ from the element of emotion, the affection.
Personally, I attach more weight to this argument
than its formal expression might seem to warrant.
I believe that the simple feelings — our experiences when we 'feel hungry,' 'feel dizzy,' 'feel
tired,' 'feel comfortable,' 'feel poorly,' 'feel first-
rate' — represent a stage or level from which
we ascend to the emotions; and that the emotions, again, represent a stage or level from which
we descend to secondary feelings: our anger
weakens and simplifies to a feeling of irritation,
our resentment to a feeling of chagrin or annoyance, our joy to a feeling of pleased content-
ment, our grief to a feeling of depression.   I
believe that we are here in presence of a general
law or uniformity of mental occurrence; that all
conscious formations show like phenomena of
rise and fall, increase and decrease in complexity,
expansion and reduction.   Nevertheless, as systematic psychology stands to-day, the argument
has no objective validity, no power to carry conviction.   It may be traversed, flatly and finally,
in two different ways: by the James-Lange

theory of emotion, and by the theory of Stumpf. If we accept a strict version of the James-Lange theory, and identify the specifically emotive or affective processes in emotion with organic sensations, then evidently we dispense, at this middle level, with the independent affective element, and the argument from continuity falls to the ground. And if we divorce the sense-feeling from the emotion, in Stumpf's way, and assert that the 'psychological nucleus' of the emotion, the central and characteristic process that makes it what it is, is altogether different from sense-feeling, — that "die Sinnesgefühle den Gemütsbewegungen heterogen sind,"—then, again, we have a sharp severance of continuity, and the argument lapses. Neither of these alternative views can be lightly brushed aside: the James-Lange theory has aroused prolonged discussion, and has gained many adherents; and the Stumpf theory, in essential points, commands the assent, e.g., of Stout and Irons.[2]

It would be interesting to take representative statements of the three views of emotion — say, the statements of Wundt, James, and Stumpf — and to estimate each one in the light of the other two. I doubt, however, whether the comparison would be profitable. Surely, if we are to reach anything like a conclusion, we must begin lower down; we must go, not to emotion, but to sense-feeling.   Is there any one who, when weighing James' theory in the balance, has not heartily wished that he had given us a chapter on the feelings?   Is there any student of the *Tonpsychologie* and of Stumpf's later work who has not felt the want of that 'Abschnitt über die durch Sinneseindrücke erweckten Gefühle' which was promised in 1883 and has delayed until 1906? [3]   Can any one doubt that the issue raised by Wundt's tridimensional theory of affections is, systematically, a more fundamental issue than is involved in the most radical doctrine of emotion?   I may be seeing things crookedly; but as I see them, the heart of the problem lies in feeling.   Let us, then, attack the problem at this point; let us consider, as critically as we may, the alleged criteria of affection.

(1) We may take up, first, the statement that sensations are the objective and affections the subjective elements of consciousness; and we will try to give these terms, 'objective' and 'subjective,' a tangible psychological meaning.

Let us be clear that the meaning must be psychological; the difference, if it exist, must be a difference that is open to introspective verification.   Anything in the way of epistemological

argument is wholly out of place. It is out of
place for two reasons. On the one hand, psychology is an independent discipline, and can
no more take dictation from epistemology than
it can from metaphysics or ethics. And, on
the other, epistemology is concerned with the
principles of knowledge — whether with the
material and formal principles together, or with
the material principles alone, is matter of definition; while the psychological element has no
part or lot in knowledge, has no reference or
meaning or object or cognitive contents of any
sort.

Let us be clear, also, that the meaning which
we give to the terms 'objective' and 'subjective'
must cover a difference in the elementary processes regarded as elementary. It has been
urged, for instance, that the sensory elements
in perception are looked upon, in ordinary
thought, as properties of external things, whereas
feeling is always personal, reflects always a state
of the mind itself. Heat seems to reside in the
burning coals; but the pleasantness, the grate-
fulness, of the warmth is in me. I will not now
dwell on the epistemological implications of this
argument, but will accept it at its face value,
as an argument from the psychology of perception and feeling. And I reply, first, that the

statement which it makes is not true, the distinction which it draws cannot be drawn. For
the pleasant or grateful feeling which is subjective, in me, is a feeling and not an affection;
it comprises certain organic sensations; and
nobody confuses organic sensations with properties of external things. I reply, secondly,
that the argument, even if it were true, would be
irrelevant. For it is an argument based, not on
introspection of the elementary processes as
such, but on the character or behaviour of these
processes in combination. We, however, are
dealing with the mental elements in their status
as elements.

There are, I think, three interpretations of the
terms 'objective' and 'subjective' that have
claims upon our attention. (*a*) The first is
that of Wundt. In a recent study of Wundt's
doctrine of psychical analysis, Hollands has made
the subjectivity of affective process, in Wundt's
system, the topic of detailed study. I need not
here attempt any summary of the discussion,
since Hollands' articles are easily accessible
in *The American Journal of Psychology.* The
upshot of the investigation is that Wundt contrasts, under the two rubrics, tendency to fusion
and persistent discreteness. "Feeling . . . is
always falling into unitary masses, it forms a

single continuum. This . . . we may take as
Wundt's final meaning in psychology for *subjective*."

What are we to say in criticism? This, evidently: that while Wundt has, as Hollands maintains, given the distinction an "introspective
definition," he has not derived it from a comparison of isolated sensation with isolated affection. A 'tendency to fusion' is not an attribute
that shows, like intensity or quality, in the single
element. Besides, there is also a tendency to
fusion in the organic sensations; they, too, are
'always falling into unitary masses.' Indeed,
if we reject Wundt's theory of the plurality of
affective qualities, the criterion becomes meaning-
less: the 'unitary masses' and the 'single continuum' formed with pleasantness-unpleasantness by excitement-depression and strain-relaxation take us out of the affective sphere and into
that of organic sensation; the subjectivity that
should characterise affection now characterises
a group of sensations. Finally, it must be
remarked that the doctrine of the *Totalgefühl*
is not universally accepted. "Es giebt," says
Saxinger, "einen grossen Kreis von Thatsachen,
welcher Zeugniss für das Vorkommen coexis-
tirender Gefühle ablegt." Here is no fusion,
no continuum, but separation and discontinuity.

Let us try another interpretation.   We might argue (*b*) that sensations are objective because they are experienced in the same way by every one, and that affections are subjective because they are experienced differently, individually, by different persons or by the same person at different times.   Here, again, however, it would be enough to point out in answer that the single elements carry no such distinction upon them. Stumpf has also brought up a factual objection: he reminds us that what is supposed to hold of the affective processes holds very definitely of sensations of temperature.   A room that seems overwarm when you come in from the outside air may seem chilly to those who have been sitting in it for some time.   Stumpf might have generalised this objection, and referred simply to the phenomenon of adaptation.   Wherever we have adaptation, there we have the possibility that like stimuli will arouse different sensations in different minds.   And if you rejoin that the sensations are, nevertheless, always the same under the same conditions, then I ask: How do you know that this rule does not also apply to affections?   The variability of affective experience may be due, precisely, to difference in affective adaptation.

There is still the third possibility.   We might

express, in the terms 'objective' and 'subjective,' the fact (c) that sensations can stand alone
in consciousness, independently of affection,
while affection never appears alone, but always
and of necessity as the concomitant of some sensation. Many psychologists, as we know, have
looked upon affection not as an elementary process, coördinate with sensation, but as an attribute of sensation; they speak of *Gefühlston*,
affective tone, feeling tone, algedonic quality.
The hypothesis that underlies these phrases I
shall discuss in the next Lecture; I am here concerned simply with the alleged fact that sensations occur in isolation, affections only in connection with sensations. If the difference exists,
it is an admissible ground of distinction; for
although it is not a difference of attribute, it is
nevertheless a difference that shows in the comparison of element with element: the attempt to
isolate an affection will result, always, in the isolation of paired sensation and affection.

But does the difference exist? Listen to
Külpe. "We find sensations present," he says,
"where feeling is absent; that is, we have
sensations which are neither agreeable nor disagreeable; and we further find (such at least
is the author's experience) feelings present where
sensation is absent; that is, we have feelings

which are not accompanied by or attached to
definite sensations, or which arise where the nervous conditions of sensation are debarred from
the exercise of their ordinary influence on consciousness." I do not think that many of the
psychologists who recognise the independence of
the affective element would subscribe, without
qualification, to this opinion. But it is by no
means uncommon — *e.g.* in experimental work
upon the association of ideas — to find cases recorded in which a feeling precedes or lags behind
or outlasts its idea. And if Külpe is too extreme,
Ladd can probably claim a widespread acceptance of his view that "in the flow of the one
stream of conscious life the feelings may assume
either one of the three possible time-relations
towards the sensations and ideas by which we
classify them; they may fuse with them in the
'now' of the same conscious state, or they may
lead or follow them." Our final possibility is
thus sufficiently disposed of.[4]

We have considered three meanings of the
term 'subjective.' We have taken it to imply
a tendency towards fusion; individual variability
of experience; and what we may call a second
remove or a higher power of conscious existence.
In every instance argument has been met by
counter-argument, authority for by authority

against. We must, I think, conclude that, if
there really is a difference between sensation
and affection, the words 'objective' and 'subjective' are ill chosen to express it.*

(2) The distinction that we have next to consider is the distinction of local and not-local.
Sensations, it is said, may be localised; affections are not localisable. The distinction is
ambiguous, since the 'locality' may be a position
in perceptual space or a place in consciousness.
We will take the question of 'outer' localisation
first.

Are all sensations localisable at some point of
space? "Allen Sinnesempfindungen," says von
Frey, "ist die Beifügung eines Lokal- oder
Merkzeichens eigentümlich." And he adds,
"für den Unbefangenen wird gerade das Lokal-
zeichen ein Beweis sein, dass der Schmerz ein
den übrigen Sinnesempfindungen gleichwertiges
Element des Bewusstseins darstellt." That is
definite enough. As usual, however, there are
statements on the opposite side. "Eine Lokalisation der Geruchsempfindungen als solcher,"

---

* In my own mind, the difference of subjective and objective
appears always as a difference of texture: affection is softer,
flimsier, more yielding than sensation, — however organic the
sensation may be. This textural difference is what I 'feel' when
I read, e.g., that "feeling as such is matter of *being* rather than of
direct knowledge."

writes Nagel, "gibt es genau genommen nicht. Ich für meine Person wenigstens vermag meine schwachen Geruchsempfindungen gar nicht zu lokalisieren." When odours are localised, they are localised because their stimuli affect more than one set of end-organs: "bei dem Geruchssinn ist das lokalisierende Vermögen gleich Null." Definite again! Angell and Fite tell us, similarly, that "genuinely pure tones are essentially unlocalisable in monaural hearing"; "it seems quite safe to say that in monaural hearing really pure tones are unlocalisable." And even with binaural hearing, it is not difficult so to arrange the conditions of observation that localisation is impossible. If you work with sounds of very low intensity, or if you work with tuning-fork tones in the open, your observer surrounded with a curtain, you will find cases in which there is sheer inability to localise. "There are sounds," says Pierce, "that prior to all accessory experience are sharply and definitely located. . . . But over against these sharply located sounds are others that can be assigned no position whatever." Finally, Orth insists that there are organic complexes, vague resultants of diffuse, weak stimulation, which cannot be localised. Not all sensations, then, are capable of localisation.

But, on the other side, is affection unlocalis-

able? Stumpf reports that the agreeableness
and disagreeableness which accompany sensations of the higher senses seem to him to have a
certain spatial moment; they are not localised,
it is true, in the colours and tones themselves,
but are felt "als im Kopf ausgebreitet." "Auch
diese etwas unbestimmte Lokalisation ist aber
Lokalisation." I have known observers to in-
sist, similarly, that the pleasantness of the taste
of chocolate cream is localised in the mouth, the
pleasantness of tones and chords in the head or
chest. Lagerborg bears witness to the same
effect: "an einem Katermorgen nehmen wir
Unlust im Kopf, im Rachen, im Magen wahr."
And Störring distinguishes a *Stimmungslust*,
"an der . . . die gesammten jeweilig vorhan-
denen Bewusstseinsinhalte teilhaben," from a
localised *Empfindungslust*, "die an die . . .
[betreffenden] Empfindungen allein gebunden
erscheint."

There remains the question of 'inner' localisation. Sensations, it is said, run their course
side by side in consciousness; affection is always
coextensive with consciousness. The argument
hinges, therefore, on the possibility of what are
called 'mixed feelings.' Can pleasantness and
unpleasantness exist simultaneously in consciousness?

If we appeal to the text-books, we find the expected divergence of opinion. "It is hardly possible in the present state of our knowledge to decide positively for or against the reality of these mixed feelings. . . . In our own view, mixed feelings are certainly less well authenticated than cancellation of feeling." This is Külpe's statement in the *Outlines*. "Just as we may sense cold in the feet and warmth in the hands at the same time, so may we experience the pleasantness of a savoury dish along with the unpleasantness of a severe headache. . . . The affective accompaniment of complex mental formations may be extremely complicated." This is Ebbinghaus' statement in the *Grundzüge*. "All the affective elements present in consciousness at a given moment connect to form an unitary affective resultant": that is Wundt. "A full sense of conflict between pleasure and pain arises when the two feelings are both present in a distinct and strong form, and are not so unequal in point of strength as to allow of one overpowering the other": that is Sully. And so we might continue.

So far as I know, the coexistence of pleasantness and unpleasantness has only in three cases been made the subject of experimental inquiry. In two, the result has been negative. Orth,

in 1903, gave seven tests to four observers with
a view to the analysis of the emotion of doubt.
He records unpleasantness ten times and pleasantness five times (in nine and four of the twenty-
eight tests, respectively) ; there is no instance
of simultaneity, but one very striking instance of
succession, in which the order is pleasantness,
unpleasantess, pleasantness again, and terminal
unpleasantness. Alechsieff, in 1907, attacked
the problem directly. He made twenty-nine
experiments with pairs of stimuli (tastes and
odours, tones and colours) so chosen that the
one, taken alone, would be pleasant and the
other unpleasant. "Aus diesen Versuchen kam-
en wir zu dem Schlusse, dass Lust und Unlust
nicht gleichzeitig in unserem Bewusstsein existieren können, sie können nicht nebeneinander,
sondern immer nur nacheinander von uns erlebt
werden." I may add that in 1906 experiments
of the same type were begun by Hayes in the
Cornell laboratory, and — so far as they went
— yielded a like result; they were, however, too
few in number to warrant separate publication.

It is, perhaps, unfortunate that Orth was a
pupil of Külpe's, Alechsieff a pupil of Wundt's,
and Hayes a pupil of my own; for all three
of us may be suspected of *parti pris*, and all
three of the experimenters may therefore have

been influenced — despite our efforts at impartiality — by what is called 'laboratory atmosphere.' It is still more unfortunate, I think, that the experiments themselves are so scanty. All the more welcome, then, is Johnston's paper of 1906. The investigation covers a period of two years; the observers are twelve graduate students in Harvard University or Radcliffe College; the paired stimuli include colours, tactual surfaces, tuning-fork tones, noises, forms filled with different colours, and odours, as well as more complicated material; and the outcome is definitely positive. We are informed, *e.g.*, that, after training, eleven of the twelve observers "were all convinced that both feeling-tones, for tactual and visual impressions, could be present at once."

I should be very sorry, now, to criticise for the sake of criticising. On the contrary, I would give a good deal, as the saying is, to have this question of mixed feelings settled in the one way or the other; it is a question that has been with me, more or less insistently, for the past dozen years; and I should have attacked it experimentally long ago, had I found an adequate method. Theories, believe me! sit more lightly on their owners than is commonly supposed ; I would cheerfully exchange all my

'views' of feeling for a handful of solid facts.
And if Johnston had proved his conclusion, I
should accept it. So far, however, is he from
proof that it is even difficult to say, in precise
terms, what his conclusion is meant to be.

Consider! There were twelve graduate observers, seven of whom "had had from one to
five or more years' training in laboratory investigations." Here is no levy of tiros, but a
band of veterans. Had they never heard of
feeling, never run across theories of feeling,
never thought out for themselves what feeling
might mean, never discussed the various definitions of feeling? Moreover, several members of
the group were available for the whole period of
two years. Did they not work out a definition
of their own, adopt some particular criterion or
criteria of feeling in the course of the period?
Not a word is said upon these two points; we
do not know what the observers meant by feeling either at their down-sitting or at their up-
rising. At the most we can guess from the introspective reports. And the very first report
cited — the description of feeling for a particular
shade of red — reads thus: "It feels as if it
would be soft." No doubt it does! But in what
sense is 'soft' a feeling?

The instruction given to the observers was of

E

a very general kind. They "were requested to give themselves up to the situation and to report as accurately as they could the kind of affective state experienced." In preliminary series, with single stimuli, the same observers had, however, been given a far more complex instruction. They had been told, in effect, to describe the feeling; to report always all concomitant organic sensations; and to distinguish the significant organic concomitants from the accidental. This is a large order! The rule of work in *Ausfrageexperimente* is, surely, to make instruction narrow and definite, for any given series, and thus to fractionate the introspections. There is no other way to secure unequivocal results. While, now, the instruction in the experiments with paired stimuli was simpler than that in the experiments with single stimuli, there can, I think, be little doubt that the habit of observation formed in the first series was carried over to the second; only thus can I account for certain of the introspections recorded. At any rate, the complexity of the original instruction was a mistake; and the general instruction of the second series should, in my judgment, have been narrowed by specific regulations concerning, *e.g.*, the direction and distribution of attention. Or if it seemed advisable to take series with general instruction, then these should have been paralleled by other series in which the instruction was variously narrowed. It is odd that Johnston says nothing, gives not a single reference, on the score of the *Ausfragemethode*.

I have sometimes been charged with preferring method to result. I do not know that that would be a crime; I do not know why the search for truth should not be the sole end of a man's endeavours. If he sinned, he would sin in good company. But on lower ground the point is, of course, that your result is, after all, a function of your method; method is the road to result; given a method, — and in fairly competent hands results will follow of themselves. Let us see, then, to what kind of result the method of which I have just spoken has led.

It is essential that the results of this form of the method of impression be stated in the observers' own words. Orth gives his complete records. Alechsieff gives complete samples. Johnston does not. While he writes out a temperamental analysis of his twelve observers, later verified by themselves, he has edited and arranged the introspections, and only occasionally mentions an initial or puts a phrase into inverted commas. The temperamental analysis does not help us; we want to know

who said what, and how often, and in what
context. Moreover, Johnston's own account is
both meagre and confused. I can find no mention of the time during which the paired stimuli
were exposed, — though this fact is of cardinal
importance when it is a question of the coexistence or succession of affective processes. I
find no mention of the number of experiments
made with each observer, or of their arrangement, or of the time-interval between them. As
for the outcome, I hope, but I cannot be sure,
that the following summary is correct.

Johnston notes (a) phenomena of complete
fusion. This appears to be identical with what
he terms "a total mood with similar or harmoni-
ous constituents." To be distinguished from
fusion is (b) summation, where, e.g., two unpleasant elements "exist throughout, each in
turn intensifying the whole undertone of feeling,
but also remaining a feeling-tone of a particular
kind." In (c) partial reënforcement, "both feeling-tones contribute to a feeling of the same kind,
yet do retain some individual characteristics
which stand out for themselves." I do not see
how this differs from (b); at most there is a
slight difference of degree. What is differentiated by Johnston as (d) partial inhibition seems
to be only a name given by certain observers to

partial reënforcement. At any rate, these four are all cases of fusion or summation, and do not directly concern us. Next comes (e) total inhibition, which does interest us here. "Cases of total inhibition . . . are by far the most frequent, as would naturally be expected[?]. When sandpaper is being applied, and no repose is felt in the body, a colour, suddenly presented, for a moment pleases the eye, but quickly loses all feeling-character, and can only be 'intellectually perceived.'" "In cases of feelings of opposite nature occurring together, the stronger generally prevails, finally in most cases effacing all specific tone for the weaker element. An odour, for example, even when always unpleasant, becomes less so when one looks at a pleasant colour, when a feeling-tone can, or often when it cannot, be detected for the colour at the time." I understand from these sentences that when two opposite feeling-tones are aroused by two stimuli, operating at the same time, the regular or usual result is cancellation; what we feel, if we feel at all, is the excess of the one over the other. But Johnston has a sixth category, of (f) merely simultaneous, independent coexistence. "When a very unpleasant form . . . is being felt, a slightly unpleasant colour tends to arouse often in this situation, as if by contrast, a simultaneously pleasant element in the total experience." "When there is a clear strife between the two [feeling-tones], they both can exist as equal partial tones with an undertone of unpleasantness in the failure to coördinate them." Now these experiences must, in the light of what has just been said, be rare. Why, then, — seeing how critical the observations are, — were not the complete introspections given? It looks to me as if, in both of the instances quoted, we were in presence of fairly complex emotive processes; the pleasure that arises 'by contrast,' and the displeasure that comes from 'failure to coördinate,' are not the feeling-tones of the stimuli. Are they feeling-tones at all? Or are they organic complexes, the organic sensations characteristic of relief and of disappointment? And again: if they are feeling-tones, were they strictly coexistent? Is it possible to experience three affective processes at once — a pleasantness, an unpleasantness, and another unpleasantness — and to hold them distinct at a given moment of time? Very little weight, I am afraid, can be attached to this imperfect report of what are, admittedly, exceptional cases. —

Let us now glance back over this whole discussion. We found that the distinction of local and not-local, as referred to sensations and

affections, might mean two different things.   It
might mean, first, that sensations are, and
affections are not, localisable in perceptual space.
We found, however, statements to the effect
that some sensations cannot be localised, while
we found also alleged instances of the localisation of affection.   We may therefore reject this
criterion, without going into the further question
whether locality, some form of *Merkzeichen*, is
an attribute that shows in the single sensation.
The distinction might mean, secondly, that
sensations run their course side by side in consciousness, while affections are always coextensive with consciousness.   The experimental
evidence, so far as it goes, appears to bear out
this contention.   Orth, Alechsieff, and Hayes
find no mixed feelings; Johnston finds that
mixed feelings are the exception and not the
rule; and we have seen that the exceptional instances are themselves not above suspicion.   On
the other hand, the experimental evidence is
scanty and incomplete; and psychological opinion at large is sharply divided.   Moreover, it
might be urged that there are occasions when
consciousness reduces to a single sensation:
pain, or a deafening noise, or a blinding glare.
So we seem to be as uncertain at the end as we
were at the beginning.[5]

(3) A third distinction, which we owe to Wundt, is that of difference and antagonism. Sensations range between maximal differences; feelings, between maximal opposites. "Allgemein werden die Empfindungsqualitäten durch grösste Unterschiede, die Gefühlsqualitäten durch grösste Gegensätze begrenzt."

I think that there has been a tendency, in the discussions of feeling, towards too cavalier a treatment of this distinction. It is really not quite easy to see what the difference means, and not quite easy to bring valid argument for or against it. Before, however, we come to details, let us notice that Rehmke refuses to connect pleasantness and unpleasantness in any way whatever. "Lust und Unlust sind 'incommensurable Grössen,' wie Ton und Farbe es sind." "Die Thatsachen des Seelenlebens . . . geben nicht den geringsten Anlass zu der Behauptung: 'Lust und Unlust sind gegensätzliche Zustände, welche durch einen Indifferenzpunkt in einander übergehen.'" "Lust und Unlust als thatsächlich besondere Bestimmtheiten der Seele haben nichts mit einander gemein." This view is, no doubt, exceptional; but it deserves consideration in the present context.

The objection usually brought against Wundt's formula is that there are sensations, too, which

range between maximal opposites. This is
probably what Stumpf has in mind when he
says that the statement is "so offenbar mit
den Tatsachen in Widerspruch, dass wir nicht
darauf einzugehen brauchen." What, then, are
the 'Tatsachen'? Orth refers to warmth and
cold: "die Empfindungen des Temperatur-
sinnes bewegen sich in derselben Gegensätz-
lichkeit." He cites also the organic complexes
of hunger and satiety, and the bodily states that
we term 'fresh' and 'tired.' Külpe, in his section on sensations of temperature, argues in the
other direction. "A simple increase or diminution of temperature can change either sensation
into its opposite, the path of change lying through
a point of indifference or zero-point. There is
no analogy to this fact in the sphere of sensation,
though there is a very complete one in that of
feeling." Ebbinghaus passes very lightly over
the 'gegensätzliche Gliederung' of the affective
processes: "sie stehen hiermit übrigens nicht
allein," he says, and quotes the three cases given
by Orth. All this seems to me rather superficial.

What we mean by maximal differences of sensation is clear enough. The attributes of sensation are, as we saw in the last Lecture, either
qualitative or intensive. If they are intensive,

they range — so to say, vertically — between
zero and infinity, or rather between a lower and
an upper limiting value. If they are qualitative,
they range — so to say, horizontally — between
extremes that are equally remote from both of
these limiting values. How can there be an
'opposition' of sensory qualities? We are referred to the sense of temperature: but there is
no sense of temperature. There are a cold sense
and a warmth sense, — different senses. The
thermometric scale is continuous; but that has
nothing to do with the case. Years ago I was
troubled by this antithetical account of warmth
and cold, and made a series of experiments,
from warmth to cold and from cold to warmth,
in order to trace the passage of the one to the
other through the point of indifference. I never
found that point. Külpe, who entirely believes
in its existence, confesses that he, too, has been
unable to verify its occurrence. The whole
construction is artificial; and the appeal to temperature is an appeal to physics, not to psychology. As for hunger and satiety, — try them!
Introspect your organic sensations in moderate
hunger and after a hearty dinner. So far from
finding opposition, antagonism, you will find a
very general resemblance. Lastly, the sensations of freshness and tiredness, in so far as they

are muscular in the strict meaning of that term,
— in so far, that is, as they belong to a single
sense, — range from bright to dull, from light
to heavy, from lively to dead: but these are
qualitative differences, akin to the differences of
black and white in vision and of high and low
in audition; there is no opposition or antagonism between them.

Now look at the other side of the shield.   Our
ordinary speech is very apt to couple words
which, in a loose way, may be considered as
'opposites.'   We speak of hard and soft, rough
and smooth, sharp and blunt, wet and dry,
strong and weak, keen and dull, light and heavy,
warm and cold; we speak of dark and fair,
hungry and thirsty,* wide-awake and drowsy,
fresh and tired, good-looking and ugly, clever
and stupid, good and bad.   The list might go
on indefinitely.   It is perfectly clear that, in
most instances, there is no real opposition between the paired terms; they stand simply for
extremes of possible difference, whether in an
attribute of sensation or in formations as complex as character and intelligence.   Why, then,
are two or three of them singled out, as express-

* When Alice tried to 'quench her thirst' with the Red Queen's
biscuit, — "and it was *very* dry," — the antagonism between
hunger and thirst was at least as real as the alleged antagonism
of hunger and satiety!

ing opposition? Why, indeed, — unless because an affective opposition is implied? Pleasant warmth and unpleasant cold; pleasant satiety and unpleasant hunger; pleasant freshness and unpleasant tiredness: is not that the opposition? I think that wherever the opposition is conscious, it is affective. Notice, too, that it is never absolute; cold may be pleasant in summer, unpleasant in winter. Hunger may be pleasant, a 'jolly' hunger. Tiredness may be a 'comfortable' tiredness. We thus oppose degrees of cold, degrees of hunger, degrees of tiredness, as well as cold and warmth, etc. On the whole, warmth and satiety and freshness are pleasant, and cold and hunger and fatigue are unpleasant; here is the general opposition to which our authorities appeal: but there are special oppositions that, if sensory at all, must be intensive and not qualitative. Notice, lastly, that other paired terms may be brought into conscious opposition if only we grant them an affective colouring; a carving-knife may be beautifully sharp or horribly blunt, a bed may be comfortably soft or dreadfully hard. And here as before there are oppositions of degree; comfortably soft may contrast with too soft, dreadfully hard with just hard enough.

This interpretation of the facts of 'sensory

opposition' squares very well with the systematic doctrine that all 'psychological' contrast —
I use Lipps' phrase — is a matter of feeling:
that the ordinary man looks small by the side
of a giant because you are disappointed, and
looks large by the side of a dwarf because you
are surprised. To that doctrine I subscribe.
But neither it nor the considerations which I
have just been urging tell us what affective
opposition is. Is it mutual incompatibility in
consciousness? Those who — like Lipps, in
his earlier writings — deny the possibility of
mixed feelings might agree to such a definition,
and we have seen that the evidence against
mixed feelings is fairly strong. Only, we saw
also that it is not conclusive.[6]

(4) A fourth criterion of affection is suggested
by Külpe. You will remember that Külpe classifies sensations as peripherally excited and centrally excited; the distinction corresponds to
that between sensation and image, and we shall
do well, perhaps, to employ the more familiar
terms. He classifies feelings in the same way,
as peripherally and centrally excited. Since,
however, very few psychologists agree with him
that affective processes can stand alone in consciousness, we shall do well, again, to phrase

the difference as that between the affection which accompanies a sensation and the affection which accompanies an image. Now the greatest disparity between sensation and image, Külpe says, shows on the side of intensity, and the intensive difference between the two processes is "normally recognised in every case by introspection." On the other hand, the affection which accompanies the image is "usually as vivid" — that means here, as intensive — as that which goes with the sensation. "Only the very highest degrees of sense-pleasure and sense-pain are now able to overpower the centrally excited, 'higher' feelings." Here, then, is our criterion. Image is weaker than sensation, but the image-affection is intensively equivalent to the sense-affection.

I wish to avoid all reference to the systematic question of affective reproduction, and I shall therefore let the phrase 'centrally excited affection' pass without comment. We know what Külpe means. But shall we accept the statement of fact upon which his criterion rests? Ladd very definitely does not. "In general," he writes, "ideal pleasures and pains, when measured by a strict standard of quantity, are much inferior to those occasioned by strong sensations." And more strongly still: "Ideal

pains and pleasures are not comparable in mere
intensity with sensuous pains and pleasures."
Contradiction could hardly be flatter. And contradiction is what we shall have, here and elsewhere in the psychology of feeling, until we can
work out an experimental control of introspection. As Wundt said long ago, "Selbstbeobachtung ist ausführbar, sie ist es aber nur unter
der Bedingung der experimentellen Beobachtung."

We cannot, however, leave the matter at this
point, since Stumpf has taken Külpe's suggestion seriously, and has brought two arguments
against it. First, of course, he rules out the
appeal to emotion; he denies the continuity of
sense-feeling and emotion. Then he says: suppose that Külpe's statement were literally and
universally true; still, the difference that he
signalises would not be very important. "Denn
wir finden unter den verschiedenen Sinnen doch
auch bei allem Gemeinsamen genug charakter-
istische Verschiedenheiten: der eine zeigt Simul-
tankontrast, der andere nicht, der eine zeigt
messbare Ausdehnungsunterschiede, der andere
nicht, u.s.w." He points out, also, that if you
regard sensation and image as the same in kind
and different only in degree, then Külpe's distinction loses its theoretical significance.

The second objection offers an alternative to Külpe's view. May it not be, Stumpf asks, that the image-affection is normally weaker than the sense-affection, — just as the image is normally weaker than the sensation, — but that the image-affection is very easily transformed into a sense-affection? In other words, may we not be liable "in ganz gewöhnlichen Fällen" to affective hallucinations, just as "unter besonderen Umständen" we are liable to hallucinatory images? No doubt, cause must be shown; but cause can be shown, Stumpf thinks, in terms of his own theory of *Gefühlsempfindungen*, — the theory which we are to discuss in the next Lecture.

I do not know how to meet the first objection. If the attributes available for definition are merely quality, intensity, extent, and duration, and if extent is not an universal attribute of sensation, then we might, certainly, classify the mental elements at large as spatial and non-spatial. The classification would, indeed, be superior to Külpe's distinction of sensation and affection, in the sense that it is based upon a difference observable in the single element, whereas Külpe's intensive criterion requires the presence, along with affection, of sensation or image. We should grow accustomed, after a while, to placing sight and touch in a class by themselves, and bracketing pleasantness-unpleasantness with tones and odours and the rest. At the same time, I hardly suppose that Stumpf meant his argument to be worked out in detail; the gist of it is, simply, that Külpe's difference is unimportant. And to that we can only reply that Külpe thinks it important, and that Ladd denies its existence.

The second objection stands or falls with Stumpf's personal views: its consideration must, therefore, be postponed.[7]

(5) It has been said that the fact of habituation, the loss or change of quality with lapse of time, marks off affection from sensation. The habitual sensation is indifferent, has ceased to affect us, while its sense-quality remains unchanged.

The obvious reply is that affective adaptation has its direct analogue in sensory adaptation. As we become adapted to colours, tastes, odours, pressures, so do we become habituated to pleasantness and unpleasantness. This is Stumpf's position. Ebbinghaus, on the contrary, finds only "eine verhältnismässig schwache Analogie" between the two sets of phenomena. We must therefore inquire further.

F

The statements in the text-books are conflicting. Külpe says that habituation means indifference. "There is no evidence that unpleasantness passes into pleasantness. Observations
that seem to point towards any such process are
referable to other causes. At least, the reverse
passage, of pleasantness into unpleasantness, will
be found to be of hardly less frequent occurrence; and no one would attempt to explain
it by habituation." Ebbinghaus declares that
"diese blosse Abschwächung der Gefühlswerte
erst eine Seite der Sache ist," and seeks to show
how, in terms of adaptation, pleasantness may
pass through indifference to unpleasantness and
unpleasantness through indifference to pleasantness, — the very occurrences that Külpe ex-
cludes. Both authors, I suppose, have Lehmann in mind; but they put a different estimate
upon Lehmann's conclusions.

Lehmann distinguishes between affective habituation to continuous and to intermittent
stimuli. Where the stimulus is continuous,
affective blunting is "ein rein scheinbares Phä-
nomen," pure illusion. You begin, we will say,
with a pleasantness. As time goes on, the sense-
organ becomes adapted; you have an "Abstumpfung der Empfindung" which naturally
means also an "Abstumpfung des Gefühls."

If the stimulus persists, unpleasurable sensations from foreign stimuli make incursion into consciousness, and the indifference becomes unpleasantness. The two factors, of sensory adaptation and foreign interference, may operate singly or in various combinations. Or you begin with an unpleasantness. This continues, with increasing intensity, until the onset of sensory adaptation in the form of nervous exhaustion. If indifference occurs, it occurs only when and because the sensory side of your experience drops out of consciousness; as soon as the sensation reappears, the unpleasantness reappears with it. You may, then, reach a stage of indifference, of forgetfulness, but the original unpleasantness never changes to the opposite quality.

Now turn to intermittent stimuli. You have, according to Lehmann, precisely the same phenomena as before: either the sensory side of the experience becomes obscure, through diversion of attention, or unpleasurable sensations from foreign sources invade consciousness, or both factors coöperate to change the original affective quality. But he goes on to point out that the intermittently repeated stimulus does not wholly lose its affective significance; there is a law of the 'indispensableness of the habitual.'

General sensory adaptation, the "Gewöhnung des Organismus," leaves a need, a "Bedürfnis." As the satisfaction of a need is pleasurable, you may have, in terms of this law, a shift of affective quality from unpleasant to pleasant; only, the shift is indirect, from unpleasantness of stimulus to indifference, from that to the unpleasantness of need, and from that again to the pleasantness of satisfaction. The converse change, from pleasant to unpleasant, is not mentioned by Lehmann.

Külpe, then, repeats Lehmann exactly. There is no evidence of the change, under habituation, from unpleasantness to pleasantness; Lehmann shows that the passage is indirect. No one would think of ascribing to habituation the change from pleasantness to unpleasantness; Lehmann says nothing of such change. Ebbinghaus, on the contrary, reinterprets Lehmann. He accepts the law of custom, of the indispensableness of the habitual, but makes the unpleasant stimulus pass directly, through indifference, to pleasantness. And he parallels this law by a law of tedium or ennui, which is realised when an originally pleasant stimulus passes directly, through indifference, to unpleasantness.

In my own opinion, affective habituation is

a phenomenon of the same order as sensory adaptation, and results always and only in indifference. Even if Ebbinghaus is correct, and quality passes into opposite quality, we have a sensory analogy in the case of vision: adaptation to yellow means blue-sightedness, local adaptation to green means a purple after-image. However, our present concern is with the difference between sensation and affection; and we have gone far enough with the phenomena of habituation to see that, in the present state of psychology, appeal to them is hopeless.[8]

(6) I have postponed to the last the discussion of a criterion which, to my mind, is the most obvious and the most important of all. It is this: that affections lack, what all sensations possess, the attribute of clearness. Attention to a sensation means always that the sensation becomes clear; attention to an affection is impossible. If it is attempted, the pleasantness or unpleasantness at once eludes us and disappears, and we find ourselves attending to some obtrusive sensation or idea that we had not the slightest desire to observe.

Külpe emphasises this difference between the elementary processes, and at the same time forestalls a misunderstanding. "A weakly pleasurable feeling," he writes, "is intensified by the direction of the attention upon its concomitant sensations, and an impression which stands on the border line between pleasantness and unpleasantness may be made unpleasant by an intense concentration of the attention upon it. In a certain sense, then, attention is a favourable condition for the feelings as it is for sensation." That is the removal of the possible misunderstanding. "But," Külpe goes on, "curiously enough, the result is quite different if attention is turned upon the feeling itself. It is a familiar fact that contemplation of the feelings, the devotion of special attention to them, lessens their intensity and prevents their natural expression. This diminution of intensity . . . [is shown by] a tendency of the affective contents to disappear altogether, to make way for the state of indifference. . . . Attention, then, is adverse to the feelings, when concentrated directly upon them." He then quotes the introspective report which accompanied certain experiments made by the method of expression. "The subject often insisted that the feeling had altogether disappeared under attention, and that it was very difficult, in any case, to attend to pleasantness or unpleasantness. Feeling has too little objectivity and substantiality for the attention to be directed and held upon it. It is focussed for a moment, and then other processes, especially organic sensations, interpose and take possession of the conscious fixation-point." And later on, when describing the effects of attention, he says: "While pleasure and pain (*Lust und Leid*) are brought far more vividly to consciousness by the concentration of attention upon their concomitant sensations, they disappear entirely when we succeed (and we can succeed only for a moment) in making the feeling as such the object of attentive observation."

I myself, in 1894, published a brief account of experiments which had led to a like result. Further evidence is furnished by Zoneff and Meumann. These investigators made experiments in which the observers were instructed to attend now to the stimulus, now to the feeling aroused by the stimulus. The instruction proved to be ambiguous. In certain cases, "man concentrirt sich, d. h. man behält das Gefühl willkürlich eine relativ längere Zeit im Blickpunkte des Bewusstseins und *analysirt* dasselbe. Es wird etwa darüber nachgedacht, ob das Gefühl mehr oder weniger angenehm bezw. unangenehm ist. Hier findet eine wirkliche Analyse des Gefühls statt, die von einer gewissen körperlichen Spannung begleitet ist." In other cases, "der

Reagent sucht sich das Gefühl möglichst *zum Bewusstsein* zu bringen, *ohne aber dasselbe zu analysiren*, oder mit anderen Worten, das Gefühl tritt in den Blickpunkt des Bewusstseins, *dabei bleibt es aber, es geschieht mit ihm nichts weiter.* Das Gefühl wird so zu sagen mit Hingebung gefühlt." As for the result: "eine blosse Richtung der Aufmerksamkeit auf das Gefühl [the second case] verstärkt dasselbe, wird dagegen das Gefühl zum Gegenstand einer psychologischen Analyse gemacht und in diesem Sinne Gegenstand der Aufmerksamkeit, so wird es bedeutend geswächt, ja sogar ganz aufgehoben."

The general sense of these passages is clear. The unpractised observers, when instructed to 'attend' to the feeling, thought that they were to do the best they could for it, to assume the mental attitude most favourable to it; to resign themselves passively to the feeling, to let it have its way with them. Under these conditions, the feeling naturally attained its fullest intensity. The more practised observers — this distinction is drawn by the authors, not by me — sought to abstract from the sensible concomitants, and to attend strictly to the affective contents as such. Under these conditions, the feeling was notably weakened, if not entirely destroyed.

I say that the general sense of the passages is

clear. The wording, however, is obscure and can be justified, if at all, only by the consideration that Zoneff and Meumann are purposely taking a non-committal position as regards systematic questions. Thus, the unpractised observers certainly did not 'direct their attention to the feeling' in the same sense that one directs one's attention to a sensation. So far from attending, reaching out to the feeling, they sat back and let the feeling come. The very fact that they did this — that they instinctively refrained from attention to the feeling itself, in order to give it first place in consciousness — shows how unnatural, not to say impossible, the literal instruction was. Again, the practised observers are said to 'analyse the feeling.' But how could they 'analyse' what a few pages back has been called an 'elementary' feeling? What they did was to ideate the feeling, to reflect upon it, to ask themselves questions about it: all this, in the vain effort to hold it as a sensation is held. Once more: what is meant by the presence of a feeling "im Blickpunkte des Bewusstseins"? The associations that come with the phrase are drawn from the sphere of sensory attention, so that here Zoneff and Meumann seem to have departed from their non-committal attitude. You cannot, after all, free yourself

from 'Voreingenommenheit' by a fiat of will;
you have approached the problem by way of
certain concepts, and though you deny them
your speech will betray you.

In his recently published *Experimentelle Pädagogik*, Meumann writes as follows: "[Es] muss
noch von emotionaler und voluntionaler [!] Aufmerksamkeit gesprochen werden, denn unsre
Aufmerksamkeit kann sich ebensogut auf Willenshandlungen und Gefühle richten und es ist
ein blosses theoretisches Vorurteil, wenn das
von manchen Psychologen geleugnet wird. Sie
können sich jederzeit selbst davon überzeugen,
dass wir unsre Gefühle einer analysierenden
Beobachtung zu unterziehen vermögen, wie
jeden anderen Bewusstseinszustand, dann richtet
sich die analysierende Aufmerksamkeit auf das
Gefühl."   I must confess that this passage stag-
gers me.   Anybody at any time may convince
himself that he can attend to his feelings?   And
yet, four years earlier, Meumann had attached a
"quite especial importance" to his and Zoneff's
experimental work on that point, and had stressed
the fact that "'die Richtung der Aufmerksamkeit' auf ein psychisches Erlebniss ein sehr
vieldeutiger Ausdruck ist, mit dem ganz hetero-
gene Vorgänge bezeichnet werden."   But, you
will say, he speaks now of 'analytical observa-

tion,' 'analytical attention.' So he does, —
without defining the adjective. And then this
analytical attention to the feelings is of the same
order as analytical attention to "any other state
of consciousness." Four years earlier we were
told that the feelings were "bedeutend ge-
schwächt, ja sogar ganz aufgehoben"! —

I began this discussion with a reference to
Külpe. I did so, because I know of no experiments earlier than his. The doctrine which I
am defending — "der Schlendrian der alten
Aufmerksamkeitstheorie" which, according to
Meumann, is a mere theoretical prepossession
— is, of course, very much older. It is aptly
phrased, *e.g.*, by Hamilton. "Reflection," he
says, "is properly attention directed to the phenomena of mind." "We are, indeed, able to
constitute our states of pain and pleasure into
objects of reflection, but in so far as they are
objects of reflection, they are not feelings, but
only reflex cognitions of feelings." It is fully
worked out by Ward. It is implicit in Wundt's
theory of feeling as the "Reaction der Apperception auf das einzelne Bewusstseinserlebniss,"
the "Reactionsweise der Apperception auf den
Bewusstseinsinhalt." Külpe's acceptance of the
Wundtian theory is grounded upon the implication; and Wundt's own language is exceed-

ingly careful. Hollands writes : "Concerning the method of feeling-analysis, we find the statement that feeling . . . cannot be isolated as an object of attention. . . . This is the invariable teaching of Wundt." Even when Wundt slips, he furnishes his own corrective. While, *e.g.*, he speaks incautiously, in one passage, of the 'apperception' of the affective tone of an obscurely perceived sensation, he explains in another that well-marked feelings may accompany a 'Vorstellungsinhalt' which "wegen der vorwaltenden Richtung der Aufmerksamkeit" is not apperceived; and the two accounts refer to the same experience.

I need not multiply quotations. No doubt, there are dissentient voices. Saxinger, for instance, cites Lehmann to the effect that we are able, by voluntary direction of attention, to bring a feeling to the forefront of consciousness. True, this is a misquotation : Lehmann speaks, in fact, of the direction of attention upon a "betonte Vorstellung," not upon a feeling; but Saxinger's words show that he, at any rate, has no difficulty in conceiving of attention to a feeling. Indeed, he speaks, a little later on, of the 'Beleuchtung' of feelings by the attention. And the authors who identify affection with sensation must, of necessity, take Saxinger's view, — unless they avoid the present issue altogether. On the whole, however, I think that this sixth criterion stands its ground more firmly than any of the others that we have considered.[9]

What, now, is to be our general conclusion? This, I think: that two of the proposed criteria of affection must probably be given up; that two others are extremely instable; and that two deserve very serious consideration. The two that we must apparently discard are those furnished by habituation and by central intensity. The two that we pronounce doubtful are those of subjectivity and of non-localisableness. The two that, at any rate, give us pause are those of qualitative antagonism and lack of clearness.

This statement is as near as I can get to an impartial verdict. The whole discussion illustrates the difficulty of discriminating between elementary processes in any other way than by appeal to experience itself. And I would ask you to remember that that appeal still remains. All of the distinctions between sensation and affection profess to be drawn from experience; the wording may be clumsy, or suggestive, or individually coloured; but the difference itself is either there or not there, in your own introspection.

I would ask you, also, to remember one other thing. A psychologist who definitely accepts any single criterion, and so makes affection an independent mental element, may very well revise our conclusion, and ascribe value to criteria that we have disputed or rejected. We have proceeded serially, taking each distinction by itself. That was necessary, in the interests of clearness; but I do not know that it was quite fair. If, for instance, we were to consider subjectivity and coextension with consciousness along with antagonism and lack of clearness, making the four characters interdependent, as, to a large extent, they really are, we could, I believe, considerably strengthen the case for an elementary affection. I can do no more than mention the point here; I shall recur to it, briefly, in my concluding Lecture.[10]

III

THE AFFECTIONS AS *GEFÜHLSEMPFINDUNGEN*

LECTURE III

THE AFFECTIONS AS *GEFÜHLSEMP-FINDUNGEN*

MANY attempts have been made, and for various reasons, to identify affection with sensation, and thus to reduce all the mental elements to a single kind. We must rule out of consideration here, as we did also in the previous Lecture, anything that savours of epistemology. For that matter, there is more than enough to occupy us on the purely psychological plane; the introspective resemblance between pleasantness-unpleasantness, on the one hand, and certain sensations, on the other, has been urged again and again in the history of psychology. I take two modern instances. Bourdon, in 1893, identifies pleasure with the sensation of tickling. "Le plaisir est une sensation spéciale et non pas une sensation commune ni une propriété de toutes les sensations; et il est de même nature que la sensation spéciale de chatouillement." "Le plaisir serait un chatouillement diffus, de faible intensité, tandis qu'au contraire le chatouillement serait en quelque sort un plaisir bien localisé et de grande intensité." [1]   In 1894 von Frey, working from the opposite direction, identifies unpleasantness with pain, while he makes pleasantness a negative matter, absence or cessation of pain. "Der Schmerz," he says, "[ist] die einfachste Form des Unlustgefühls"; and "die tägliche Erfahrung lehrt, dass es die *Aufhebung* des Schmerzes ist, welche uns Lust bereitet." [2]   Bourdon is able to quote, on behalf of his theory, authorities as high as Descartes and Bain; [3] and von Frey, though he does not say so, is championing a doctrine of pleasure which is as old as Plato. [4]

I do not, however, intend to enter upon the history of our subject; that would take me too far afield. I intend only to expound and criticise one notable attempt, made very recently, to bring the sense-feelings, all simple affective experience, under the rubric of sensation. I refer to Stumpf's paper *Ueber Gefühlsempfindungen*, which was read before the Society for Experimental Psychology at Würzburg in April, 1906, and was published in December of the same year, with slight additions and modifications, in the *Zeitschrift für Psychologie*. [5]

The range of Stumpf's inquiry is limited to what are ordinarily called the 'sense-feelings,' *die sinnlichen Gefühle.* These include, "first, the purely bodily pains (that is, those which appear without any essential concernment of intellectual functions *), whether they are set up from without or from within the organism; secondly, the feeling of bodily well-being in its more general and its more special forms, the latter including the pleasure-component in tickling, the feeling produced by itching, and the sexual feelings; and lastly the agreeableness and disagreeableness that may be connected, in the most various degrees or gradations, with the sensations of all or nearly all the 'special' senses, with temperatures, odours, tastes, tones, colours." The point of view which the inquiry adopts is primarily descriptive.[6]

We begin with a discussion of the three possible views of elementary affective process.[7] The affection may be an attribute of sensation, — an 'affective tone' of sensation. Or the affection may be a mental element, distinct from and coördinate with sensation. Or, lastly, the affection may be itself a sensation, a sensation of a special kind, like the visual or the kinæsthetic.

The first of these three views Stumpf disposes of as it deserves. It is a view which received its

---

* I take this to be the meaning of the phrase "ohne integrierende Beteiligung intellektueller Funktionen."

coup de grâce at the hands of Külpe in 1893,[8] —
the year of publication, be it remembered, of
the fourth edition of the *Physiologische Psychologie*, in which affection still figures as a 'third
attribute' of sensation.[9] Külpe points out that
affection cannot be an attribute of sensation of
the same sort as the recognised attributes, because it has attributes of its own. Sensations
show differences of intensity, quality, time, and
(in some instances) space; affection shows differences of intensity, quality, and time. Ziehen,
in the 1906 edition of his *Leitfaden*, seeks to meet
this argument. "Dem gegenüber verweise ich
Sie auf das Beispiel eines chemischen Prozesses
(z. B. einer Oxydation), welche selbst eine bestimmte Intensität und Qualität hat und oft
zugleich noch von einem Licht von bestimmter
Intensität und Qualität begleitet ist."[10] Stumpf
replies, rightly, that the attribute of an object,
as these terms are employed in everyday life,
is one thing; and that the attribute of a sensation, as these terms are employed in psychology,
is another and a very different thing. An
'object' is an empirical collocation of attributes
which are themselves sensations or sense-deriva-
tives; we can think away the scent of a flower,
and leave the flower a concrete object as it was
before. But the attributes of sensation are

known only by abstraction; they are the modes
of variation of a wholly simple contents; we
cannot think any one of them away without at
the same time thinking away the sensation.[11]
Stumpf's rejoinder thus leads us to Külpe's
second argument: that the annihilation of an
attribute of sensation carries with it the disappearance of the sensation, whereas a sensation
may be non-affective, indifferent, and still be
far removed from disappearance. I do not see
how these arguments can possibly be answered,
and I agree with Stumpf that "man sich wundern
muss, wie [die betreffende Anschauung] immer
noch von manchen festgehalten werden kann." [12]
Yet we find Marshall, in January of the present
year, positing an 'algedonic quality' of sensation:
"each elementary presentation must display
either agreeableness or disagreeableness, or
indifference which is a mode of transition between the other two." [13]   What is this 'mode of
transition'?   If it is really indifference, neither
pleasantness nor unpleasantness, it is nothing
at all; and how can nothing at all be a 'quality'?   If it is indifference in the affective sense,
the indifference of satiety, of 'having had enough
of a thing,' of 'being tired of it,' then — as
Ziegler says — "hat das Gleichgültige stets etwas
vom Unangenehmen an sich"; [14]   indifference

is a stage on the road to aversion, nausea, disgust; it is already unpleasant, not a 'mode of transition' from pleasantness to unpleasantness. I have been told that, in philosophy, errors never die; and it may be that they die hard, in psychology, because that earlier habit of immortality is still strong upon them.

There remain, then, the alternatives: that affection is a second mental element, and that it is a kind of sensation. Stumpf here throws the burden of proof upon the advocates of affective independence. Unless the differences between sensation and affection are primary and universal, the separation of the processes runs counter to the scientific principle of economy.[15] He accordingly reviews the three principal arguments of his opponents: the relation of sense-feeling to emotion, the subjectivity of feeling, and its lack of spatial localisation and extension.[16] What he has to say on these topics we already know; his objections were mentioned and allowed their due weight in the preceding Lecture. You will remember that he makes a sharp division, in his own system, between sense-feeling and the higher, intellectual feelings, the *Affekte oder Gemütsbewegungen*, and that he definitely rejects the two remaining criteria. I will only add now that he has, in my opinion, passed too

lightly over certain other proposed criteria; and
that the appeal to a 'principle of economy' is
worth very little, because the appeal in science
lies always to the facts of observation. However, it is precisely to the facts that Stumpf
next takes us.

He opens with a section on 'sensations of
pain, and the sensations of pleasure (*Lustempfindungen*) that take their origin from cutaneous
stimulations or from vegetative states.'[17] And he
makes every effort, at the outset, to prove that
pain is a department of sense, and the pain-quality a quality of sensation. "Es ist also die Isolie-
rung dieser Empfindungsqualität, sozusagen die
Reinzüchtung des Gefühlssinnes, gelungen."[18]
"Die principielle Frage, auf die es für uns
gegenwärtig ankommt, ist . . . ob es Schmerz-
empfindungen in der gleichen Bedeutung wie
Farbenempfindungen,   Geruchsempfindungen
gebe, als echte und eigentliche Sinnesquälita-
ten."[19] Let me say at once that nobody, who
knows anything at first hand of the psychology of
cutaneous sensation, would be tempted nowadays
to traverse this position. That there is a sense
of pain is a fact as well established as that there
is a sense of pressure. So far, I agree entirely
with Stumpf. Nevertheless, there are two points
in his exposition, two very closely related points,

that seem to invite criticism. The first concerns
the nature of the pain-quality, and the second
the nature of the unpleasantness of pain.

Stumpf is fully convinced of the painfulness
of the pain-quality. "Der Schmerz ist eben
schmerzhaft, dass ist seine berechtigte Eigen-
tümlichkeit, daran kann, glaube ich, selbst die
feinste Psychologie nichts ändern." [20] Believers
in a separate affective process regard the underlying sensation in the experience of pain as painless, *schmerzlos;* "während wir uns zu der
Ansicht geführt sehen, dass das sogenannte
Schmerzgefühl die sinnliche Qualität selbst ist,
und dass der Schmerz in jener angeblichen
nur zugrundeliegenden Sinnesempfindung schon
durchaus komplett gegeben ist." [21] A difficulty
arises, of course, in connection with the sensation
of prick or sting. Goldscheider expressly remarks that his 'secondary sensation' need not
be painful; under the most favourable conditions
it is a "fein-*stechendes* Gefühl von nicht schmerz-
haftem Charakter." [22] And the 'Stichempfind-
ungen' aroused directly by cutaneous stimulation
are not painful. Stumpf meets the difficulty by
suggesting that the sensations in question may
belong to the sense of pressure. But he does
not, in any case, regard it as momentous; whether
the 'Stichempfindung' is mediated by the nerves

of pressure or by the nerves of pain, the important thing is the appearance of pain as a sensible quality.

That is the first point. In the second place, Stumpf looks upon the unpleasantness of pain, not as concomitant affective process, but as the qualitative character of pain itself. To add an affective tone of unpleasantness, he says, "scheint mir zwecklos." [23] Why should you call upon a second genus of mental elements to make a thing what it is in its own right, — to make a pain painful? [24] We hear sometimes of pleasurable pains; but the phrase is misleading. You may, perhaps, have pain-sensations and agreeable sensations at one and the same time from different regions of the skin, and the two qualities may possibly enhance each other, "by a kind of contrast"; but that is not the same thing as feeling an agreeable pain. The pleasures of asceticism and of martyrdom are matters of emotion; the sensible pain either persists, but is held in check by intellectual rapture, or disappears in the analgesia of the ecstatic state. Pain, then, falls into line with the other sensations just by reason of the fact, paradoxical as it may seem, that it has *no* affective tone.[25]—

I pointed out in my first Lecture that stimulation of a pain-spot gives qualitatively different

sensations, according to the intensity of the
stimulus.   At a very low intensity we have itch;
then prick or sting; and lastly, at higher intensities, pain.   The observation demands a certain
amount of technical skill, and calls for a responsive pain-spot; but I cannot doubt its accuracy.
It seems, then, doubly unfortunate that Stumpf
has claimed the sensation of itch as a sensation
of *pleasure*.[26] Psychophysically, it is a weak
sensation of pain; itch passes into sting, and
sting into pain, within the same peripheral
organ.   Psychologically, itch is not pleasure,
but itch; its quality is not pleasurable, but
itchy. The psychophysical question was raised
by Stumpf only in order to be dismissed, and
I do not wish on my side to intrude psychophysical considerations into a piece of
descriptive psychology.   I merely note that
"identische Nervenfasern" [27] presumably mediate 'Lustempfindungen' as well as pain and
painless sting.   But the psychological argument is important. In a passage already
quoted, Stumpf speaks of "das durch Jucken
entstehende Gefühl" and of the "Lustkom-
ponente des Kitzels."   In both expressions,
the pleasure seems to be something additional
to, superadded upon, the sense-quality proper.
The feeling produced *by* itching, or arising

through itch, is not — if language means anything — the itch-quality itself; and if itch is a
special form of pleasurable sensation, there
must be some mark or sign upon it to inform
us of the fact. In pain, the quality tells its
own story; pain is painful. How does itch
— which, by the same reasoning, is just itchy
— tell us that it is pleasant?

Let us see how the psychologist of affection
would read the facts. Itch, he would say, is a
sensible quality which is ordinarily attended by
pleasantness. Itch passes into sting, which
may be weakly pleasant, or indifferent, or slightly
unpleasant. Sting passes into pain, which is
ordinarily attended by unpleasantness. Under
certain circumstances, itch may be unpleasant;
an itch that is widely diffused over the skin, or
that persists for a long time, and more especially
an itch that is both widely diffused and of long
duration, may be distinctly unpleasant. Here,
as elsewhere in sensation, space and time may
produce the effect of intensity.[28] Pain is, of
course, always painful, in the sense that it always
shows the pain-quality; it is painful, that is,
just as sting is stinging and itch is itchy. I
cannot understand how Stumpf reaches the conclusion that, for the advocates of an independent
affective process, the pain-quality ceases to be

pain, becomes *schmerzlos*. But the pain-quality need not always be unpleasant, — that is the point upon which issue must be taken with Stumpf. It is not easy to find instances, though I think that they are not uncommon in daily life. Ebbinghaus cites the scratching of an irritated area of the skin: [29] and it is true, in my observation, that if you rub the nails of the right-hand fingers briskly up and down over the back of the left hand you get, particularly when the hand is dry and the skin a little rough, lines of pain that are undeniably pleasant; though the consequent after-image is sore, and undeniably unpleasant. Kelchner says, apropos of one of her experiments: "hier macht Vp. die Angabe, dass das Abklingen des physischen Schmerzes von schwacher Lust begleitet sei, — ein Ausspruch, der wieder den *Empfindungscharakter* des Schmerzes zu bezeugen scheint." [30] The sensory character of pain is above the need of witnesses; but the testimony to the possible pleasantness of weakly intensive pain is valuable. Stumpf's illustration of pain-sensations (*i.e.* disagreeable sensations) and agreeable sensations, set up simultaneously at different parts of the skin, and enhancing each other by a sort of contrast, is, of course, hypothetical only; it is not intended to describe an experience of his own. For that reason, and also because it raises further questions of the distribution of attention and of the nature of the contrast-effect, we need not seriously consider it.

Which, now, has made out the better case? Stumpf, who terms itch a *Lustempfindung* and pain an *Unlustempfindung*, or the affective psychologist who declares that both itch and pain may be, according to circumstances, pleasant, indifferent, or unpleasant? —

I may pass over Stumpf's mention of the internal, organic pains.[31]   When we turn to his discussion of the sensations of pleasure, we find the same general difficulty that I have just remarked in the special instance of itch. "Annehmlichkeit, Wohlsein," he says, "[ist] die zweite Hauptqualität des Gefühlssinnes." [32] And he distinguishes, among cutaneous pleasures, tickling, itch, and lust; among vegetative pleasures, satiety, repose, and general comfortableness (*allgemeines Wohlbehagen*). Yet he says that the question of the "Gleichartigkeit aller Lustempfindungen" may be left open! [33]   Now, if *Annehmlichkeit* is a sensible quality, there must obviously be different kinds of it; how do we distinguish itch from tickling, tickling from lust, lust from satiety, and so on, save by their qualitative differences?   If, on the other hand, all the sense-pleasures are of the same kind, then certainly such diverse things as lust and satiety cannot be exhaustively described as 'sense-pleasures'; they are that, and they are something that is qualitatively differentiated as well. Is it not clear that, with the best will in the world, Stumpf cannot wholly rid himself of the doctrine that he is combating, — that this doctrine creeps into the argument with all the seeming inevitableness of fact? [34]

Stumpf's second section deals with the 'affective tone' of the remaining senses, the agreeableness and disagreeableness of temperatures, pressures, odours, tastes, colours, tones.[35] He begins by drawing a valid distinction between very intensive and moderate or weak stimulation. Where the stimulus is very strong, or abnormally strong, he says, it is likely to involve pain-organs, over and above the organ to which it is specifically addressed. Temperature-pains and pressure-pains are pains proper, due to stimulation of the cutaneous pain-spots. The pains of blinding light and of deafening noise are, introspectively, of essentially similar character, and may be referred, with a high degree of probability, to contraction of the iris and of the muscles of the middle ear.[36] All this we may cheerfully grant; and its result is that certain experiences, which at first thought would seem to fall within the sphere of pressure or temperature, sight or hearing, are in reality phenomena of cutaneous or organic pain, and thus have already received implicit consideration in the foregoing section. We stand, theoretically, where we stood at the completion of that section. "Aehnliche Betrachtungen," Stumpf goes on, "lassen sich auch über die peripherisch durch starke Reizungen erregten Lustempfindungen anstellen." [37] Here, I think, he falls into that schematism as regards pleasure which is one of the besetting sins of the sensationalists. Are they not all apt to give full details concerning pain, and then to say, offhand, 'Just the same thing holds, *mutatis mutandis*, of pleasure'? The passage must mean that pleasures of touch or temperature, sight or sound, aroused by intensive peripheral stimulation, depend for their pleasurableness upon the coexcitation of the organs of tickling, itch, lust, etc. What is Stumpf thinking of? The 'feel' of silk next the skin is exceedingly pleasant, — but largely so, most of us would say, because it does *not* tickle. And silk is not an intensive stimulus. It is pleasant to come into a warm room when one is chilled with the cold. But while, under such circumstances, we may get circulatory sensations of tingling, it is not necessary, in my experience, that we have either tickle or itch.　It is pleasant to turn the eyes from the white glare of snow to the dull green of fir, and it is a relief to the ear when a factory whistle ceases to sound.　But the evergreens and the silence are not intensive peripheral stimuli.　Perhaps Stumpf has in mind such things as the pleasure of violent bodily exercise and the supreme comfort of a Turkish bath, — organic rather than peripheral pleasures.　But where is the analogue of these pleasures in the domain of sight or hearing ? —

We come now to the crux of the whole argument: to the explanation of the agreeableness and disagreeableness of moderate or weak stimulation in the departments of vision and audition, taste and smell.　This 'affective tone' Stumpf regards as a 'concomitant sensation' ("das Wort Mitempfindung im weitesten Sinne genommen").[38]　Psychologically, a concomitant sensation is, of course, a sensation like any other, an elementary mental process with a certain status in consciousness and a certain set of attributes.　We should therefore expect, since on Stumpf's own admission there is no such thing, in strictness, as indissoluble association,[39] that he would at once cast about for instances of dissociation, and would seek to show us the 'affective sensation' in isolation. Instead of doing this, he offers us reasons for shifting the scene of our debate from sensation to idea. Why is it, he asks, that we can *not* sense the agreeableness of a colour or a scent alone, without being obliged at the same time to sense the colour as visual and the scent as olfactory quality? [40]

Well! Stumpf replies, there might be anatomical reasons. It might be a matter of physiological fact that the excitation underlying agreeableness cannot be set up independently of the excitation underlying colour or odour. And after all, it was only the other day that physiologists succeeded in separately stimulating the cutaneous pain-organs; here too, then, the future may bring results that we cannot now foresee. Or, again, we might think that colour and the agreeableness of colour are intimately fused, as are, *e.g.*, taste and smell, or the two tones of the octave. Or, lastly, it is possible, even probable, that the concomitant sensations of agreeableness and disagreeableness are sensations of central origin. In that case, we can separate them from their companions, if at all, only by change of central conditions, not by modification of peripheral stimulation.

I would call your attention to the fact that two

H

of these arguments are psychophysical, and that
the third, if it is not psychophysical, is irrelevant.
To talk of anatomical reasons for the conjunction of colour with agreeableness of colour, and
to talk of that agreeableness as a centrally excited
concomitant sensation, — to talk in this way is
to leave the field of descriptive psychology for
the field of psychophysics.   And it seems to me,
in general, that Stumpf is inclined to bar out
psychophysical reference where it does not support his views, and to bring it in, without apology,
wherever it can furnish him with even a speculative confirmation.[41]   I know very well that
sweeping criticism of this kind is likely to be both
unfair and ineffective.   I have, however, too
much respect for Stumpf to be consciously unfair, and too serious a concern for my own position to be consciously ineffective.   My general
impression is as I have stated; and I believe that,
if you read Stumpf's paper for yourselves, you
will come to the same conclusion.   At all events,
the appeal in these two cases lies, frankly, to
psychophysics.   So it does also in the third
argument, if that is relevant.   Psychologically,
the fusion of the octave, under the most favourable conditions, is analysable into its two constituent tones: here, then, is no analogy.   Psychologically, the blends of taste and smell are

not analysable; the most experienced psychologist cannot tell, by introspection, that the 'taste'
of his coffee is partly taste and partly smell.
Only by psychophysical procedure — by holding the nose, or what not — can the components
in the blend be separated. In other words, it
is only as subject-matter of psychophysics that
the taste-smell blend may be termed a fusion.
And the analogy that it affords to the fusion of
colour and agreeableness of colour is, therefore,
a psychophysical analogy. There remains the
possibility that we may some day isolate the
pleasure-organs of vision as we have already isolated the pain-organs of the skin. How serious
that is, I leave you to judge for yourselves.

My objection is not by any means to psychophysics as such. I do object, however, to the
basing of a psychological argument upon a
speculative psychophysics. And we have a
peculiar right to object, in the present instance,
because Stumpf promised us a descriptive psychology. "Wir wollen nicht," he says, "Behaupt-
ungen über die anatomischen Gebilde oder die
physiologischen Prozesse aufstellen, die den
sinnlichen Gefühlen zugrunde liegen."[42] What
else, then, is he now doing? His text stands as
I have given it; psychological considerations are
relegated to a footnote. In the text, Stumpf has

accepted the inseparability of colour and agreeableness of colour as a fact; in the note, he cites
four cases which appear to tell against the fact,
— though he himself practically reduces them to
two.   Scripture infers, from his experiments on
association of ideas, that feeling may stand alone
in consciousness; but the results, we are told,
admit of very various interpretations. Vogt
reaches the same conclusion by way of his method
of hypnotic suggestion; "über die Brauchbar-
keit dieser Methode," says Stumpf, "habe ich
kein Urteil."   There remain Kiesow's investigation of the taste-feelings, in which sensible
was paralleled by affective discrimination, and
Stumpf's own work with beating and dissonant
tones.   Kiesow, however, was simply attempt-
ing a quantitative form of the method of impression; and Stumpf's experiences simply illustrate the occurrence of affective habituation or
adaptation.[43]

We are still only on the threshold of the discussion.   The essential thing in Stumpf's view,
you remember, is not that colour and agreeableness of colour should be separable in sensation,
but that they should be separable in idea.   He
clearly sees — no doubt, he saw very early in
the course of this inquiry — that the agreeableness and disagreeableness of tone and colour,

taste and smell, cannot possibly be constituted a class of sensations in the ordinary meaning of that term, — cannot possibly be put on a level with pain and tickle and itch. The psychophysical hypotheses which I have just been criticising are therefore introduced to explain how two mental processes, possibly separate in idea, may be altogether inseparable in sensation. If the explanation is accepted, if we waive the objection that something which is termed a sensation cannot be separately sensed, then we are free to enter upon the argument which will lead us through separateness in idea to the theory of central concomitance. You see, I hope, how pivotal those psychophysical hypotheses were, although Stumpf brings them in as it were parenthetically, by way of excursus. A little speculative physiology — and we are prepared to revise our definition of sensation, and to look for proof of sensory character in the realm of ideas!

This whole question of ideation, or (to put it in more elementary terms) of the existence of an affective image, is very thorny. More than a decade ago I argued, as against Ribot, that there is no such thing as affective reproduction, but only affective renewal or revival.[44] I should argue to the same effect to-day, though with greater caution in statement and with less as-

surance of carrying conviction. For before the
question can be settled, we must, I think, know
a great deal more than we do of sense-imagery,
and particularly of the range of images of organic
sensations. In an early number of Woodbridge's *Journal* I gave an account of my own
organic images, such as they are; expressed
myself as rather sceptical of any great freedom or
variety of organic imagery in general; and urged
the importance of further work.[45] Let me repeat
here that further work — systematic observation by competent observers — is badly needed.
Stumpf, now, takes a positive attitude, while
he admits the fact of individual differences.
"Die Schmerz- und Lustempfindungen, die
durch Hautreizungen oder durch die Tätigkeit
der vegetativen Organe bedingt sind, hinterlassen
zweifellos auch Gedächtnisbilder, blosse Vorstellungen." [46] He is apparently speaking from
personal experience, since he says later: "auch
mir scheint z. B. die Vorstellung eines Stich-
schmerzes möglich, und zwar mit dem Charakter einer reproduzierten Vorstellung in demselben Sinne, wie wir von Farben- und Tonvorstellung reden." [47] I wish that we had been
given more details. The passage from which the
first quotation is taken goes on to point out the
occurrence of hallucinations of pain, — another

subject, surely, which invites psychological investigation. The paragraph ends, rather curiously, with the words, "ähnliches auch bei den Vorstellungen der Wollüstigen." I say 'curiously,' because the words ought to mean that the voluptuary has images, or even hallucinations, of his own lust-sensations, whereas it seems obvious that the images must be images of some voluptuous situation, and that lust itself is present, not as image, but as sensation.

On the topic of what I should call the affective image proper, the image or reproduced idea of the agreeableness and disagreeableness that attach to scents and colours and tones, Stumpf's attitude is similarly positive. He speaks again from personal experience; the affective image which accompanies the memory-image of a major triad or of a Böcklin picture seems to him to be distinct and vivid.[48] Since he says on the same page, "natürlich müssen die Fälle, in denen offenbar Denktätigkeiten und Affekte mit im Spiele sind, wie das Wohlgefallen an einer Melodie oder einem Bildwerk, beiseite bleiben," we must suppose that he is, in reality, thinking of the constituent tones in the chord and the constituent colours in the picture, not of the chord as harmony and the picture as work of art. He further remarks that these affective images "sehr leicht in Gefühlsempfindungen übergehen"; that is, that we are ordinarily liable in their case to affective hallucinations, such as occur only occasionally in the case, *e.g.*, of peripheral pain. If you ideate the sound of a friend's voice, or of a musical chord, the affective quality may be as vivid as in actual hearing, while the tonal quality has all the marks of a representation.

There are, then, images of the agreeableness and disagreeableness which come with the sensations of the higher senses. They are fleeting; to illustrate them, Stumpf has to cite complex ideas like those of a chord or a picture: [49] but they exist. Now, then, we may raise the critical question, and ask whether colour image and image of agreeableness are separable, — whether, as we put it just now, a colour and its agreeableness are separate in idea.

We need not expect, Stumpf says, that the separation will be easy. Think of odours: the people who have smell-images can rarely evoke them without at the same time evoking the memory picture of the flower or fruit or whatever it is that the scent connects with in sensation. "Ich selbst kann mir u. a. den Heliotropgeruch gut vorstellen, aber nur unter dieser Bedingung." The separation, then, will be difficult: only, it should not be impossible.[50]

Let us look at the senses in order. For most
men, the single colour and the single tone are, in
sensation, practically indifferent. "Es wird uns
oft recht schwer, zu sagen, ob eine Farbe mehr
angenehm oder mehr unangenehm ist, oder ob
sie angenehmer ist als eine andere." [51] Individual organisation and temporary disposition
may afford exceptions to this rule: "aber im
ganzen sind die rein sinnlichen Gefühlswirkungen
isolierter Farben (einschliesslich der Graunu-
ancen) und isolierter Töne (einschliesslich der
Geräusche) relativ gering." I think that Stumpf,
even with the allowances that he makes, is here
arguing too schematically. No doubt, a patch
of red on the book-shelf and the sound of middle
C from the piano, as they break into our everyday
consciousness, leave us "most uncommon calm."
But many men — Wundt is an example, among
psychologists — are extraordinarily sensitive to
the affective value of single colours and single
tones; and one is surprised that Stumpf himself
should so lightly brush aside the *Tongefühle*.
Again, when colours and tones are presented
methodically, as by the serial method or the
method of paired comparisons, it is the exception that they are indifferent; the rule is
definitely the other way. Perhaps, however,
this is what Stumpf has in mind, when he

refers to "augenblickliche Nervendisposition," as he may have Wundt and himself in mind when he refers to "individuelle Organisation." Take, then, more obvious cases. If isolated patches of colour and isolated tones are usually indifferent, what of masses of colour: the carmine or purple or orange sweep of an uniformly coloured sunset sky? the high blue of a tropical sea, the white of extended snow, the yellow-brown of a sandy shore, the dull lead or slate of lake or ocean? I am not thinking of landscape and seascape, of emotion and reflection, but of the colours themselves, given sensibly to the eye. And what of certain noises: harsh, rough, grating, scraping, crunching, sickening noises? Surely, there is case upon case, instance upon instance, in which colours and sounds possess a high degree of agreeableness or disagreeableness. Stumpf ignores them all, and concludes that the affective tone is too weak, in sensation, to come separately into consciousness as idea. But — cannot weak sensations, then, be ideated? Fechner believed and Ebbinghaus believes that you can ideate the just noticeable sensation and the just noticeable difference between sensations; [52] is there anything weaker? And apart from that, which is a technical matter, is it not a fact of daily experience that weak sensations may be imaged?

Think now of a *diminuendo* on the violin, of the
faint anticipatory glow of a rising moon, of the
suspicion of a breath of garlic in a savoury salad :
if you have images in these sense-departments at
all, you will have no difficulty in imaging such
weakest sensations.

Stumpf, nevertheless, has disposed of sight and
hearing. He turns to taste and smell, and first
of all quotes Nagel's very definite statement with
regard to smell. "So leicht es mir ist," we read
in the *Handbuch*, " das mit einer Geruchsemp-
findung verbundene Lust- oder Unlustgefühl
zu reproduzieren, so unmöglich ist es bezüglich
der eigentlichen Geruchsqualität." [53] The statement is definite, but none the less ambiguous ;
for the term 'reproduction' may cover a multitude of possible experiences. Stumpf finds, by
personal inquiry, that Nagel's 'reproductions' are
always mediated by association ; Nagel can call
up, *e.g.*, the agreeableness of the smell of tar,
without reproducing that odour itself, but the
pleasantness appears to depend "auf den, wenn
auch unbewussten, Nachwirkungen von Schif-
fahrtserlebnissen." [54] The revised statement is
not wholly clear ; but Stumpf concludes that the
feeling in question is rather a mood, a *Stimmung*, than an elementary *Gefühlsempfindung*,
and so rules it out of the discussion. Nagel's

reproductions of the disagreeableness of odours are always connected with other images (the disagreeableness of ammonia, *e.g.*, with pricking and stinging in the nose), so that they furnish no proof of separability in idea. And notice that, all through, we have no strict guarantee of the arousal of an affective *image;* Nagel's 'reproductions' may very well be renewals, reinstatements of feeling, — what Stumpf calls 'hallucinations.'

That is all that we hear about smell. As for taste, Stumpf suggests that the mere sight or name of oysters may arouse in the epicure "einen Anflug des körperlichen Wohlbehagens, das sonst mit dem Genuss verknüpft ist, ohne dass der Geschmack selbst ihm zum Bewusstsein kommt." [55] It might, of course, be objected that the feeling in this case is not separately ideated; it is ideated along with visual sensations, the sight of the shell-fish or of the printed word. Stumpf replies, and from his standpoint justly, that at all events the feeling is ideated separately from the taste, and that that is the important point. [56] However, he invalidates his own example in a way that, I confess, I should not have thought of: "es ist mir nicht sicher," he says, "dass das nämliche Gefühl, wie es an die Geschmacksempfindung oder Geschmacks-

vorstellung geknüpft ist, auch die blosse Gesichts-
vorstellung begleitet";[57] he is not sure that the
affective image aroused by sight is the same affective image that accompanies taste. My own
objection would be, again, that there is no evidence of affective image, but only of affective
reinstatement. Be this as it may, we hear no
more of taste.

In his eagerness for further instances, Stumpf
quotes the colour-feelings aroused in the artist
by the sight of an etching, the feelings which
attach to poetic expressions, and various experiences of himself and of his co-workers in the
sphere of tones, — feelings accompanying the
sight of musical phrases and harmonies and
rhythms, the effort to recall a modulation, the
mere thought of the tone-colour of different
pianos.[58] Now it is perfectly clear that in most
of these cases we are dealing, not with the affective tone of sensation, but with something much
more complicated, — with *Affekt* or *Gemüts-
bewegung*. Stumpf, it is true, avers that the
look of a "nichtswürdige Tonverbindung" gives
him "einen Stich" of sensory disagreeableness,
and that the look of "langgehaltene konsonante
Akkorde" affects him in somewhat the same way
as a warm bath. But it is, surely, very difficult
to think that we are here in presence of anything

else than æsthetic feelings, — feelings that, from long and expert familiarity with the subject-matter, have the promptness and immediacy of sense-feelings, but that nevertheless are in origin æsthetic. How can you tell, by eye, that a *Ton-verbindung* is *nichtswürdig*, save as the result of musical training? The *Tonverbindung* is not a sensation, and no amount of practice can make it a sensation. And how can you recognise long-drawn consonant chords in the musical score? Not by sensation. Stumpf, however, is very far from dogmatic. "Alle diese Beobach-tungen führe ich mit einer gewissen Reserve an, da in Fällen, wo die Tonvorstellung nicht merk-lich ist, doch auch das sinnliche Gefühl meist nur flüchtig und schwer zu fassen ist," and contrari-wise.[59] Affective image, that is, is at least very largely a function of tonal image; clear-cut separation of the two is doubtful.

I conclude, then, — I have no choice but to conclude, — that the proposed demonstration of the separateness, in idea, of sensation and sense-feeling has broken down. There is no atom of reliable evidence. Remember that the refusal to consider the 'higher' feelings, the rigorous restriction of the argument to the isolated, single sensation, are Stumpf's refusal and Stumpf's restriction, not the critic's. Stumpf marked out his own ground; and though, in my judgment, he has more than once shifted his position,[60] he finds himself obliged to retire. He retires, however, with a very clever riposte. There are psychologists, he says, — Külpe is one of them, — who posit a simple duality of feeling, a single quality of pleasantness and a single quality of unpleasantness. Now we have seen that cutaneous pain, which is unpleasantness, may be isolated and imaged; and we have seen that the cutaneous pleasure-sensations may be isolated and imaged. *Ergo*, these psychologists must admit, in general, the possible occurrence of the separate affective image as of the separate affection itself; when they reproduce the unpleasantness of a bad smell, they have an image of cutaneous pain; and if they wish to know, precisely, what the unpleasantness of a bad smell is, *per se*, they have only to isolate a cutaneous pain-sensation.[61] It is needless to work out the reply. Pain and itch, for these psychologists as for Stumpf himself, are sensations. Only, for that very reason, they are not affections. Stumpf has covered his retreat; but we must not let ourselves be blinded to the essential thing, — the fact that he has retreated.

Now for the rally! Stumpf rallies — on what? on descriptive psychology? Not at all! — on

psychophysics.   Our principle of scientific economy forbade us to make a separate class for the
affective elements unless the facts positively
constrained us to that conclusion.   Now let us
grant that the agreeableness of colours and tones
and scents is separable from the colours and tones
and scents themselves neither in sensation nor in
idea.   We are not really forced to the admission; but let us bow to the equivocal nature of
the evidence, and make it.   Are we thereby constrained to recognise the independence of the
affective process?   Surely not: the purporting
affective element may still be a concomitant or
accessory sensation of central origin.[62]   The
central physiological mechanism may be of
such a kind that the excitation of colour-feeling
necessarily implies the coexcitation of colour-
sensation.   This view becomes, indeed, physiologically probable if we assume, as many do,
that the feeling-qualities of any one sense-department are different from the feeling-qualities
of the rest, that the colour-feelings and the tone-
feelings are qualitatively distinct.   Ebbinghaus,
who places the affective elements in a class of
their own, nevertheless regards them, physiologically, as "Nebenwirkungen derselben Ursachen, die den begleitenden Empfindungen und
Vorstellungen zugrunde liegen." [63]   It is but

a short step from this to the view that makes them sensations, "zentrale Mitempfindungen."

To appreciate this final stand, we must look back over Stumpf's whole essay. He started out on a question of descriptive psychology; we were to hear nothing of genetic psychology or of psychophysics. He began by examining three of the alleged criteria of affection — the three that he himself took to be the most noteworthy — and found them wanting. He then turned to the consideration of the sense-feelings in detail; dealing first with pain, and the cutaneous and vegetative pleasures, and secondly with the 'affective tone' of the remaining senses. He had no difficulty in showing that pain, itch, tickle, lust, and so forth are sensational in character, — though, as I pointed out, his interpretation leaves many facts out of account (the varying pleasantness and unpleasantness of itch, the possible pleasantness of pain, etc.). He had no particular difficulty, on the side of pain, with the affective tone of intensive sensations of the other senses, — though I showed that there were distinct difficulties on the side of pleasure. His real difficulty, the difficulty which he himself feels and acknowledges, arose in connection with the affective tone of moderately and weakly intensive sensations of sight and sound, taste

I

and smell. And this difficulty, insurmountable on the plane of descriptive psychology, is twice avoided by appeal to speculative psychophysics. Now, then, if I ask you: 'What is Stumpf's psychological evidence for the existence of a class of *Gefühlsempfindungen* which shall replace the affective elements of current psychology?' — what have you to reply? Stumpf offers his whole article in evidence. I grant that the article is subjectively persuasive and objectively important; otherwise I should not have devoted this hour to its criticism. But I affirm that, when critically reviewed, it contains no stronger evidence than the principle of economy and the demonstration that, as our knowledge of nerve-physiology goes, the existence of centrally excited accessory sensations is a psychophysical possibility. The persuasiveness of the essay, then, I discount altogether. Its objective importance lies, I think, not in what it has shown, but in the example which it has set. Stumpf lends the weight of his name to a sensationalistic theory of affection; and we may expect in the near future, both from adherents and from opponents of that theory, an industrious collection of psychological facts, psychological observations, which will finally sway the balance in the one direction or in the other.

However, the proof of the pudding is in the eating. Stumpf adds a final section, in which he deals with 'applications' of his psychophysical theory.[64] In the domain of sensation we have, he says, well-developed methods and well-established results. If, then, we can only bring ourselves to look upon affections as sensations, we can attack them directly by sensation-methods, and can check or control our data by sensation-results. In particular, we may expect by this means to bring light into the dark places of genetic psychology.[65]

The point is well taken. If, as a matter of fact, the theory of central concomitant sensations helps us to a stable affective psychology, then let us welcome it gladly, without waiting to ask whether its foundation is in psychology or in physiology, and whether its author has or has not adduced at the outset valid arguments in its favour. A good working hypothesis is valuable for its own sake, and the facts whose discovery it assures soon become strong enough to furnish the required corrective. Stumpf, now, devotes seven pages — one-seventh of his whole paper — to the test of the theory from this point of view. Let us see what the outcome is.

In the first place, Stumpf points out that the theory accounts for the various analgesias, for the cases of anæsthesia in which pain-sensation persists, and for the occurrence of 'unnoticeable' sensations of pain and pleasure, — sensations which are above the limen of stimulus but below the limen of attention.[66]   As we agree that pain, itch, tickle, etc., are sensations, we have no quarrel with him on their behalf.   It need only be said that his theory has, here, no advantage of any kind over the orthodox affectional theory.

Secondly, Stumpf instances the fact of 'indifferent' sensations.   An affectional theory, he says, has, by a sort of *a priori* necessity, to postulate the presence of affective process in consciousness, even where introspection is unable to discover it, — witness Lotze's doctrine of the "Allgegenwart der Gefühle."   If, on the other hand, that process is an accessory sensation, "so liegt nicht der mindeste Grund vor, warum eine solche Begleitung völlig allgemein und ausnahmslos den Empfindungen zukommen müsse"; while we can readily understand how it comes about that extensive and intensive stimulation of any sort brings the accessory sensation into consciousness.[67]   This argument, however, is unconvincing.   An affectional theory is a theory of affective facts; and the fact that some sensations are indifferent is ordinarily explained by reference either to habituation or to insufficient intensity of stimulus.

It seems to me that there is small choice, on this topic, between the opposing views. One might argue, against Stumpf, that a concomitant sensation which is rarely if ever isolable in consciousness, which can hardly be separated from its companion, whether as sensation or as image, ought *a priori* always to accompany its pair; and, indeed, I am inclined to think that this objection is stronger than that which Stumpf urges from the other side. Lotze's view is introspectively grounded, and may, perhaps, have been due to "individuelle Organisation." [68]

Thirdly, Stumpf declares that his theory accords better than its rival with the facts of the dependence of affective tone upon the quality of sensation, as set forth, *e.g.*, by Ebbinghaus.[69] I might reply that this dependence is itself in dispute; Külpe, *e.g.*, denies it.[70] All that Stumpf could then assert would be that his theory accords with a particular view entertained by Ebbinghaus, — a view, be it remembered, which Ebbinghaus himself regards as compatible with an affectional theory. If, however, this is unduly to press the sense of the term 'dependence,' — though Ebbinghaus heads his section, 'Die seelischen Gefühlsursachen"! [71] — and if Stumpf has in mind simply the factual connections of sensation and affection, then I do not see, and

Stumpf makes no effort to show, in what way his theory is superior. The facts are "eine weitgehende Konstanz, . . . aber doch wieder Ausnahmen von dieser Regelmässigkeit." To say: "die Auffassung der Sinnesgefühle als Mitempfindungen . . . fügt sich diesen Bedingungen ohne weiteres," as if there were something in the very nature of concomitant sensations that indicated a rule with salient exceptions, is of little avail; we must know in detail the conditions of the rule and the conditions of the exceptions.

The argumentation on these two points is very much 'in the air.' It may well be the case that Stumpf has thought out his position with all necessary fulness, and that as he writes a crowd of confirmatory associations press in upon him. But the statements actually made are schematic to a degree. I have tried, working on the hints which Stumpf has earlier given, to think out a physiological mechanism that should behave, naturally and normally, as the substrate of the concomitant sensations is required to behave: but the deeper I go, the farther do I seem to travel from anything like our current conception of the substrate of sensation.

There is a fourth point. Stumpf thinks that his theory brings us nearer than any other to an understanding of the vast and unsettled problems of affective genesis, of the individual development and generic evolution of the sense-feelings, — and also of the related problem of the striking diversity of affective reaction to the same stimulus.[72] He illustrates this thesis by reference to the senses of taste [73] and hearing.[74] As the psychology of tone is Stumpf's special field, and as he gives more space to hearing than to taste, I may confine myself to his discussion of the tonal feelings.

We have at our disposal a mass of facts from history, from individual psychology, and from ethnography. We have also a number of facts gained from psychological experimentation : "the existence and the peculiar character of the 'feeling of purity' with consonant intervals, the shift of this feeling within certain limits under the influence of æsthetic and other motives, as well as its dependence upon recently formed habits; the great secular changes as regards the pleasantness of consonances at large, the origin and development of the modern feeling of harmony, the possibility of its temporary annulment by intensive occupation with divergent tone-structures." [75] Now, Stumpf says, the theory of concomitant sensation gives us the right attitude to all these facts. For brief periods of time, the same stimuli will evoke a constant affective

reaction; but in long periods of time the sense-
feelings are exposed to transforming influences,
both of an individual and of a generic sort, more
especially to the influence of habitual direction
of attention, of disposition of judgment, of habits
of all kinds. Let such factors operate through
generations, and we may have inheritance, connate peculiarities of feeling-effect. These peculiarities are perhaps, in some instances, residua
of sense-feelings which originally appeared in
connection with emotions; and Stumpf here
broaches a subject of fascinating interest, — the
possibility of expert reconstruction of those
emotions themselves. "Die Ausführung muss
freilich einer anderen Gelegenheit vorbehalten
bleiben." [76]

Here I am less inclined to criticise than to re-
gret. We are given a skeleton, an outline —
less than that: a bare suggestion of Stumpf's
doctrine of the 'Ton- und Musikgefühle.' [77]
Would that we had the completed work! Until
that appears, it is hopeless to argue under this
heading, whether for the affective element or for
the concomitant sensation.

The paper ends with a brief comment on the
inadequacy of the teleological principle as a
principle of explanation.[78] On this matter I
not only agree with Stumpf, but I should even

be inclined to go farther, and to rule the teleological principle out of affective psychology
altogether. —

Has, then, this section on 'applications' shaken
our previous conclusion ?   My own feeling is that
Stumpf's presentation would have been stronger
without it.   These brief and summary statements
read like the formularies of a faith; their dogmatism stands in marked contrast to the careful
and elaborate argument that has gone before.
On the evidence, we must still say that the
theory of concomitant sensation, as a psychological theory, has little to commend it.   When
the evidence is all in, and the explanatory power
of the theory has been tested along the whole
line of observed fact, then I, for one, shall be
ready to revise, and if necessary to reverse, this
judgment.   May the day come quickly that
brings us the long-delayed volume on the *Tongefühle!*

THE TRIDIMENSIONAL THEORY OF FEELING

LECTURE IV

THE TRIDIMENSIONAL THEORY OF FEELING *

A LECTURER who had expounded Wundt's elementary doctrine of feeling in the year of grace 1893 would have called attention to two principal points: the status of feeling in consciousness, and the number and nature of the affective qualities. Feeling, Wundt says in the fourth edition of the *Physiologische Psychologie*, is a third attribute of sensation, "eine dritte Eigenschaft der Empfindung." "Neben Intensität und Qualität begegnet uns mehr oder minder ausgeprägt in jeder Empfindung ein *drittes* Element. . . . Wir nennen diesen dritten Bestandtheil der Empfindung den *Gefühlston* oder das *sinnliche Gefühl.*" And feeling or affective tone ranges between qualitative opposites, which "wir als *Lust-* und *Unlustgefühle* bezeichnen." Pleasantness and unpleasantness are the ultimate simple forms of sense-feeling, the irreducible qualities of the pure affective tone which is immanent in the simple sensation. At the same time, the terms 'pleasantness' and 'un-

* This Lecture has been printed in the *American Journal of Psychology*, April, 1908.

pleasantness' are not adequate to describe the affective tone of any and every sensation that we obtain by psychological analysis. The qualities of the higher senses, sight and hearing, play an important part in the compound ideas which appeal to the æsthetic side of our nature. Probably for this reason, their affective colouring is approximately, *annähernd*, identical with that of such compound ideas; they have taken on a *Stimmungscharakter*, "der nicht mehr schlechthin auf Lust und Unlust zurückgeführt werden kann, sondern in andern, in gewissen Affecten deutlicher ausgeprägten Gegensätzen einen adäquateren Ausdruck findet." Tones, *e.g.*, may be grave or cheerful, colours may be calming or exciting. The passage from pure affective tone, pleasantness or unpleasantness, to these æsthetic, emotional shades of feeling may be traced through the series of the senses. Touch and the common sensations show pleasantness-unpleasantness with only a trace of "qualitative Färbung"; tastes and smells are predominantly pleasant or unpleasant, but nevertheless admit of "verschiedenartigere Gefuhlsfärbungen." Tones and colours, which are strongly pleasant or unpleasant to children and savages, have almost lost these attributes for the civilised adult, —though even for us the seriousness of deep

tones and of black surfaces leans towards unpleasantness, and the excitement of high tones
and of white towards pleasantness, — and have
assumed an affective colouring whose general
affinity to pleasantness-unpleasantness is, in
extreme cases, proved only by its movement
between qualitative opposites.[1]

That, then, was Wundt's doctrine, taken at the
purely descriptive level: sensations with an
immanent attribute of pleasantness-unpleasantness, the original simplicity of which appears
clearly enough in the lower sense-departments,
but in the higher is obscured by æsthetic or quasi-
æsthetic reference.

Now suppose that, as the novelists say, three
years have elapsed, and that the same lecturer
is discussing the same subject in 1896. He has
in his hands the first edition of Wundt's *Grundriss der Psychologie*. And there he reads of
"zwei Arten psychischer Elemente, die sich als
Producte der psychologischen Analyse ergeben,
. . . Empfindungselemente oder Empfindungen
[und] Gefühlselemente oder einfache Gefühle."
The constitutive attributes ("unerlässliche Be-
stimmungsstücke") of sensation are quality and
intensity. Affection, too, possesses these attributes. But there is a difference. While sensible
qualities are limited by maximal differences,

affective qualities range between maximal opposites. While the number of sensible qualities is fixed, by the differentiation of the sense-organ, the number of affective qualities is indefinitely large; for simple feelings are the subjective complements, not only of simple sensations, but also of compound ideas and of still more complicated ideational processes. And while sensations fall into a number of separate systems, there is but one affective system; tone and colour, warmth and pressure, are disparate, but "alle einfachen Gefühle bilden eine einzige zusammenhängende Mannigfaltigkeit, insofern es kein Gefühl gibt, von dem aus man nicht durch Zwischenstufen und Indifferenzzonen zu irgend einem andern Gefühle gelangen könnte."

Do, then, all these many affective elements fall within "dem allgemeinen Rahmen einfacher Lust und Unlust"? By no means! There are three *Hauptrichtungen der Gefühle*, three dimensional categories, "innerhalb deren unendlich viele einfache Qualitäten vorkommen." These are pleasantness-unpleasantness, excitement-inhibition or excitement-tranquillisation, and tension-relaxation. As a rule, Wundt says, psychologists have paid regard only to pleasantness and unpleasantness, and have relegated the other two affective classes to the emotions.

But as emotions arise from the combination of feelings, the fundamental types of emotion must be preformed, *vorgebildet*, in the affective elements.[2]

In cases like this, I always want to trace the motive. Like the lawyer in *David Copperfield*, I assume that in all such cases there *is* a motive. What ,was it, then, that led Wundt to his change of opinion ?

If my reading of Wundt is correct, the changes that he has made, from time to time, in his various systematic works have never been due, in any real way, to external causes, but have always represented the climax or culmination of a stage of internal development. The germs of the changes are invariably, I think, to be found in the prior Wundt, and the changes themselves are but the full and self-conscious maturity of ideas that had long been 'incubated,' had long been held in the obscure margin of consciousness. On the other hand, it is possible, at least in most cases, to point with a fair degree of probability to the external cause that brought these obscure ideas to the attentive focus. In the present instance, that external cause appears, very obviously, in the publication of Külpe's *Grundriss*. Let me be clear on this matter, even if I am repe-

K

titious! I believe that Wundt would have formulated his new affective theory in any event;
the theory was implicit in him and in his previous writings. If Külpe had not given the
touch that led to crystallisation, some one else
would, sooner or later, have performed the same
office. In fact, however, Külpe undoubtedly did
furnish the external stimulus, — so that, indeed,
we have to thank him, not only for his own
Grundriss, but in a certain special and limited
sense for Wundt's as well.[3]

Let me take you, now, to the first edition of the
Physiologische Psychologie, the edition of 1874.
In general, the exposition is very like the exposition of 1893. But, in 1893, we are told that the
affective tone of sensations of the higher senses
is a *Stimmungscharakter*, a colouring that they
have 'taken on' in virtue of their constant par-
ticipation in æsthetic ideas. In 1874, the reference to æsthetics comes at the end of the discussion; the fact that sight and hearing have
freed themselves of sense-pleasurableness and
sense-unpleasurableness fits them to serve as
elements in æsthetic effect. They are not grave
and dignified and happy and cheerful because
they have been æsthetically employed, but their
gravity and cheerfulness are what enables us to
employ them with æsthetic result. "Lust und

Unlust," Wundt concludes, "sind, wie es scheint, nur die von der *Intensität* der Empfindung herrührenden Bestimmungen, während an die *Qualitäten* Gegensätze anderer Art geknüpft sind, welche zwar zuweilen in eine gewisse Analogie mit Lust und Unlust sich bringen lassen, an sich aber doch von diesen letzteren nicht berührt werden." Here is the doctrine of the plurality of affective dimensions plainer and more definite than it was twenty years later; here is, evidently enough, the germ of the doctrine of 1896.[4]

Once more: the chapter from which I have been quoting is entitled, in 1893, "Gefühlston der Empfindung," — in 1874, "Sinnliche Gefühle." Is not that significant also? Affection, in 1874, is not an attribute of sensation; it appears in that rôle for the first time in 1880. Affection, in 1874, is a relation, the relation which sensation sustains to consciousness at large. "Als ein nach Qualität und Intensität bestimmter Zustand ist die Empfindung nur im Bewusstsein gegeben; in Wirklichkeit existirt sie daher auch immer nur in ihrer Beziehung zu demselben. Diese Beziehung nennen wir das sinnliche Gefühl."[5]

Clearly, then, the whole of the new affective theory is implicit in the original edition of Wundt's great work. So far from suddenly

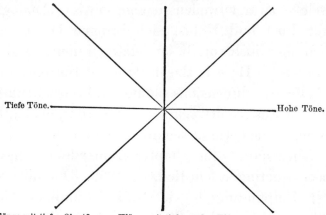

FIG. 3. Wundt's Schema of the 'System der Klanggefühle': *Physiologische Psychologie*, 1874, 446. "Jedem dieser Ton- und Klanggegensätze entsprechen Contraste des Gefühls, die allmälig durch vermittelnde Zwischenstufen einem Indifferenzpunkt sich nähern, durch welchen sie in einander übergehen. Den tiefen Tönen und Klangfarben zur linken Seite entsprechen die ernsten, den hohen zur rechten die heiteren Stimmungen, bei grösserer Klangstärke sind alle Stimmungen mit einem gehobenen, energischen, bei geringerer Klangstärke mit einem gedämpften, sanften Gefühlston verbunden. Da zwischen den hier herausgegriffenen Strahlen alle möglichen Uebergänge sich denken lassen, so kann man sich vorstellen, alle durch die Klangfarbe bestimmten Gefühlstöne seien in einer Ebene angeordnet, deren eine Dimension, dem Continuum der einfachen Töne entsprechend, die Contraste von Ernst und Heiterkeit mit ihren Uebergangsstufen enthalte, während die zweite, welche die Stärke der Theiltöne abmisst, die Gegensätze des Energischen und Sanften vermittelt." — Cf. *ibid.*, ii., 1902, 327 f.

reversing his attitude to affective processes, he
has, in reality, returned to his first systematic
position. In other words, the problem with
regard to Wundt is not so much that he now
makes affection an independent element with a
plurality of dimensions and qualities, as rather
that he ever did anything else. This problem,
too, can be solved; but it is foreign to our present consideration.

We are to examine, in this Lecture, the theory
which I briefly outlined a moment ago on the
basis of the *Grundriss* of 1896. The theory has
been widely and variously discussed, and I cannot attempt to cover the whole of the relevant
'literature.' I shall refer, for the most part, to
the earliest statements of it, in the *Grundriss*
of 1896 and the *Vorlesungen* of 1897, and to the
latest systematic statement in the *Physiologische
Psychologie* of 1902.

First of all, then, how does Wundt arrive at
his three affective dimensions? How does he
prove that there are three, and that these three
are pleasantness-unpleasantness, excitement-inhibition, and tension-relaxation? Well! his
main reliance is on his own introspection.
Wundt is a man of keen sensibility. He writes
of feeling *con amore;* he is fond of quoting

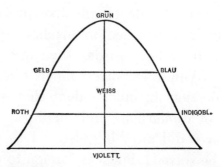

FIG. 4. Wundt's Schema of the 'System der Farbengefühle': *Physiologische Psychologie*, 1874, 448. The affective opposition, "der einerseits im Gelb, anderseits im Blau am stärksten ausgeprägt zu sein scheint, . . . ist der der Lebhaftigkeit und der Ruhe . . . Zwischen dem Gelb und dem Blau gibt es aber *zwei* Uebergänge : der eine durch das Grün, der andere durch die röthlichen Farbentöne. . . . In dem Roth und den ihm verwandten Farben ist die Bewegung des Gelb und die Ruhe des Blau zu einem zwischen Bewegung und Ruhe hin- und herwogenden Zustand der *Unruhe* geworden. Diese Vermittlung durch den Zwiespalt ist am deutlichsten in den blaurothen Farbentönen, wie im Violett, repräsentirt. Das Grün dagegen drückt ein wirkliches Gleichgewicht aus. Im Vergleich mit dem erstarrenden Blau und dem erregenden Gelb verbreitet es ein befriedigendes Ruhegefühl." These two modes of transition make the series of simple colour-feelings a closed curve, analogous to the 'colour triangle.' "Mit Rücksicht auf ihre Bedeutung als Uebergangsstimmungen wird aber hierbei dem Grün angemessener das Violett als das Purpur gegenüberzustellen sein, und es werden dem entsprechend Roth und Indigoblau, Gelb und Blau einander gegenüber zu liegen kommen. . . . Denken wir uns die den verminderten Sättigungsgraden der Farben bis zum Weiss entsprechenden Gefühle ähnlich angeordnet, so bilden sie alle zusammen die von der Farbencurve umschlossene Ebene, in welcher der Punkt des Weiss die indifferente Stimmung bezeichnet, wie sie die einfache, weder durch besondere Stärke noch durch Schwäche des Lichts noch durch einen Farbenton modificirte Lichtempfindung hervorbringt. Rings herum liegen die matteren und darum auch durch kürzere Uebergänge vermittelten Gefühlstöne der weisslichen Farben." "Für jede Farbe gibt es also *drei* Uebergänge der Stimmung zu einer Farbe von entgegengesetztem Gefühlston : der harmonische durch das ruhige Grün, der contrastirende durch das zwiespältige Violett und der indifferente durch das gleichgültige Weiss." The complete schema of visual sensations is, however, tridimensional; the vertical axis shows the colourless sensations aroused by the "Intensitätsgrade des Lichts." These have their own feelings. "Zwischen den Gegensätzen der Helligkeit, dem ernsten Dunkel und dem heiteren Lichte, existirt nur der *eine* Uebergang durch das indifferente Weiss von mittlerer Helligkeit. Indem die Lichtstärke der Farben zu- oder abnehmen kann, können sie auch an diesen Gefühlstönen der Helligkeit Theil nehmen."— Cf. *ibid.*, ii., 1902, 329 f.

Goethe's *Farbenlehre;* feeling has played a
larger and larger part in his psychological system as time went on; as early as 1874 he had
systematised, thrown into diagrammatic form,
his affective reactions to colours and tones. So
the new theory appears in the *Grundriss* without
preface or apology, — "wird einfach als Tatsache eingeführt," Orth plaintively remarks,[6] —
takes its place in the exposition with all the
assurance of established fact. Remembering
its genesis, its deep-rooted and slow growth in
Wundt's mind, we need not be greatly surprised.
Wundt had said in 1874, "Gelb . . . regt an,
blau stimmt herab "; and had emphasised
"das eigenthümliche Gefühl des Aufmerkens"
which appears "im Zustande des Besinnens
oder der Spannung." [7] No doubt it seemed
obvious to him in 1896 that the introspective
evidence, though not expressed, would be understood, — if indeed the thought of expression
ever occurred to him. Now, after several years
of criticism, he is more explicit; the *Physiologische Psychologie* introduces the theory by way
of definite introspective analysis.[8]

Even in the *Grundriss*, however, Wundt is not
simply dogmatic. He explains (*a*) that a triple
classification of the affective elements is required

for the distinction of the fundamental types of emotion. Later on, it is true, he declares that a psychological classification of the emotions "nur auf die Qualität des Gefühlsinhaltes gegründet werden kann." The argument has a circular look: affections are classified by reference to emotion, emotions by reference to affection. I think, however, that it is formally sound. Theoretically, emotions may be classified by quality, by intensity, and by temporal course. In practice, intensity and temporal course fail to furnish reliable criteria: hence emotions must be classified by quality. Qualitative analysis then reveals certain fundamental types of emotion, which must, of course, be preformed in the affective qualities. Emotive classification thus points us back to a particular classification of affections, while affective classification, to be adequate, must necessarily point forward to emotion. Formally, this reasoning is rather a matter of what Fechner would call the 'solidarity' of a system than an instance of merely circular argumentation.[9] Whether it is materially sound is another question, — a question which Stumpf, e.g., would answer with an emphatic negative.[10]

Wundt also brings evidence of an objective sort, the evidence (b) derived from the method of expression. He lays but slight stress on pulse-correlation in the *Grundriss*: "es ist unzulässig, die Ausdrucks- der Eindrucksmethode in Bezug auf ihren psychologischen Werth gleichzuordnen." [11] In the *Vorlesungen*, too, the pulse-records are introduced to prove the physiological relationship of the 'lower' to the 'higher' feelings, some time before we reach the distinction of the three affective dimensions.[12] It is not until 1900, in the *Bemerkungen zur Theorie der Gefühle*, that the changes in innervation of heart, vessels, and respiratory mechanism — "ein überaus feines Reagens auf die leisesten Aenderungen der Stärke wie Richtung der Gefühle" [13] — are given anything like an independent place in Wundt's argument. Do not fear, now, that I shall plunge you into the technical intricacies of the expressive method, and that the remainder of the hour will be filled with sphygmograph and plethysmograph, pneumograph and dynamograph! Even if that method came into our discussion, I could pass it over with the reminder that, not so long ago, I gave a critical review of it from this platform.[14] But it does not come into our discussion. Grant everything that the most ardent disciples of the method demand, and then ask yourselves: Where is the evidence, in these correlations, that

we are dealing with elementary mental processes? What have pulse-curves to say to the
question of the irreducibility, the ultimateness
in consciousness, of the experiences of excitement-inhibition, tension-relaxation? Wundt himself is careful, in psychological connection, to
differentiate "specifische Beschaffenheit" and
"elementare Natur." [15] How can pulse and
breathing be relied upon to make the same distinction? [16]

Let us, then, dismiss the expressive method,
and come back to the *Grundriss.* Had Wundt
stopped short at the point which we have now
reached; had he stated his theory, shown its
usefulness in systematic regard for the classification of emotions, and indicated the correlated
differences in the pulse-tracings: his position
would, I think, have been stronger than it actually is. But he attempts, further, (*c*) to connect
the three dimensions of affection with the three
relations in which a given feeling may stand to
the temporal course of mental processes at large.
Pleasantness and unpleasantness denote a determinate modification of our present mental
state; excitement and inhibition exert a determinate influence upon the next succeeding
state; and tension and relaxation are qualitatively determined by the preceding state. "Diese

Bedingungen machen es zugleich wahrscheinlich, dass andere Hauptrichtungen der Gefühle
nicht existiren." [17] And yet — quality is the
criterion for the classification of emotions, and
the classification of the emotions requires three
ultimate affective dimensions! Here, surely, we
have the fallacy of too many proofs! Wundt,
it is true, offers in the *Bemerkungen* a defence
of his dual argument. "Es handelt sich hier
um Momente, die selbst wieder mit einander
zusammenhängen:" " [es] kommt hier überall
nicht ein Verhältniss von Ursachen und Wirkungen, sondern lediglich ein solches von Beziehungen und Bedingungen in Frage, die sich
wenigstens vorläufig durch eine vollständige
Analyse aus der Gesammtheit der complexen
Bedingungen nicht isoliren lassen." [18] If I understand these passages aright, Wundt's meaning
is as follows: 'Consciousness is always exceedingly complex, so that the affective processes are
given in complex relations and appear as variously conditioned. Causal analysis is, at present, beyond our powers. We can, however,
trace certain relations and follow up certain
part-conditions; and our results, different or
even incompatible as they may look, are really
abstractions from — represent moments of — a
single system of causal interrelations. Hence

they may safely be set down side by side.' In the abstract, all this may be granted. Still, however, I do not see, in the concrete, how the three affective dimensions can be guaranteed *both* by temporal relation to the course of consciousness *and* by qualitative differences in emotion. The latter are enough, in themselves: the former is, at the best, a matter of reflection, of analysis above the elementary level; and its obvious superfluity tends to cast doubt upon the results of qualitative analysis proper, with which it is brought into agreement. For the rest, it is significant that, in his later writings, Wundt has dropped this principle of temporal relation as a means of affective classification.

In the *Vorlesungen* of 1897 a new principle makes its appearance. After distinguishing the three dimensions of pleasantness-unpleasantness, excitement-tranquillisation, tension-relaxation, Wundt says: "dass es noch andere Hauptrichtungen ausser diesen gebe, scheint mir nach der subjectiven Beobachtung nicht wahrscheinlich. Auch dürften die genannten den allgemeinsten Bedingungen entsprechen, unter denen Gefühle überhaupt entstehen." [19] The dimensions are guaranteed first by introspection, and secondly (*d*) by the threefold character of affective conditions. The conditions are found

in the "Empfindungs- und Vorstellungsele-
mente, an die [die Gefühle] gebunden sind." [20]
Pleasantness-unpleasantness represent a quality-
dimension; excitement-tranquillisation, an in-
tensity-dimension; tension-relaxation, a time-
dimension. "Die Bedeutung von Lust und
Unlust als 'Qualitätsrichtungen' liegt darin, dass
vorzugsweise in ihnen die Wirkungen der quali-
tativen Eigenschaften des gesammten Bewusst-
seinsinhalts zum Ausdruck kommen": and
similarly with the other two dimensions.[21] Intrinsically, of course, every affection is a quality,
qualitatively different from every other. But
the affective qualities of the three dimensions
reflect, express, are determined by the quality,
intensity, and temporal properties of sensations
and ideas.

I am not here concerned with the correctness
or incorrectness of Wundt's correlation. He has
himself changed it, in the *Physiologische Psychologie* of 1902, where pleasantness-unpleasantness represents an intensive, and excitement-
tranquillisation a qualitative dimension,[22] — just
the reverse of what was said in 1897. I am concerned with the correlation as a principle of
classification. There are, Wundt declares, three
general conditions of the arousal of feeling: the
quality, the intensity, and the temporal relations

of conscious contents. And the threefold character of the conditions furnishes, along with introspection, evidence that there are but three dimensions of affection. What, then, has become of the spatial relations of conscious contents? The chapter-headings of the *Physiologische Psychologie* tell us that *Sinnesvorstellungen* are of three kinds: intensive, spatial, temporal. Spatial and temporal ideas may be grouped together as extensive; intensive ideas differ from sensations by the composite nature of their intensity and quality.[23] These intensive ideas are therefore responsible for two affective dimensions, the intensive and qualitative; the temporal ideas are responsible for a third dimension, the temporal; only the spatial ideas are excused from affective duty. I argue, then, in this way. In so far as affective classification is dependent upon the various forms of idea, in so far Wundt's classification is inadequate; for the spatial form of idea is as important, in the mental life, as the intensive or the temporal.[24] And if there is no such thing as a spatial dimension of affective qualities, then we may justly doubt whether the principle of classification is sound, and whether any conclusion as to the number of affective dimensions may be deduced from it. Remember, I am not arguing on a matter of fact; I am considering the application of a principle.

Wundt replies, in the *Bemerkungen*, that he has left spatial ideas out of account for two reasons: first, "weil sich mir Beziehungen derselben zu bestimmten Gefühlsrichtungen weder in der unmittelbaren subjectiven Beobachtung noch bei der Analyse der Ausdrucksbewegungen darboten;" and secondly, "weil es mir scheint, dass man sehr wohl bei jedem Affect qualitative, intensive und zeitliche Eigenschaften unterscheiden kann, während ich mit dem Ausdruck, der Zorn oder die Freude habe irgend eine räumliche Ausdehnung, keinen rechten Sinn zu verbinden weiss." [25] The first of these arguments misses its mark for the reason that, in the *Vorlesungen*, the distinction of three general conditions of feeling, their connection with three forms of idea, is offered as *additional* evidence, over and above 'subjective Beobachtung,' for the finality of Wundt's classification. "*Auch* dürften die genannten Hauptrichtungen den allgemeinsten Bedingungen entsprechen, unter denen Gefühle überhaupt entstehen." I object to Wundt that the one of his two criteria is invalid, and he rejoins that the other is valid! The second argument goes equally wide. I did not assert that an emotion possesses spatial attributes, that an affection may be 'extended,' but that certain ideas possess spatial attributes and relations, — and that, if we are classifying affections by reference to the forms of ideas, then these spatial characteristics must be taken into account, as well as the intensive, qualitative, and temporal. I use the phrase 'spatial dimension of affective qualities' precisely as Wundt uses the phrase 'temporal dimension,' — to signify affective qualities that are dependent upon ideational extension. I acquitted Wundt, just now, of the charge of circularity; I am afraid that I must here charge him with the logical error which is known in the vernacular as 'missing the point.'

In sum, therefore, Wundt's three affective dimensions are supported, primarily, by his own introspection, while he has appealed, further, to the necessities of emotive classification; to the results of the method of expression; to the temporal relations of the affective processes; and to their general conditions in consciousness. The first use of these arguments I take to be sound, both formally and materially, though I do not arrive by it at the conclusion which Wundt has reached. The second must be pronounced irrelevant; the third has been given up by Wundt himself; the fourth we have seen to be logically defective and psychologically indefensible.

We have now to consider the theory on the basis that remains for it: introspection of the simple sense-feelings and qualitative analysis of the emotions. I find a difficulty, at the outset, in Wundt's terminology. You may have been surprised that, when I have had occasion to mention Wundt's category of 'excitement,' I have paired it with 'inhibition' or 'tranquillisation,' rather than with the more usual term 'depression.' I have, throughout, been quoting Wundt's own words; but it is true that, in the *Grundriss*, 'depressing' is given as an alternative to 'tranquillising,' and that in the *Physiologische Psychologie* 'Depression' is suggested for the higher degrees of 'Beruhigung.' [26] Wundt can, of course, do no more than take language as he finds it. But I think that his actual choice of words bears witness to a conflict, in his thought, between two purposes: the purpose of transcribing his introspections, and the purpose of maintaining the typical affective movement between opposites. Pleasantness and unpleasantness, *Lust* and *Unlust*, are opposite in name, as well as in nature. What of *Spannung* and *Lösung?* In English, 'relaxation' — which, I suppose, is the nearest equivalent of *Lösung* — suggests rather the remitting or resolving of tension than its qualitative opposite: this latter

L

would be better expressed by 'relief.' Possibly *Lösung* has for Wundt an implication of positive relief, of *Erleichterung*, — though it has not for me, nor for German friends of whom I have made inquiry. Wundt speaks also of the *Befriedigung*, the fulfilment, of expectation;[27] but that term brings us perilously near to *Beruhigung*. The chief difficulty, however, arises in connection with the remaining dimension. What is the opposite of *Erregung?* Sometimes Wundt says *Hemmung*, sometimes he says *Beruhigung*, sometimes *Depression*. The antithesis *Erregung-Hemmung* comes from nerve-physiology;[28] *Erregung-Depression* comes, evidently, from observation of the emotions, normal and pathological; *Erregung-Beruhigung* appears to be the analogue of *Spannung-Lösung* and to convey the same suggestion. But what is, in introspection, the *felt* opposite of *Erregung?* I cannot myself identify the feelings of *Hemmung*, *Depression, Beruhigung;* I cannot feel them as degrees of the same thing, as lying in the same affective dimension; I cannot always distinguish between *Beruhigung* and *Lösung*. *Erregung*, 'excitement,' seems to me to feel very differently in different contexts, to be an equivocal term. It is easy to say that such considerations are mere 'Wortklauberei': but I am trying to express a real introspective difficulty.

If, then, I am to judge others by myself, this uncertainty in the meaning of terms may be at least a partial reason for the fact that Wundt's classification, despite its claim to finality, does not always command the assent even of those who agree with its spirit and intention.   Gure-witsch, *e.g.*, in his *Theorie der sittlichen Gefühle*, makes a fourth affective category for *Streben-Widerstreben*.[29]   Vogt, again, ranges feelings of activity and passivity alongside of pleasantness-unpleasantness, arousal-depression, tension-re-laxation.[30]   Wundt identifies *Strebungsgefühl* with *Thätigkeitsgefühl*, which he regards as a total feeling, compounded of strain and excite-ment.[31]   Royce, on the other hand, is disposed to think that two dimensions — pleasantness-unpleasantness and restlessness-quiescence — are adequate to the facts of the affective life.[32]   I do not at all mean that these differences of opinion are fatal to the theory.   But they testify — do they not? — to a lack of precise formula-tion.   Royce throws two of Wundt's dimensions into one; Vogt and Gurewitsch split the same two into three.

The single dimension about which Wundt himself seems, from the first, to have felt no doubt is that of *Spannung-Lösung*.   The other two dimensions, as I pointed out just now, have actually exchanged places in his system. And the same uncertainty characterises certain of his observations in detail. Let me give you an instance. In the *Bemerkungen* of 1900, Wundt writes: "ich wüsste . . ., wenn ich vor die Wahl gestellt wäre, irgend einen dieser Eindrücke dem andern vorzuziehen, absolut nicht zu sagen, ob mir das rein spektrale Blau oder das Roth . . . angenehmer sei." This does not mean that the two colours would be equally pleasant. "Ich würde eben einem solchen Verlangen immer nur die Aussage gegenüberstellen können, dass diese Eindrücke an sich mit Lust und Unlust nichts zu thun haben." [33] The passage is a little startling, when one remembers that work had already been done upon colours — and colours that were not spectral colours — by the method of impression! [34] Two years later, now, we have the following: "wenn ich zuerst ein spektralreines leuchtendes Roth und dann ein ebensolches Blau im Dunkelraum betrachte, so kann ich nicht umhin, beide als im hohen Grad erfreuende, also lusterregende Eindrücke zu charakterisiren." [35] True, the sentence is concessive; the next begins with a 'gleichwohl'; but it is, nevertheless, in flat contradiction to the former quotation. If two impressions are highly pleasant, they *can* be com-

pared as regards pleasantness, and a judgment
of greater, less, or equal can be passed upon
them.   Similarly conflicting statements are made
concerning high and low tones.[36]   I readily
acknowledge, again, that these minor incon-
sistencies are in no sense fatal to the theory;
indeed, Wundt has so often emphasised the importance for feeling of the "ganze Disposition
des Bewusstseins" [37] that I feel reluctant, as it
were a morsel ashamed, to dwell upon them.
Still, they are there !   And it is not reassuring to
find that the dimension *Spannung-Lösung* owes
its exceptional position, the stability of which I
spoke above, to its systematic connection with
the doctrine of apperception.   It must have
occurred to many of you, when, earlier in the
Lecture, I was arguing the claims of space as a
condition of feeling in consciousness, to ask:
What, then, after all, are the claims of time?
Since, in the psychology of sensation, duration
and extension are, both alike, to a very large
extent equivalent to, interchangeable with, intensity, why should they not be bracketed with
intensity as the conditions of one and the same
affective dimension?   We should then have
something like Royce's classification: pleasantness-unpleasantness, conditioned upon all the
'qualitative' attributes of sensation, and ex-

citement-quiescence, conditioned upon all the 'intensive.' Now Wundt recognises the equivalence, under certain circumstances, of intensity and duration. "Insbesondere kann die Lust-Unlustcomponente [bei längerer Einwirkung auf das Bewusstsein] ganz dieselben Veränderungen erfahren, die auch die Steigerung der Intensität mit sich führt." [38] But feelings of *Spannung* and *Lösung* are "die specifischen, für die Aufmerksamkeitsvorgänge charakteristischen Elemente." [39] "Da aber Apperception und Aufmerksamkeit zeitlich sich entwickelnde Vorgänge sind, die zugleich in einer bestimmten zeitlichen Folge wechseln, indem jede Lösung eine vorangegangene Spannung fordert, und eine neue Spannung wiederum nur auf Grund vorangegangener Lösungen einsetzt, so sind diese Gefühlscomponenten enger als die übrigen an den zeitlichen Ablauf der Bewusstseinsvorgänge gebunden." [40] Any serious doubt, therefore, about Wundt's doctrine of attention and apperception must at the same time jeopardise this third dimension of simple feeling.

So far, I have spoken only of the three affective dimensions; I have said nothing of the multitude of elementary qualities which the dimensions are held to include. "Die qualitative

Mannigfaltigkeit der einfachen Gefühle ist un-
absehbar gross und jedenfalls viel grösser als die
Mannigfaltigkeit der Empfindungen." [41]   So the
Grundriss, — which proceeds to give two reasons. First, every sensation of the multidimen-
sional sensation-systems belongs to more than
one affective dimension. Secondly and more
importantly, the feelings that attach to sensation-complexes, intensive, spatial, and temporal
ideas, and to certain stages in the temporal course
of emotion and volition, are nevertheless themselves irreducible, and must therefore be counted
among the elementary affective processes. You
will notice that these reasons are phrased in the
language of a special psychological system,
though the appeal to introspection is implied.
Later on, the appeal becomes explicit; we are
reminded that, *e.g.*, the feeling of gravity, *Ernst*,
"in verschiedenen Fällen in seiner Qualität
wieder variiren kann." [42]   In the *Vorlesungen*,
the doctrine of the multiplicity of affective qualities follows naturally from the doctrine of the
Totalgefühl.[43] The *Physiologische Psychologie*
relies upon an 'aufmerksame Selbstbeobachtung.'[44]   We are apt to overlook the great variety
of the feelings, partly because they are intimately
bound up with the objective contents of consciousness, partly because we have no words to

express them. "Angesichts der [an der Hand des vergleichenden Verfahrens der Eindrucksmethode] ausgeführten Analyse scheint es mir in überwiegendem Masse wahrscheinlich, dass die sechs Grundformen . . . eben nur *Grundformen* sind, von denen jede einzelne eine sehr grosse Mannigfaltigkeit im ganzen verwandter, aber dabei doch von Fall zu Fall nuancirter Einzelgefühle unter sich begreift." [45]

There can be no manner of doubt that, in this matter of the number of the affective qualities, the psychological pendulum has been swinging, of recent years, in the direction that Wundt has taken. Ladd emphatically repudiates the view that "'pleasure-pains' are exhaustive of the entire quality of the feeling-aspect of consciousness." The theory is simplicity itself: "but simplicity, in the interests chiefly of biological and experimental psychology, 'gone entirely mad.'" [46] I do not know whether Ladd felt pleased or pained that he had written this last sentence, when two years later he read Wundt's *Grundriss.* He says himself, however, that "almost all mental states which are marked by strong feeling in the case of developed minds are *mixed* feelings." [47] At any rate, he works resolutely through the sense-departments, in 1894, and makes out a long list of elementary

processes.   James, in the same year, remarks
that "there are infinite shades and tones in the
various emotional excitements, which are as distinct as sensations of colour are, and of which
one is quite at a loss to predicate either pleasant
or painful quality." [48]   This position is, of
course, entirely compatible with a dual view of
Lust-Unlust, of "the primary *Gefühlston*"; indeed, the two doctrines seem to me to appear,
side by side, in James' own exposition.   Nevertheless, the passage may fairly be cited in the
present connection.   Lipps, again, working as
it were from the opposite pole to Wundt, has
arrived, as we all know, at a very complicated
classification of the feelings.[49]   Stumpf has expressed the opinion, as against Külpe, that
"sinnliche Annehmlichkeit" and "sinnliche Unannehmlichkeit" cover "eine grössere Mannigfaltigkeit von Gefühlsqualitäten." [50]   This array
of convictions is imposing, even if there are
authorities — Höffding, Külpe, Jodl, Ebbinghaus, Lehmann, Rehmke [51] — upon the other
side.

The fact is, of course, that the ultimate question of our second Lecture, the question of the
criteria of affection, has not been settled.   The
parties to the present controversy do not really
'feel' differently; but they approach the problem

with a certain attitude towards affective process, with a certain general view of the status of feelings in consciousness. Ebbinghaus says outright that Wundt and Jodl, *e.g.*, are 'not talking of the same things.'[52] Orth believes that Wundt's theory is the outcome "seiner ursprünglichen Auffassung des Verhältnisses zwischen Empfindung und Gefühl."[53] Ladd writes with a sort of ethical, even religious, atmosphere upon him: how can you compare the pleasure of cheese and beer with the pleasure of seeing a good *Hamlet?*[54] Lipps considers the feelings as modes of reference to the self; feelings are "Ichinhalte oder Ichqualitäten."[55] Stumpf adopts a sensationalist view of the sense-feelings; and in sensation qualitative differentiation is obvious enough. James is concerned with the varieties of emotive experience, and his protest against the 'hackneyed psychological doctrine' that pleasure and pain are the essence of emotion comports, as I have pointed out, with a strictly dualistic view of the affective qualities proper. It is not that our affective experience is radically different, but that we approach it from different directions, see it under different angles, assimilate it in terms of our systematic associations.

I do not mean that the point at issue is a mere *Etikettenfrage.* It is much more than that.

Our decision 'makes a difference,' as the prag-
matists say, to the whole structure of our psychological system. And it must be remembered
that Wundt does not acknowledge any other
methods than those employed by the dualists,
and would not acquiesce in the statement that
his results are of another order. He comes
within our universe of discourse; he invites argument. I therefore proceed to argue; and I take
as ground for argument an illustration which
he employs on more than one occasion, — the
feeling which attaches to the common chord
c–e–g.[56]

Let me remind you, first, of Wundt's doctrine
of the *Totalgefühl*.[57] A compound feeling, a
feeling due to the confluence of a number of
elementary feelings, is always psychologically
simple in the sense that it has its own irreducible
quality, but may also permit the distinction of
its various components. "In jedem derartigen
Gefühl lassen sich *Gefühlscomponenten* und eine
Gefühlsresultante unterscheiden." The components Wundt terms 'partial feelings,' the resultant, 'total feeling'; we have had an instance already in the 'feeling of activity' which
results from the compounding of tension and
excitement. The compound feeling thus bears
a close resemblance to the formation which, in

the sphere of tonal sensation, is called a fusion; Wundt speaks, in the *Physiologische Psychologie* of 'affective fusions.' There are degrees of affective, as there are degrees of tonal, fusion; the partial feelings may appear simply as an undifferentiated colouring of the resultant, or may maintain their individuality, though in a subordinate position, alongside of the total feeling.

After this preface, we are ready to listen to the three tones. To prevent a swamping of the partial feelings by the total feeling, — the highest degree of affective fusion, — we take the tones separately in succession, and observe how they 'feel' in isolation. The tone c, heard by itself, affects us, Wundt says, by way of a 'calm seriousness' or a 'quiet cheerfulness'; it brings out feelings of two dimensions, pleasantness-unpleasantness and excitement-tranquillisation. The other two, e and g, will do the same, — though the affective qualities will be somewhat different. If, now, we put the tones together in pairs, every pair will give us a compound feeling: we have the three total feelings of ce, eg, cg, accompanied or coloured by the partial feelings which we have compounded. And if the conditions are favourable for observation, we should be able to distinguish a fivefold feeling in connection with every pair; the two dimensions of the two partial feelings, and the total feeling. Now let us sound all three tones simultaneously. We have the total feeling of *c–e–g*; we have three relative total feelings, or 'partials of the second order,' as Wundt calls them, — the feelings of *ce*, *eg*, *cg*; and we have the 'partial feelings of the first order,' the six elementary feelings aroused by *c*, *e*, and *g*. The feeling of *c–e–g* is a tenfold complex. Do not forget that such a feeling is, for Wundt, an "einheitliche Mannigfaltigkeit"; do not forget that the partial feelings may, more or less completely, have forfeited their independence. But, with all allowance made, ask yourselves if you experience anything like the body of feeling that, on Wundt's theory, you 'ought' to experience. Suppose that, in spite of our precautions, affective fusion has reached its highest degree; let the partials of the first order disappear altogether, as separate components, and let them remain only as a vague colouring of the whole affective impression. Now your compound feeling should be a fourfold complex. Surely, it is not; surely, the feeling lacks the depth, the solidity, that a feeling thus compounded must possess; surely, you can describe the chord in no other terms than 'slightly pleasant,' 'moderately agreeable.'

I think that it is fair to test the theory in this way, by the judgment of a group of psychologically trained observers, seeing that Wundt has laid the observation before the psychological public in two of his books. I have, for myself, repeated the test often and again, and have varied it in half-a-dozen ways: always, while the chord remains a single impression, a sensible fusion out of musical setting and so far as possible freed from musical significance, I get the same meagre affective result.[58]

If, now, Wundt retorts that in this and like instances we are feeling-deaf and feeling-blind, may we not suggest, on our side, that he is organically anæsthetic? The lack of interest that Wundt shows in the organic sensations has always been a source of wonderment to me. Take the new edition of the *Physiologische Psychologie*. Here is a total of 2035 pages. Of these, 45 are given to *Tast- und Gemeinempfindungen;* the *Gemeinempfindungen* alone, which I now have principally in mind, receive four, two and a half of which are devoted to pain![59] Of course, there are all sorts of scattered references. But look in the index under *Organempfindungen, Gemeinempfindungen, Niedere Sinne, Gelenkempfindungen, Muskelsinn,* — what you can think of. Aside from *Bewe-*

gungsempfindungen and *Augenbewegungen* there
is surprisingly little.   Meumann makes a similar
complaint with regard to Nagel's *Handbuch*.
"Vermisst hat der Referent, dass den inneren
Empfindungen (Organempfindungen) kein aus-
führlicheres Kapitel gewidmet wird; die gegen-
wärtige Physiologie scheint sich mit der Frage
der Sensibilität der inneren Organe nicht mehr
viel zu beschäftigen." [60]   Now I personally believe that the organic sensations play an important part, not only in feeling and emotion,
but in many other departments of the mental
life: in the formation of sensory judgments, in
the mechanism of memory and recognition, in
motives to action, in the primary perception of
the self.   It is true that, as compared with what
we know of sight and hearing, our knowledge of
the organic sensations is scrappy in form and
small in amount; that is why I have said, in
another connection, that "of all problems in
the psychology of sense which are now before
us, the problem of the nature, number, and laws
of connection of the organic sensations appears
to me to be the most pressing." [61]   Let me add,
now, that if any one of you is thinking of a piece
of work in this general field, he would do far
better, in my opinion, to start out from the side
of the organic sensations than to succumb to

the fascinations of pneumograph and sphygmograph.

Well! I believe that organic sensations are responsible for the dimensions of excitement-depression and tension-relaxation. On this point I can claim the support of Ebbinghaus [62] and, I suppose, of all those who accept the James-Lange theory of emotion. Stumpf, too, declares that he cannot regard them as "Elementarerscheinungen," though he offers no further analysis.[63] But I believe, also, that organic sensations are responsible in certain cases for a *Nuancirung*, a shading and colouring, of feelings in the dimension of pleasantness-unpleasantness. I say 'in certain cases,' for two reasons. First, it is entirely possible that this *Nuancirung* is a matter, not of simple sense-feeling, but of association, of emotive residua.[64] Secondly, however, I do not think that the colouring and shading is as universal as Wundt asserts. Vogt, whose method of suggestion led him to the distinction of four pairs of feelings, is unable to discover it.[65] Orth cannot find it, in the introspections that he educes by the *Reizmethode*.[66] Störring's observers, on the other hand, report a qualitative difference between *Stimmungslust* and *Empfindungslust;* but though this is, so to say, a gross difference, the expressions used are

singularly disappointing. We read, in some
detail, of extensive differences, differences in
intensive fluctuation, differences of excitement
and passivity; but on the side of quality we
have only "Stimmungslust ist gleichartiger," and
the dogmatic statement "Zwischen Stimmungslust und Empfindungslust besteht *qualitative
Differenz.*" [67] I myself have never observed a
qualitative differentiation of pleasantness-unpleasantness, under experimental conditions;
and when I observe a difference in everyday
life, — a difference on the level of the sense-feeling, — I seem to find a reason for it in concomitant organic sensations.

I have sought, on two occasions, to put
Wundt's theory to an experimental test. The
method employed was the method of impression,
in Cohn's form of paired comparisons. The
procedure, in brief, is as follows. A series of
stimuli — tones or colours or rhythms — is laid
out, and the stimuli are presented to the observer
two at a time, care being taken that every member of the series is paired with every other member. The observer has to decide which of the
two stimuli shown him is the more pleasant, the
more unpleasant, the more exciting, the more
depressing, and so on. If colours are exhibited,
he points to right or left, as the case may be;

M

if tones are used, he notes down '1' or '2,' according as the first or second stimulus is preferred. The work is laborious, and the method consumes a large amount of time. We have, however, the great advantage of a twofold control, objective and subjective.

The subjective control is afforded, of course, by the introspection of the observers. The introspective task is extremely simple; the observer has merely to be passive, to let himself go, to allow the stimuli to take affective possession of him; and then to indicate, in the particular instance, which of the two makes the stronger impression. Moreover, since the introspective experience within a series is cumulative, all of the same kind, the observer is able, in the intervals between successive series, to give a general account of his method of judgment, of the nature of his affective reaction. The objective control is afforded by the course of the affective judgments themselves. If, *e.g.*, pleasantness and unpleasantness are really affective opposites, then the 'curves' or tracings which indicate the distribution of judgments in parallel 'pleasant' and 'unpleasant' series should be diametrically opposed: a colour which stands high on the scale of pleasantness should stand low on the scale of unpleasantness, and contrariwise.   If excitement-depression and tension-relaxation also denote affective opposites, then their 'curves' should be similarly opposed.

The stimuli chosen were colours, musical tones, and groups of metronome beats given at varying rates.   The two former had been specified by Wundt as productive of excitement-depression, the latter as productive of tension-relaxation.   My idea was, on the subjective side, to test by their means the immediacy of reaction in these dimensions.   In the case of pleasantness-unpleasantness, you cannot say what the basis of your judgment is, otherwise than that it resides in the stimulus; the one of two colours or two tones *is* more pleasant than the other, just as directly as it is bluer or louder. Suppose, then, that colours and tones bring out equally prompt and unmediated judgments of excitement-depression, and that metronome intervals bring out equally prompt and unmediated judgments of tension-relaxation : then we shall have some ground for the acceptance of the two new affective dimensions.   Suppose, on the other hand, that the judgments of excitement and tension are forced or difficult, mediated by associations or by organic sensations : then we shall have an introspective differentiation of these judgments from those of pleasantness-unpleasantness.

On the objective side, I argued in much the same way. Suppose that the curves, of which I spoke just now, show typical differences, — so that the distribution of judgments of pleasantness takes one course, that of judgments of excitement another, and that of judgments of tension a third, — while still the curves of pleasantness and unpleasantness, of excitement and depression, and of tension and relaxation are related as opposites: then, again, there will be ground for the acceptance of Wundt's dimensions. Suppose, on the contrary, that the curves of excitement and of relaxation agree with the curve of pleasantness and the curves of depression and of tension with the curve of unpleasantness: then, since the pleasant-unpleasant dimension is not in dispute, we have a strong indication that that alone is fundamental and that the other two dimensions are affective only because and in so far as pleasantness and unpleasantness are involved in them.

The results of the first investigation, in which colours and musical tones were tested for pleasantness-unpleasantness and excitement-depression, and metronome intervals for pleasantness-unpleasantness and tension-relaxation, were

published in the Wundt *Festschrift;* those of
the second, in which the same tones and intervals
were tested for all three of the Wundtian dimensions, were published by Hayes in the *American
Journal of Psychology.* They may be summed
up under three headings.[68]

(1) Judgments of pleasantness and unpleasantness are direct, easy, and natural. The
qualities themselves appear to the observers to
be simple and homogeneous, identical throughout the experiments. Their opposite character
is vouched for both by introspection and by the
course of the curves.

(2) Judgments of excitement are less direct,
and the term is equivocal. If it is taken as the
opposite of depressing melancholy, its curve
agrees with that of pleasantness; if it is taken
as the opposite of tranquillity or soothing calm,
its curve agrees with that of unpleasantness: the
reverse curves then agree with those of unpleasantness and of pleasantness, respectively.
If, in default of special instruction, the observer
vacillates between the two meanings of the word,
the curve shows a vacillating character, — partly
'pleasant' and partly 'unpleasant'; the period
and nature of the affective oscillation are vouched
for by introspection. Judgments of depression
are, in their turn, distinctly less direct than those

of excitement, and are often associatively mediated. There is no evidence of a dimension of excitement-depression, still less of a number of exciting and depressing qualities.

(3) Judgments of tension are easy; but tension is described, throughout, in kinæsthetic terms. Increasing tension means, uniformly, increasing unpleasantness, and the curves of the two classes of judgment correspond. Relaxation may be taken as the opposite of unpleasant tension, in which case its curve agrees with the curve of pleasantness, or may be identified with depression. Nowhere is there evidence, in this third case, either of a new affective dimension or of specific qualities.

Naturally, these results are not 'conclusive.' For one thing, the experiments are too few. For another, they were obtained in a single laboratory, and that a laboratory from which criticism of Wundt's doctrine had already proceeded. For a third, the argument upon which the experiments rest is not demonstrably valid. It would, I think, be a very strange thing if three sets of stimuli should affect a number of observers by way of excitement-depression (or tension-relaxation) precisely as they do by way of pleasantness-unpleasantness, — but nobody can prove that such a state of affairs is, on the plural theory, impossible. Were I a champion of affective plurality, I should unhesitatingly urge these objections to the work, and I have no desire to slur them over because I am on the other side. Nevertheless, the results are experimental evidence; Wundt cannot, in the future, appeal to the method of impression as confidently as he has appealed in the past.[69] And if our investigations are compared with those of Brahn and Gent, upon which Wundt relies in the *Physiologische Psychologie*, it will appear, I am very sure, that the critical sauce meted out to the goose must be considerably strengthened for the gander.[70]

If now, in conclusion, I may give, with all due modesty, my own reading of the situation,[71] it is this: that Wundt's tridimensional theory of feelings shows, as it were in typical form, the peculiar features that distinguish his psychology at large. Wundt has, in an eminent degree, the power of generalisation, and his generalisations cover — as generalisations oftentimes do not! — an encyclopædic range of detailed knowledge. But the exercise of this very power leads him to put a certain stamp of finality upon his theories, as if questions were settled in the act of systematisation. You know what I am thinking of:

the theory of space perception, the theory of attention, the definition and demarcation of psychology itself. The affective theory which we have been discussing is typical, then, both for good and for bad. It is good, in that it gives rounded and complete expression to a psychological tendency that, in many minds, has been struggling for utterance. It is bad, in that it offers a solution, ready-made, of problems which in actual fact are ripe only for preliminary and tentative discussion. Like those other theories of attention and of space-perception, it represents the culmination of an epoch of psychological thought; but, like them again, it is rather the starting-point for further inquiry than the statement of assured psychological result. On the whole, I take it as matter of encouragement that generalisation has been at all possible. What has been done, provisionally, at a lower level of knowledge, can be done again, and better done, at a higher. In the meantime, we must not be dogmatic, we must not be too impatient for results, we must not set theory above observed fact; recognising to the full the difficulty and the merit of constructive effort, we must use all the weapons in our critical armoury against ourselves as against others, and against others as against ourselves.

V

ATTENTION AS SENSORY CLEARNESS

LECTURE V

I SUPPOSE that every experimental psychologist has, at one time or another, been confronted with the sceptical question : 'What, after all, has the experimental method done for general psychology ?' As a rule, it is not easy to find an answer : first, because the questioner, both by the fact and by the manner of his asking, betrays an ignorance of psychology at large; but secondly, and more especially, because the influence of the experimental method has, as a matter of fact, made itself felt over the whole extent of the psychological system, and instances fail you by the very number and urgency of your associations. "Wenn ich zusammenfassend sagen soll," — this is Wundt's reply to the question, — "was ich selbst an psychologischen Einsichten der experimentellen Methode verdanke, so kann ich nur antworten : Alles, was ich auf diesem Gebiete für richtig und zum Theil für unumstösslich halte." [1] That is largely and positively said. But if we want details, I think that the experimentalists may justly point to three principal achievements: the complete recasting of the doctrine of memory and association,[2] the creation of a scientific psychology of individual differences,[3] and the discovery of attention.[4]

To say, however, that experimental psychology 'discovered' attention is to make a fairly sweeping claim, and a claim that you may reasonably incline to dispute. What of Hamilton? You will remind me that Hamilton gives a long discussion of "attention as a general phenomenon of consciousness";[5] you may even recall the fact that I myself, in a previous Lecture, quoted this discussion.* What of James Mill, and the twenty-fourth chapter of the *Analysis?*[6] What of Bain, and the theory of attention that we find in *The Emotions and the Will?*[7] Well! I make you a present of Hamilton and Mill and Bain. I will do more; I will cite a strongly worded sentence from Braunschweiger. "It would be hard," says this author, a special student of the history of attention, "to find a single idea or thought that can contribute in any sort of way to the solution of this important problem, which does not appear at least *in nuce* during the eighteenth century."[8] No doubt! — and we are told, in the same manner, that Darwinism goes back to the philosophy

* P. 75.

of Ancient Greece.   But what I mean by the 'discovery' of attention is the explicit formulation of the problem; the recognition of its separate status and fundamental importance; the realisation that the doctrine of attention is the nerve of the whole psychological system, and that as men judge of it, so shall they be judged before the general tribunal of psychology.

In this sense, surely, experimental psychology discovered attention.   And as we connect the name of Helmholtz with the doctrine of sensible quality, and the name of Fechner with that of sensible intensity, so must we connect the name of Wundt with the doctrine of attention, — which, as I see it, is that of sensible clearness. The experiments which Wundt carried out in the early sixties are the beginning of the whole matter; [9] and the system which Wundt has wrought out is informed and infused with attentional theory.   The veriest beginner knows that, if he goes to Wundt, he must read about apperception! [10]

It is true that the discovery of attention did not result in any immediate triumph of the experimental method.   It was something like the discovery of a hornets' nest: the first touch brought out a whole swarm of insistent problems. We have only to travel beyond the limits of

Wundt's system, and we find that 'chaos' of which Pillsbury complains. "Die Aufmerksamkeit," says Ebbinghaus, "ist eine rechte Verlegenheit der Psychologie." [11] I think that he has felt the *Verlegenheit* himself; there is a marked difference between his accounts of sensation and association, on the one side, and his treatment of attention, on the other. A characteristic feature, both of Ebbinghaus' sections and of Pillsbury's recent book, is the constant appeal to casual introspection, to the occurrences of everyday life; and though the appeal is useful, as sustaining the reader's interest, it is none the less a confession of scientific weakness. We expect the illustrations in a modern work on electricity to lead us, beyond themselves, to a severely technical exposition; we do not expect to stop short with the illustrations.

I shall begin my own discussion of attention with an attempt to lay a very ancient ghost, — the ghost that stalks through current statements of psychological method. Kant told us, more than a century ago, that psychology could never rise to the rank of an experimental science, because psychological observation interferes with its own object.[12] We have bowed down before this criticism; and, because the facts were continually against it, we have tried in all sorts of ways to get round the facts, and to save Kant's infallibility while we still went on with our experiments. Let us, now, look the objection squarely in the face. Is there anything peculiar, anything fatal, about attention to mental processes?

We are agreed, I suppose, that scientific method may be summed up in the single word 'observation'; the only way to work in science is to observe those phenomena which form the subject-matter of science. And observation means two things: attention to the phenomena, and record of the phenomena; clear experience, and communication of the experience in words or formulæ. We shall agree, further, that, in order to secure clear experience and adequate report, science has recourse to experiment, — an experiment being, in the last resort, simply an observation that may be repeated, isolated, and varied. What, then, is the difference between natural science and psychology? between experimental inspection and experimental introspection?

We may set out from two very simple cases. (1) Suppose that you are shown two paper discs, the one of an uniform violet, the other composed half of red and half of blue. Your problem is, so to adjust the proportions of red and blue in the second disc that the violet which appears on rotation exactly matches the violet of the first disc. You may repeat this set of observations as often as you will; you may isolate the observations by working in a room that is free from other, possibly disturbing, colours; you may vary the observations by working towards the equality of the violets first from a two-colour disc that is distinctly too blue, then from a disc that is distinctly too red: and so on. (2) Suppose, again, that the chord *c–e–g* is struck, and that you are required to say how many tones it contains. You may repeat this observation; you may isolate it, by working in a quiet room; you may vary it, by sounding the tones first in succession and then all together, or by striking the chord at different parts of the scale. It is clear that, in these cases, there is no difference between introspection and inspection. You are using the same method that you would use for counting the swings of a pendulum, or for taking the readings from a galvanometer scale, in the physical laboratory.

Now let us take some instances in which the material of introspection is more complex. (3) Suppose that a word is called out to you, and that you are asked to observe the effect which this stimulus produces upon consciousness: how

the word affects you, what ideas it calls up, and
so forth. The observation may be repeated;
it may be isolated, — you may be seated in a
dark and silent room, free from disturbances;
and it may be varied, — different words may be
called out, the word may be flashed upon a
screen instead of spoken, etc. Here, however,
there does seem to be a difference between introspection and inspection. The observer who is
watching the course of a chemical reaction, or
the movements of some microscopical creature,
can jot down from moment to moment the
successive phases of the observed phenomenon.
But if you try to report the changes in consciousness, while these changes are in progress, you
interfere with consciousness; your translation
of the mental processes into words introduces
new factors into the experience itself. (4) Suppose, lastly, that you are observing a feeling or
an emotion: a feeling of disappointment or
annoyance, an emotion of anger or chagrin.
Experimental control is still possible; situations
may be arranged, in the psychological laboratory,
such that these feelings may be repeated, isolated
and varied. But your observation of them
interferes, even more seriously than before, with
the course of consciousness. Cool consideration
of an emotion is fatal to its very existence;

N

your anger disappears, your disappointment evaporates, as you examine it.

To overcome this difficulty of the introspective method, students of psychology are usually recommended to delay their observation until the process to be described has run its course, and then to call it back and describe it from memory. Introspection thus becomes retrospection; introspective examination becomes *post mortem* examination. The rule is, oftentimes, a good one for the beginner; and there are cases in which even the experienced psychologist will be wise to follow it. But it is by no means universal. For we must remember, first, that the observations in question may be repeated. There is, then, no reason why the observer to whom the word is called out, or in whom the emotion is set up, should not report at once upon the initial stage of his experience : upon the immediate effect of the word, upon the beginning of the emotive process. It is true that this report interrupts the observation. But after the first stage has been accurately described, further observations may be taken, and the second, third, and following stages similarly described; so that presently a complete report upon the whole experience is obtained. There is, in theory, some danger that the stages are artificially separated; consciousness is a flow, a process, and if we divide it up, we run the risk of missing certain intermediate links. In practice, however, this danger has proved to be very small, — witness the stress laid by many psychologists upon 'fringes' and 'relational feelings'; and we may always have recourse to retrospection as an auxiliary method, and compare our partial results with our memory of a like experience unbroken. Moreover, — and this is a point too often lost sight of, — the practised observer falls into an introspective attitude, has the introspective habit, so to say, ingrained in the texture of his mind; so that it does become possible for him, not only to take mental notes while the observation is in progress, without interfering with consciousness, but even to jot down written notes, as the histologist does while his eye is still held to the ocular of the microscope. Let me cite a parallel case. All of us who are engaged in intellectual work, in the study and the teaching of a science, are obliged to read a very great deal, and to read critically and discerningly, in the state of selective attention. Now the experience that I wish to bring to your minds is this: that, as one is reading, one is able to take mental note of passages to be remembered and employed, without appreciable pause in the process of reading itself, and without even momentary loss of the thread of the writer's argument. I am not concerned here with the analysis of this experience, but with the mere fact, — with the fact that, when we close the covers of a book after two or three hours' reading, we have marked down half-a-dozen passages for further use without interruption of the main current of consciousness. That is the technical, critical attitude; and the introspective attitude is akin to it. There can be no doubt, again, from the results of such experiments as those of Solomons and Stein,[13] that the writing of notes, brief catchwords and symbols, need not in any way interfere with the introspection of the moment. And if we refer the disappearance of affective processes to the incompatibility of affection and attention, — I have spoken of this matter earlier, — rather than to the impossibility of direct introspection in general, we have, I think, made out our case all along the line; there is no difference, in principle, between inspection and introspection.[14]

So far, then, as my own psychological thinking is concerned, I do not believe that that ghost will walk again. Attention in psychology and attention in natural science are of the same nature and obey the same laws. But now — what is attention?

The analytical study of attention has been subject to two adverse influences: the pressure of popular psychology, and the obviousness of application. Popular psychology regards attention, indifferently, as faculty and as manifestation of faculty. It is a faculty, whose operation produces or prevents certain changes in the mental life; it is also the activity or the state — the activity of remarking, noticing, observing; the state of sustained concentration — which manifests and attests that operation.[15] Scientific psychology has, in very large measure, fought itself clear of the theory of faculties; but the influence of the popular conception is still shown in the tendency to treat the attentive consciousness as a whole, to synthetise objective and subjective, incidental and essential, in a single view. There is, of course, a typical attentive consciousness, as there is a typical memorial or imaginative or expectant or habituated consciousness. Nevertheless, the road to assured result lies through the elements of consciousness, and has consciousness itself as its goal; [16] short cuts to synthesis, however promising, end always in one-sided theory.

The intrinsic tendency of psychology to deal with attention in the large has been further strengthened by the practical importance of

attention, its importance in educational regard.
Here, if anywhere, the passage from theory to
practice has seemed to be short and easy; here,
if anywhere, a sound psychology might be of
immediate service to the responsive teacher.
Since, however, the problems of education are
necessarily formulated in terms of a completed
psychological system, and since they are of the
kind that requires speedy solution, this obviousness of application has been a real hindrance
to psychology; it has held us to the old paths,
and has discouraged that work of scattered
exploration by which alone a science is enabled
to advance.

I think that these two things — tradition and
application — are mainly responsible for the
unsettled state of attentional psychology. But I
think also that, in spite of these two things,
analysis has gone far enough to furnish us with a
clue to the attentional problem. It seems to me
beyond question that the problem of attention
centres in the fact of sensible clearness. Let me
call my witnesses!

There are two men who have a special claim
to be heard in this matter. The first is Wundt,
and his claim is of long standing. Now Wundt
declares that there are two "wesentliche Bestandtheile," two essential factors — and the word

'essential' is used in the sense of 'necessary,' not of 'important' — in every process of attention: first, the increased clearness of a particular idea or group of ideas, which is connected with the characteristic feeling of activity; and secondly the inhibition of other available impressions or memory-images. Attention, in other words, means a redistribution of clearness in consciousness, the rise of some elements and the fall of others, with an accompanying total feeling of a characteristic kind. That is the statement of the *Physiologische Psychologie* of 1903; and the discussion of attention in 1874 opens, in the same spirit, with the now familiar analogy of the *Blickfeld* and *Blickpunkt*.[17] Our second witness is Pillsbury, who writes, without theoretical prepossession, from a general review of what had been said and done in the field of attention up to 1903. Pillsbury's statement is that "l'attention accroît la clarté des sensations sur lesquelles elle porte." He goes on: "il est très difficile de préciser . . . ce que l'on entend par clarté. Pourtant tout le monde sait ce que le terme signifie et tout le monde a éprouvé le changement qui s'opère pendant l'attention." [18] If, however, we rank clearness as one of the intensive attributes of sensation, this difficulty is accounted for; we can no more define clearness, in the strict sense of definition, than we can define intensity itself.

You will not thank me, now, if I bring up a regiment of psychologists, in single file, each to deliver his testimony and disappear. I will follow a less tedious method. Baldwin's *Dictionary* distinguishes five types of attentional theory[19]: let us, then, find a typical definition of attention, under each one of these five headings, and see if our emphasis of clearness is confirmed.

First come the affectional theories, represented by Ribot. What is the definition? "L'attention," says Ribot, "consiste en un état intellectuel, exclusif ou prédominant," — "est un monoïdéisme intellectuel," — "avec adaptation spontanée ou artificielle de l'individu." A monoideism with adaptation implies, of course, a good deal more than clearness, but it very certainly implies clearness; and we read in Ribot's text of 'une idée maitresse,' 'une représentation vive,' 'un état de conscience devenu prépondérant,' — phrases in which the reference becomes explicit.[20] The theories of 'psychical energy' or of 'original activity' come next in order; here we may quote Ladd. An 'act of attention in its most highly complex form' is defined as "a purposeful volition, suffused with peculiar feelings of effort or strain and accompanied by a changed condition of the field of discriminative consciousness, as respects intensity, content, and clearness." Later on Ladd speaks of a "focussing of psychical energy upon some phases, or factors, or objects, of consciousness, and the relative withdrawal of such energy from other phases, factors, objects."[21] So Stumpf, while he defines attention as a special kind of feeling, 'die Lust am Bemerken,' notes that the primary effect of attention is "die längere Forterhaltung [des bezüglichen Inhaltes] . . . und die aufmerksame Fixirung während dieser Dauer"; or, rather, the primary effect is "ein Bemerken," while the longer duration is "ein selbstverständliches Mitergebnis der fort-gesetzten Urteilstätigkeiten, in welche der In-halt verflochten wird." [22] This *Fixirung, Be-merken* is, evidently, our 'clearness.' Thirdly, we have the 'conative' or 'motor' theories. Stout says that "attention is simply conation in so far as it finds satisfaction in the fuller presentation of its object, without actual change in the object."[23] Baldwin defines attention as "the act of holding a presentation before the mind"; it increases the intensity of sensation and "the vividness of representative states."[24] The next group, theories of 'intensity' and 're-enforcement,' is represented by Bradley. "At-tention (whatever it may be besides) at any rate means predominance in consciousness. . . . Not theorising but applying descriptive metaphors, we may call attention a state which implies domination or chief tenancy of consciousness. Or we may compare it to the focussing of an optical instrument, or to the area of distinct vision in the retinal field." [25] Lastly, for the theory of 'inhibition,' we may quote Ferrier. "Just as we can at will fix our gaze on some one object out of many appealing to our sense of vision, and see this clearly while all others are indistinct or invisible, so we can fix our intellectual gaze, or concentrate our consciousness, on some one idea or class of ideas to the exclusion of all others in the field of intellectual vision." [26]

You will understand that I am not here concerned with the validity of the classification of theories given in the *Dictionary*, or with these theories themselves considered as explanations of the attentive consciousness, or with the authors' total descriptions of the state of attention. My point is simply this: that, wherever you look, you find some form of reference to clearness; clearness is, so to say, the first thing that men lay hands on, when they begin to speak about attention. I do not want to press the point *ad nauseam*. I will add, only, that if you take the quite recent books, those that have appeared since Pillsbury completed his review, you will find just the same thing. "Die Aufmerksamkeit," says Ebbinghaus, "besteht in dem lebhaften Hervortreten und Wirksamwerden einzelner seelischer Gebilde auf Kosten anderer, für die gleichwohl auch gewisse Veranlassungen des Zustandekommens vorhanden sind."[27] "The fact that consciousness always has a focal point, which reveals the momentary activity of the mind, is what is meant by the fact of attention, so far as it can be described in terms of the *content* of consciousness"; that is Angell's statement.[28] And Judd, though his standpoint is different from ours, comes to the same conclusion. "The word 'attention' refers more especially to the selective character of the organising process, whereby one particular group of sensory factors is emphasised more than any other group"; "attention is merely a name for various phases of selective arrangement within experience."[29] Emphasis and selective arrangement are, again, our fact of 'clearness' translated into systematic terms. Finally, Meumann describes the 'Grunderscheinung des Aufmerksamkeitsvorganges' as follows: "in dem Masse, als einige bestimmte Bewusstseinsinhalte oder Tätigkeiten in den Aufmerksamkeitszustand geraten, haben *diese* höhere Klarheit, höheren Bewusstseinsgrad, werden vorübergehend der Mittelpunkt des ganzen psychischen Lebens . . . während in demselben Masse der übrige Bewusstseinsinhalt in niederem Grade bewusst ist und seinen Einfluss auf den Gang der psychischen Tätigkeit verliert."[30]

All this cataloguing is dry work; I can plead only that it was necessary. Indeed, I may claim your gratitude that there is not more of it; for I have, myself, been obliged to turn up a small library of references, in order to make sure that my position is well taken. With that assurance gained, let us proceed to the study of clearness as an attribute of sensation. Under what conditions does a sensation appear with maximal clearness in consciousness?

We shall do best to approach this question empirically, without theoretical bias, and without attempt at a systematic classification. Beginning in this way, we find the most obvious condition of clearness in (1) the *intensity* of stimulus, and its sensory equivalents. Loud sounds, bright lights, strong tastes and smells, severe pressures, extreme temperatures, intense pains, — all these things are clear in virtue of their intensity; they attract or compel our attention, as the phrase goes, in spite of ourselves; they force their way to the focus of consciousness,

whatever the obstacles that they have to overcome.   A like value attaches to long durations
and wide extensions, in so far as these are the
equivalents of a high degree of sensible intensity.
The qualification is important, because it reminds
us of the phenomena of adaptation and fatigue.
The first really hot days of summer, and the first
really cold days of winter, constrain our attention; but we soon grow accustomed to summer
heat and winter cold.   Enter a family circle,
one member of which is partially deaf, and you
are embarrassed by the loudness of the voices;
but at the end of a week you will cease to notice
anything unusual.   Tire yourself out, and a
stimulus that would ordinarily attract your attention passes unregarded; under the conditions,
it is no longer an intensive stimulus.   Duration,
then, if it is to mean clearness, must be the psychophysical equivalent of intensity, as it is, *e.g.*,
in certain forms of auditory rhythm.[31]   And the
same thing holds of extension.

I said just now that the appeal to casual introspection is a confession of scientific weakness,
and the remark applies in the present connection.
We do not know at what average degree of intensity clearness makes its appearance, and we do
not know within what quantitative limits the
psychophysical equivalence of intensity and du-

ration, intensity and extension, obtains. The general dependence of clearness upon intensity of stimulus is an evident fact, but it is a fact that we must leave in the rough.[32]

It is natural to pass from intensity, duration, and extension to the quality of stimulus. And I think it cannot be denied that (2) form or quality of stimulus is one of the conditions of clearness of sensation. I gave some illustrations in my first Lecture. There are certain pains, by no means intensive, that are nevertheless urgently, insistently, importunately clear, — pains that we 'cannot get away from' by any ordinary distraction of attention. There are certain organic complexes, also, which in my own experience have this power to compel the attention; they are intimate, worrying, wicked things.* The taste of bitter, the smell of musk, the sight of yellow belong, for me, to the same category; the least trace of them fascinates me. No doubt, there is here a wide range of individual difference. But I cannot doubt that some sensible qualities are, intrinsically, clearer than others. James comes at least very close to this doctrine

* My general name for all these experiences is 'quick' — not in the sense of 'fast,' but in that of 'intimately vital.' In my child-hood's speech 'the quick' was the tender flesh beneath the finger nails, and the wider use of the term is evidently based upon this association.

in his chapter on *Instinct*, and Müller in his references to *Eindringlichkeit*. "Es erscheint möglich, dass sich zwei Empfindungen, falls sie von *verschiedener* Qualität sind, hinsichtlich der Eindringlichkeit anders zu einander verhalten, als hinsichtlich der Intensität. . . . Man kann zwei Empfindungen verschiedener Qualität, z. B. eine Rotempfindung und eine Grauempfindung, zwar hinsichtlich ihrer Eindringlichkeit einigermassen mit einander vergleichen, hat hingegen nicht in gleicher Weise ein Urteil darüber, ob der Abstand vom Nullpunkte für diese oder jene beider Empfindungen grösser sei." Ebbinghaus brings the facts under the heading of interest, the "Gefühlswert der Eindrücke"; but the category is evidently too large for them.[33]

In the third place we may consider (3) the temporal relations of stimulus, and especially repetition and suddenness. A stimulus that is repeated again and again is likely to attract the attention, even if at first it is altogether unremarked. Pillsbury instances the case of a man absorbed in work; you may call his name once, and he will not hear you, — but call again and again, without raising your voice, and he will presently respond. Experiences of this sort are common enough, though their analysis is not quite easy. There is always the possibility, *e.g.*, that the stimulus may operate at a moment when consciousness is free, so that it produces its effect less by sheer repetition than by suddenness or intensity. On the other hand, there seems to be no reason à *priori* why summation of stimuli should not be a condition of clearness. Ebbinghaus cites, in this connection, the fact of practice; but that is, surely, a phenomenon of a very different order. "Der geübte Kliniker sieht an einem neuen Fall, der geübte Techniker an einer neuen Maschine sofort eine Menge von ihm bekannten und geläufigen Dingen, die der Ungeübte erst allmählich oder auch gar nicht bemerkt." But the previous cases and the older machines were *attentively* examined. No amount of repeated visual stimuli would make a surgeon or a technician; expert knowledge presupposes attention. The question here, however, is whether repetition as such renders a stimulus clear, brings it to the focus of attention. I think that it may; but I should like to have experimental proof. It would also be interesting to know at what point the summation-effect gives way to habituation, and whether habituation itself is ever possible without foregone attention.[34]

Sudden stimuli and sudden changes of stimulus exert a familiar influence upon attention. As regards the latter, Stern tells us, "ganz allgemein,

dass die Veränderungserregbarkeit mit abneh-
mender Geschwindigkeit abnimmt." "Lang-
same Veränderungen sind weniger geeignet als
schnelle, . . . eine Reaction der Aufmerksamkeit . . . herbeizuführen." The law rests upon
a fairly large body of experimental results,, obtained in various sense-departments.[35]

The mention of change leads us, however,
(4) to a fourth condition of great moment, the
condition that Pillsbury sets in the first place:
movement of stimulus. I quote a few instances
from Stumpf. "Sternschnuppen, deren Bild
auf seitliche Netzhautteile fällt, werden doch in
Folge ihrer raschen Bewegung sofort bemerkt.
Hält man einen Bleistift in solcher Entfernung
von einer brennenden Lampe, dass sein Schatten
auf einer weissen Papierfläche auch im directen
Sehen eben nicht mehr erkennbar ist, so wird er
sofort wieder erkennbar, wenn man den Bleistift
bewegt. Beim Tastsinn fand E. H. Weber, dass
innerhalb der sg. Empfindungskreise, in welchen
gleichzeitige Berührungseindrücke nicht mehr
unterschieden werden, doch Bewegungen noch
leicht wahrnehmbar sind." Movement, indeed,
is a stimulus of such individuality that some
authors — Exner, *e.g.*, — speak outright of movement sensations, and Heller and Stern distinguish direct and indirect touch, as we all dis-

tinguish direct and indirect vision, in terms of sensitivity for resting and moving stimuli. At all events, there can be no doubt that the stimulus which moves in the field of vision or of touch has a remarkable power to draw the attention.

Since our classification is empirical only, we may follow Stumpf's example, and include under the present rubric the phenomena that Külpe describes as 'partial tonal change,' the "continuous or discrete intensive and qualitative variation of a tone or clang within a connection of tones or clangs." A tone that beats, or recurs intermittently, or fluctuates in pitch, within a chord or compound clang stands out clearly from its background. "Everyone must have noticed how strongly the attention is attracted in a concert by the voice which carries the melody. The singer's voice, even if comparatively weak, can be heard without special effort above a full orchestral accompaniment, in passages where it alone has to rise and fall, to execute trills and runs. . . . The same voice is obscured at once, if it is allowed to rest upon a single note." [36] —

We began our list, naturally enough, with a reference to the attributes and elementary relations of stimulus. It is clear, however, that we are breaking away from stimulus. If the 'moving' tone can be so named only by analogy to touch and sight, 'movement' itself has a psychological significance that extends far beyond its formal definition in terms of space and time. And 'suddenness,' in the same way, is more than a temporal relation; the sudden stimulus is likely to be the surprising, the unexpected stimulus. These remarks apply, now, with still greater force to the fifth condition of clearness, — (5) the novelty, rarity, unaccustomedness, strangeness of stimuli. The value of this category is not undisputed. "Ein ungewöhnlicher Sinnesreiz," says Müller, "muss, um in besonderer Weise auf uns zu wirken, in Folge seiner Stärke oder anderer Momente die sinnliche Aufmerksamkeit bereits auf sich gezogen haben, so dass er und seine Neuheit und ungewöhnliche Eigenthümlichkeit uns zur Wahrnehmung kommt." While, however, there is truth in this statement, I think that the truth is partial. Novelty and unaccustomedness mean, in psychological terms, 'non-associatedness.' The novel impression is the impression that lacks associative supplements in consciousness; that stands alone, in isolation. Such an impression, provided that it is at all intensive, seems to me to become clear in its own right; it is 'startling,' just as the sudden stimulus is 'surprising' and the moving stimulus 'disturbing.' For the rest, the effect of novelty is acknowledged by James, Külpe, Ebbinghaus, and Pillsbury.[37]

A sixth condition of clearness, a condition of the very widest range, is (6) that described by Ebbinghaus as "the presence in consciousness of corresponding, *i.e.* similar ideas," and by Müller — under two separate headings — as "the likeness of the incoming sensation to the idea, sensation, or image already present in the mind" and the "associative relationship between the incoming sensation and the existent idea, or more generally between the sensation and the whole circle of ideas dominant at the moment." The condition is of great systematic importance, since, for some psychologists, it forms the bridge that leads from passive to active, from involuntary to voluntary attention. It is also, as I said, of the very widest range; for it covers all cases, from precise duplication, so to say, of incoming sensation by preëxistent image, up to the appeal of stimulus to a dominant psychophysical tendency which, at the time, may be unrepresented in consciousness.

Classical illustrations of the first kind are afforded by Helmholtz' experiments upon stereoscopic vision and the hearing of partial tones. Helmholtz found that, when the two halves of a stereoscopic slide were illuminated in a dark chamber by the electric spark, he was able to see double images at will, "wenn ich mir vorher lebhaft vorzustellen suche, wie sie aussehen müssen." So, in the case of partial tones, he devised a method to "obtain a series of gradual transitional stages between the isolated partial and the compound tone, in which the first is readily retained by the ear. By applying this process I have generally succeeded in making perfectly untrained ears recognise the existence of upper partial tones." Apart from these experimental results we know that, in everyday life, the man who finds is the man who knows what to look for; the sailor at the masthead, the hunter on the trail, the pathologist at the microscope, are all cases in point.

At the other end of the scale stand the permanent adult interests, connate or acquired, which — even when not represented in idea — are ready to be touched off by a casual stimulus. The collector, the inventor, the expert are aroused to keen attention by stimuli which the rest of the world pass without notice. I have already mentioned the psychological attitude, the introspective habit, which so grows on one with time and experience that at last everything — novels and games and children's sayings and the behaviour of an audience in a lecture-room — becomes tributary to psychology, and one can no more help psychologising than one can help breathing. "Some years ago," Jastrow writes, "I became interested in cases of extreme longevity, particularly of centenarianism, and for some months every conversation seemed to lead to this topic, and every magazine and newspaper offered some new item about old people. Nowadays my interest is transferred to other themes; but the paragrapher continues quite creditably to meet my present wants, and the centenarians have vanished." It is the vanishing, of course, that is the source of danger. If you are 'favourably impressed' by a scientific theory, the facts that support the theory crowd in upon you, while the outstanding facts, those that cannot connect with the trend of consciousness, fail to present themselves; you mean to be impartial, and the conditions of attention make you one-sided. I said, in a previous Lecture, that scientific theories sit more lightly upon their defenders than opponents are apt to suppose.*   I must add, then, that this result is secured by the cultivation of the critical attitude, the scientific habit *par excellence*, which becomes as potent as any other in the control of attention.[38]

* P. 48.

Our list of conditions has led us from attributes of stimulus to psychophysical disposition. We might, possibly, bring under this latter heading (7) the accommodation of the organs of sense, though I incline to think that an empirical classification would rank it as a separate factor. Wundt gives fixation as one of the external conditions of visual clearness. Külpe expresses himself more sceptically. "We shall, perhaps, be more correct in supposing that [these motor conditions] are only indirectly conducive to the apperception of particular contents, as determining the attributes of the contents themselves." But is not clearness precisely one of these attributes? It is true that the accidental convergence of the eyes upon some object in the field of vision, while we are mentally occupied with other things, does not bring that object to the focus of consciousness. Nevertheless, in so far as the phenomena of 'fluctuation of attention,' of which we speak later, are referable to peripheral conditions, we must admit that accommodation of the sense-organ is at least a negative condition of peripheral clearness.[39]

I come, finally, (8) to the much-discussed cases in which the absence or cessation of stimulus constrains the attention. We do not notice the ticking of the clock upon our wall, but we notice its silence. We do not notice the ordinary noises from the street, but we notice the unusual quiet after a snowfall. Fechner gives some salient instances. "Der Müller erwacht, wenn der Gang der Mühle stockt, der Schläfer in der Kirche, wenn der Prediger zu sprechen, das von der Amme eingesungene Kind, wenn die Amme zu singen aufhört, der bei Nachtlicht zu schlafen Gewöhnte, wenn das Nachtlicht erlischt, der im Wagen Fahrende, wenn der Wagen still steht." How are these effects to be explained?

Notice, first, that they are not simply instances of the cessation of unnoticed stimuli. In every case, foregone attention, and prolonged or frequent attention, is presupposed. We do, *e.g.*, attend to the ticking of the clock, again and again, in the course of the day; we hear it when we look up to see the time, and we hear it, with all plainness, in intervals of thinking and reading and writing. The miller is interested in the running of his mill; he has listened, often enough, to make sure that things are in good order. The traveller, before he dozed off to sleep, was made very uncomfortable by the jolting of the coach; he wished more than once that he was at home in his comfortable bed. On the other hand, the cessation of an unnoticed stimulus, of a stimulus that you have not attended to, is not necessarily remarked. Flowers may be put upon your mantelpiece, curtains hung across your windows, — put in place, and taken away again, — without your observing either their coming or their going.

But more than this: I doubt if any really unnoticed stimulus attracts the attention by its cessation. The appeal to sleep is very doubtful, and Fechner's examples are general at the best. Suppose that the maid breaks an ornament in the drawing-room, an ornament that you have long ago ceased to think of; you do not notice its absence. If it was large, and stood in a conspicuous position, you are struck by the novel look of that part of the room, and you cast about for an explanation. If it was small and inconspicuous, you do not discover your loss until some chance association recalls it to mind, and you search and fail to find it.

Once more: if objective cessation may attract the attention, subjective cessation may persist under circumstances that would normally bring the stimulus to clear consciousness. Delbœuf tells us that he was once staying at a country house which stood near a waterfall. The noise was so great that, on the first day of his stay, he was hardly able to follow the conversation at table. However, he soon grew accustomed to it.

Waking up one night, about a week after his arrival, he was surprised to find that he could not hear the water, "même en y prêtant une attention soutenue"; only after he had got up and looked out of window did he succeed in recovering the auditory perception of the fall. Here was psychophysical disposition, but no clearness! And Delbœuf reminds us of a very common experience of the same kind: the experience of waking at night, and listening for the tick of the clock. Is there anybody who has got out of bed, under these circumstances, in the assured conviction that watch or clock has stopped?

Evidently, these several cases must be clearly distinguished, and referred each to its own special set of conditions. If we go back to our original instances, the ticking of the clock and the noises from the street, it seems to me that we notice their cessation, for the most part, only when we are looking for them; as we glance towards the clock, as we pause in our work and listen for the familiar noise, we become aware of the silence. It is not that the absence of stimulus commands attention, but that an expectant attention, a psychophysical predisposition, is disappointed, baffled by the silence. This view is borne out by the observation that the clock may have been silent for a long while before we notice that it has stopped.   If, however, you think that the explanation goes too far, let us try another. It has been shown, experimentally, that we attend best under a slight distraction; maximal clearness requires a little 'effort,' as we say, for its attainment.   The clock and the street noises may be considered as distractions, stimulating distractions, of this kind.   Their removal would then, after the current 'spurt' of energy had ceased, make itself felt as a general restlessness or unsteadiness, a widespread complex of organic sensations.   I think you will agree that this general restlessness sometimes appears, and that we work from it to the cessation of the familiar stimulus; though I myself do not find it as frequently as I find a baffled expectation.   A third and very similar interpretation derives from Lehmann's law of the 'indispensableness of the habitual.'   According to that law, you will remember, the removal of an accustomed stimulus leaves a need, a *Bedürfnis*.   This comes to consciousness, in organic terms, as uneasiness or discomfort; and again we have a positive starting-point for the attention.[40]

We must content ourselves with general explanations, since this little group of facts has never been brought under experimental control. Indeed, what impresses one most strongly, all through the review which we have now completed, is the need of detailed experimental work. I have, of course, omitted a good many experimental references that I might have given; but those of you who know what I have left out will realise how very much more there is that I could not put in. Even as things are, however, there is a ray of daylight. Just as we found the various theories of attention held together by the central fact of clearness, so we find that all these empirical conditions of conscious clearness may be grouped together as conditions of a powerful impression of the nervous system. Let us look at them in order.

Intensive stimuli — and their equivalents in space and time — must, naturally, set up psychophysical processes of relatively great strength; and intensive excitations will not be easily inhibited or obscured by the other excitatory processes of the moment. So the qualitative stimuli that are effective for clearness must make appeal to some peculiar susceptibility of the nervous system, general or individual. — Repeated stimuli produce a cumulative effect, and thus take their place, as regards nervous excitation, alongside of intensive. Sudden stimuli impinge upon nervous elements that have hitherto been free from stimulation of their particular kind, *i.e.* upon nervous elements of a high degree of excitability;

and it is probable that the excitations which they set up suffer less dispersion and diffusion, within the nervous system, than the excitations resulting from gradual application of stimulus. — Moving stimuli arouse different nervous elements in quick succession, so that there is no possibility of fatigue or of sensory adaptation; in a sense, therefore, the effect of the moving stimulus is cumulative.— Novel stimuli are isolated stimuli; they have neither to share their effect with associates nor to hold their own against rivals. The excitation set up by the novel is thus of the same order as that set up by the sudden. — As for the effect of the anticipatory image, it is clear that, the more nearly the excitation correlated with the given stimulus coincides with a psychophysical excitation already in progress, the more easily will it make its way within the nervous system and the more dominant will it become. And, in the same way, excitations that coincide with modes of excitatory activity habitual to the particular nervous system, excitations that are in the line of a 'psychophysical disposition,' will evidently have a greater effect than others that are less accustomed. — Lastly, peripheral accommodation opens the gateway to the cortex, and permits the stimulus to operate at its full strength from the first.[41]

I do not think that it is worth while, in an elementary discussion, to go further into physiological theory.   Nor shall I attempt to recast our empirical classification of conditions, and make it scientific.   The list stands very much as Lotze left it.   It is true that Lotze himself, and later psychologists from Wundt to Pillsbury, draw a distinction, in more or less definite lines, between physiological and psychological, external and internal, objective and subjective conditions.   But what is external in one system becomes internal in another, and it is not difficult to argue either that all alike are objective or that all alike are subjective.   All are objective, in that they operate by way of the nervous system; all are subjective, in that the specific organisation of the nervous system determines their effect.   I will only suggest, then, that the common element which, empirically, holds all the conditions together — the ultimate condition of clearness at large — may be designated as nervous disposition, predisposition of the nervous system and its sensory attachments.[42]   It is the task of genetic psychology to classify the determinants of attention in the order of time, as ordinal, generic, individual; it is the task of experimental psychology to delimit and quantify their influence; and it is the task of physiology to exhibit the mechanism of their nervous operation.

VI

THE LAWS OF ATTENTION: I

LECTURE VI

THE LAWS OF ATTENTION: I

MY last Lecture was, in effect, a plea for a simplification of the psychology of attention. Külpe tells us, in his *Grundriss*, that psychologists have tended to find "the real object of investigation into the psychology of space, not in the spatial attributes, but in the spatial relations. . . . The result has been an almost total neglect of the perception of extension and figure, and an almost exclusive regard of the perception of distance and position." And he remarks further that, in the psychology of time, "interval has been given the preference over duration with as perplexing results as follow from the preference of distance over extension in the psychology of space." [1] I believe that much of our difficulty in the psychology of attention arises, in the same way, from our concessions to tradition and to practical demands; and that we should do well to sit down in serious earnest to a psychology of clearness, — considering clearness as an attribute of sensation, conditioned upon nervous predisposition, just exactly as quality is an attribute of sensation, conditioned upon nervous differentiation. How far this elementary psychology of attention could be carried it is, evidently, impossible to predict; but the number of experimental problems suggested by the preceding Lecture shows that there are many and definite points of attack.

However, a science does not advance according to any prearranged logical plan, but haltingly and unevenly, as the interests of individual workers prompt, or the claims of practical utility dictate. And the experimental psychology of attention centres, as a matter of fact, about some half-dozen large problems, — in part relatively new; in part handed down from the empirical psychology of the eighteenth century, — which have been discussed again and again, to the neglect of other and equally important questions. We are still inclined to speak, not of 'the' experimental psychology of attention, but of Wundt's or Stumpf's or James' or Müller's views upon attention. I shall not attempt, now, to lay out an ideal programme for further work; the attempt would be overbold, and the programme would not be followed. I desire rather to review what we know, what has already been done; and I shall therefore treat the elementary psychology of attention topically, under those half-dozen headings. For the sake of clearness, I shall throw each heading into the form of a law, a general statement of the behaviour of conscious contents given in the state of attention. But the statement is not to be understood dogmatically, for we shall be largely occupied with arguments and results that make against its universal validity; the 'law' is rather a challenge, an appeal to the bar of fact.

My first 'law,' in this sense of the term, runs as follows: (1) *clearness is an attribute of sensation*, which, within certain limits, may be varied independently of the other concurrent attributes. What are the facts?

In the first place, there can be no doubt of the independent status of clearness as sensation-attribute. As Wundt says: "Klarheit und Stärke der Eindrücke sind durchaus voneinander verschieden"; "das Klarer- und das Stärker-werden eines Eindrucks sind . . . subjectiv wohl zu unterscheidende Vorgänge." [2] There are, in my experience, very few departments of psychological observation in which the distinction of clearness from the other attributes of mental processes offers appreciable difficulty.

Nevertheless, independent status does not necessarily mean independent variability. It is true that most sensible qualities may be present at any degree of clearness; but, as I have already pointed out, the rule is not universal, — there are qualities that appear to be bound up with a determinate clearness, or at any rate to admit of only a very narrow range of clearness-degree. And when we turn to intensity, we are upon debatable ground from the start. Is clearness ever independent of intensity? or, in popular phrase, do we ever attend to a sensation without thereby making it stronger?

You will find all sorts of opinion: that attention intensifies sensation, that attention leaves sensible intensity unaffected, that attention reduces the intensity of sensation. On the whole, however, the trend of psychological belief just now seems to favour an interdependence of the two attributes. Pillsbury, who devotes a good part of his first chapter to a balancing of the evidence, *pro* and *con*, ends with a *non liquet:* "il semble donc que cette discussion sur les rapports entre la clarté et l'intensité reste sans conclusion."[3] I think, though, that his own leanings — if one may presume to read between the lines — are towards a coupling of the two attributes, at least within certain limits. This is also Külpe's view in the *Grundriss.* "Within certain narrow limits, . . . contents are really intensified in the state of attention." "The sensation of a loud sound, inattentively experienced, may seem equal . . . to that of a faint sound, attentively experienced. Again, it is interesting to note that the alteration of judgment by inattentive observation is always precisely the same as the alteration produced by a reduction of the intensive, spatial, or temporal values of the impressions, except that it is somewhat more uncertain. . . . This fact requires further investigation." [4] Wundt writes, to the same effect, "dass beide [Eigenschaften] einen gewissen Einfluss auf einander äussern können. . . . So bemerkt man, wenn ein Reiz das Bewusstsein bei grosser Unaufmerksamkeit trifft und dann in gleicher Stärke wiederholt wird, wie z. B. beim unerwarteten Stundenschlag einer Thurmuhr, dass der zweite Eindruck entschieden nicht bloss deutlicher, sondern scheinbar auch intensiver wahrgenommen wird. Das nämliche zeigt sich, wenn man sich willkürlich anstrengt, Erinnerungs- und Phantasiebilder zu erwecken und möglichst intensiv im Bewusstsein festzuhalten." [5] Ebbinghaus admits that the experimental evidence is doubtful, but argues, from general experience, that "eine allgemeinen Erhöhung der Empfindungsstärke durch Zuwendung der Aufmerksamkeit durchaus wahrscheinlich ist." He gives the illustrations that Wundt had

given before him: the varying intensity of the bell
strokes, heard with attention and with inattention, and the hallucinatory character of images in
a state of sustained and concentrated attention.[6]
Pillsbury and Ebbinghaus both reply to the objection that an intensifying effect of attention
would falsify our perceptions, would jeopardise
the validity of Weber's Law. Pillsbury suggests
that the increase of intensity is not absolute, not
the addition of a constant amount, but relative,
proportional to the intrinsic intensity of the
stimulus; and Ebbinghaus points out that normal intensity is, after all, intensity in the state of
attention. "[Es] beziehen sich alle genaueren
Angaben über Empfindungen, über ihre Eigenschaften, Schwellenwerte u. s. w., . . . durchweg
auf eine erhöhte ihnen zugewandte Aufmerksamkeit. Verschiedenheiten aber, die nun noch
etwa durch verschiedene Grade einer solchen er-
höhten Aufmerksamkeit hervorgebracht werden
könnten, werden als unerheblich betrachtet werden dürfen." My impression is that views of this
sort are gaining ground in psychology, as against,
e.g., Stumpf's doctrine that only weak sensations
are intensified by attention. Stumpf, you will
remember, looks at the operation of attention
from the negative side; the weak sensation rises,
by the removal of counter-influences within the

nervous system, to the full (or approximately the full) intensity which it would have possessed in its own right had those adverse influences been absent.[7] However, I will quote an authority on the opposite side. "[Eine] verstärkende Funktion der Aufmerksamkeit," says Münsterberg, "giebt es nicht; neuere Experimente bestätigen die schlichte Erfahrung, auf die schon Fechner hinwies, dass ein graues Papier an der Stelle, der sich die Aufmerksamkeit zuwendet, nicht heller erscheint; das schwache Licht wird nicht intensiver, ein Gewicht nicht schwerer, eine Linie nicht länger, ein Ton nicht lauter, wenn unsere Aufmerksamkeit die Vorstellung erfasst."[8] Münsterberg's statement is in flat disagreement with those which I have just been reading.

Experiment must decide; but direct experiment is very difficult. Let me remind you of an historical incident which has always seemed to me to be characteristic for psychology at large, and — if looked at in the right way — encouraging to the student of psychology. Mach and Stumpf sat down together before a harmonium, in the physical laboratory at Prague, to decide the question whether attention to one of the component tones in an ordinary musical chord does or does not strengthen that particular tone. The chord was sounded, and the two men listened.

"Während Mach die Verstärkung ganz deutlich zu hören angab," says Stumpf, who tells the story, "konnte ich nichts davon finden." "Soviel ist sicher, dass bei ganz unveränderten Umständen eine Verstärkung starker Töne neben anderen gleichzeitigen starken Tönen für mich nicht wahrnehmbar ist, während Mach sie auch dann wahrzunehmen erklärt." And he concludes, resignedly, that individuals differ.[9] I do not know about the individual differences: but I call the observation characteristic, because it may stand as a typical instance of divergent introspections; and I call it encouraging, because the student may take heart from it to hold by his own introspective conviction on unsettled points. No doubt, both Mach and Stumpf heard what they say they heard. 'No doubt,' I say, though I myself cannot hear as Mach hears. But since we have, in science, to pass beyond individual experience, the direct method must be given up for an indirect; we must seek to arrange conditions in such a way that the introspective discrepancies disappear.

The experiments made by the method of distraction are exceedingly interesting.[10] But though they are not very numerous, I cannot here attempt to review them. Criticism of opinion may be condensed into relatively few words;

criticism of experimental method needs time and detail. I will rather give you a brief account of experiments recently carried out in the Cornell Laboratory by my colleague Professor Bentley,[11] — experiments which point quite definitely to the positive conclusion that, even in the case of strong stimuli, attention has an intensifying effect. The stimuli, which were presented in pairs, were the sounds produced by the ordinary gravity phonometer. To the one stimulus of each pair, the observer was maximally attentive; from the other he was distracted. The distraction was effected by means of odours, which we had found in previous investigations to be superior to such things as counting, adding, multiplying, etc. Suppose, then, that two sounds, a weaker and a stronger, are given; and that the weaker is the sound attended to, the stronger the sound distracted from. If the observer judges the two sounds to be of equal intensity, still more if he judges that the objectively weaker sound is the more intensive of the two, we have an overestimation of intensity in the state of attention.

Out of 300 preliminary experiments, 285 were successful. Of these 285 judgments, 136 showed an overestimation of the stimulus attended to, 40 showed an underestimation of that stimulus, and 109 reported the relation of the two stimuli correctly. Further experiments came out in the same way. And experiments with two pairs of intensive stimuli, weak and loud, which might be supposed — under Weber's Law — to measure equal sense-distances, gave almost identical results; the overestimations with the loud stood to the overestimations with the weak stimuli in the ratio 39 to 40. Pillsbury's conjecture is thus confirmed. Lastly, it was found that the percentage of 'right cases' with distraction was practically the same as that with continuous attention. Puzzling at first, this result becomes clear if we remember that the error of distraction would operate as often to increase as to decrease the differences of sensible intensity; so that its effect must appear rather in the distribution than in the number of incorrect judgments, rather under the headings of overestimation and underestimation than in the column of wrong cases.

It is clear, then, that strong as well as weak sounds are intensified by attention, or, if you prefer the negative statement, are reduced in intensity by distraction. What this precisely means, physiologically and psychologically, it is at present impossible to say. Professor Bentley's observers certainly did not confuse intensity with clearness; and the intervention of reproductive or affective influences seems to be ruled out both by the conditions of the experiments and by the introspections. So far as they go, the results tell directly for what I have called the current psychological view of the relations of intensity and clearness.—

What, then, of our law? Why, the law stands, under the conditions and with the limitations of which we have spoken. Clearness is an independent attribute of sensation. It is also, in some measure, an independently variable attribute. It may vary in entire independence of most sensible qualities; it may vary also independently of intensity, in the sense that a very weak sound may be as clear as a very loud sound. Only it seems bound up with intensity to the extent that change of clearness involves always a change of intensity as well; very weak clear sounds are not as weak as they would be at a lower degree of clearness. How far the converse of this statement is true, within what limits a change of intensity brings with it, normally, a change of clearness, cannot be said, though the correlation probably extends beyond those extremes of intensive stimulation which we discussed in the preceding Lecture. I may add that there is nothing surprising, from the psychophysical point of view, in an intimate relation between clearness and intensity; all the conditions of maximal clearness are also, as you will remember, conditions for the powerful impression of the nervous system.

I turn, in the second place, to the law which I have named — and the name shows my own bias and opinion — (2) *the law of the two levels.* It is generally agreed that increased clearness of any one part-contents of consciousness implies the decreased clearness of all the rest; the 'energy of attention,' as we say, is limited and practically constant. So the question arises: how many levels or degrees of clearness may coexist in the same consciousness?

Opinions are widely divergent. Baldwin, *e.g.*, gives in his *Senses and Intellect* a 'graphic representation of area of consciousness, after analogy with vision,' in which no less than four levels are distinguished. At the very centre of consciousness stands apperception. Beyond that lies active consciousness or attention; beyond that, again, passive or diffused consciousness; and beyond that, the subconscious. The whole series of concentric circles is then enclosed by the unconscious or physiological, a region of uncertain boundary. "It is well," Baldwin says, "to note the play of ideas through all these forms of transition, from the dark region of subconsciousness, to the brilliant focus of attention [*i.e.*, to apperception]. Images pass both ways constantly, acting varyingly upon one another and making up the wonderful kaleidoscope of the inner life." [12] There is no question that images pass through a large number of degrees of clearness — certainly many more than four — in their passage from maximal to minimal attention; the question is, however, whether they show all these degrees within a single consciousness.

Angell seems to accept Baldwin's view in this strict interpretation. "The field of consciousness," he says, "is apparently like the visual field. There is always a central point of which we are momentarily more vividly conscious than of anything else. Fading *gradually* away from this point into *vaguer and vaguer* consciousness* is a margin of objects, or ideas, of which we are aware in a sort of mental indirect vision." [13] Baldwin's diagram is printed in illustration.

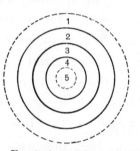

Fig. 5. Area of Consciousness. — J. M. Baldwin, *Handbook of Psychology: Senses and Intellect,* 1890, 68.

Külpe takes the opposite standpoint. He begins his article on *The Problem of Attention* by

* Italics mine.

contrasting physiological with psychological clearness. "[As I sit] looking at the flowered pattern of the paper on the wall in front of me, . . . I notice that around the spot of clearest vision the pattern loses in clearness, at first slowly, then more and more quickly, until I reach the limit of my field of vision, and cannot make out any pattern whatsoever. If I did not know that the whole wall is covered with the same paper, I should suppose that the paper-hanger had chosen less and less pronounced patterns, the farther he moved from the point upon which my eyes are fixed, until finally all pattern and colour were lost in an indifferent gray." I must interject here that I cannot, personally, verify the details of this observation; I think that Külpe has read into the wall-paper a good deal of his own knowledge of sense-psychology. But, at any rate, he refers the observation itself to physiology, and does not use the analogy as Baldwin and Angell use it. On the contrary, he writes of the attentive consciousness as follows: "When we ask how the degrees of consciousness are related to one another, we find, not an uniform gradation from the highest to the lowest, but, in most cases, a fairly sharp line of distinction. Certain contents stand at the level of clear apprehension ; and from them our consciousness drops away, without transition, to the level of obscure general impression, above which the other contents of the time are unable to rise. And the clearer the first group of contents, the more indistinct are all the rest. . . . If, therefore, at any given moment we make a cross-section of the stream of consciousness, we shall find represented on it, not all conceivable degrees of clearness, but as a rule just two groups of processes separated from each other by a considerable interval." The statements are cautious; Külpe puts in the qualifying 'in most cases,' 'as a rule'; but the caution is plainly due to the lack of experimental evidence, and cannot obscure the writer's own opinion.[14]

Six years earlier, Külpe had argued in a similar spirit against Kohn. "Die Klarheit und die Unklarheit wachsen in entgegengesetzter Richtung, und die Zustände, die ihnen entsprechen, können somit um so leichter voneinander unterschieden werden, je ausgeprägter die Aufmerksamkeit ist. Diese Erscheinung zwingt uns geradezu statt von einer einförmigen quantitativen Abstufbarkeit des Bewusstseins von zwei gesonderten Zuständen desselben zu reden." Külpe distinguishes here also between physiological and psychological distribution of clearness.[15]

Ward posits three grades of consciousness in

the wide sense: "a centre or focus of consciousness within a wider field, any part of which may at once become the focus," and a third grade of 'subconsciousness.' This subconsciousness is, however, literally sub-conscious. The threshold of consciousness "must be compared to the surface of a lake, and subconsciousness to the depths beneath it." "Presentations in subconsciousness have not the power to divert attention, nor can we voluntarily concentrate attention upon them." "This hypothesis of subconsciousness . . . is in the main nothing more than the application to the facts of presentation of the law of continuity." [16]   Consciousness has, then, not three experienceable levels, but two only; Ward's subconscious presentations are simply Fechner's negative sensations.[17]   Marshall, if I understand him aright, inclines to go a little farther.   "In the moment of reflection," he says, "we find in all cases what have been called the fields of Attention and of Inattention. We find them and nothing more."   Nevertheless, "the field of inattention seems to resolve itself into an *aura*, as it were, which aura has now a 'feel' of being fuller, and now of being narrower. . . .   The observation that this aura at times seems to be fuller, and again narrower, surely points to the existence of something psy-

chic beyond either the fields of attention or of
inattention, points to the existence of mentality
out of which consciousness whether of attention
or of inattention arises." [18] I do not find that
Marshall is more logical than Ward, — though
he does not follow Ward's example of including
in consciousness what is by definition below the
level of consciousness, — for a 'feel' of fulness
and narrowness must be a conscious feel, and
observation of the feel must be introspective
observation. However, both Ward and Marshall are arguing theoretically: Ward for the law
of continuity and Marshall for a form of psychophysical parallelism; they are not directly facing
our present problem.

Helmholtz, who does face that problem in a
particular case, affirms that "wir für das Be-
wusstwerden einer Empfindung zwei verschiedene Arten oder Grade unterscheiden müssen,"
the kinds or degrees which Leibniz named perception and apperception.[19] And this is, of
course, the doctrine that we also associate with
the name of Wundt. Indeed, the representation of consciousness in two levels, clear and
obscure, is so characteristic of Wundt's psychology that I think we sometimes tend to credit
him with its invention, — just as we credit him
with the metaphor of the *Blickfeld* and the *Blick-*

Q

punkt, although Wundt, I suppose, took that from Fortlage, and Fortlage may have taken it from Lotze, and Lotze from some earlier writer; for it goes back at least as far as Tucker! [20] The metaphor itself, with its direct implication of the two stages of consciousness, stands in 1874 at the very beginning of Wundt's section on attention, and in 1903 stands second only to the *Thätigkeitsgefühl*.[21] "Sagen wir von den in einem gegebenen Moment gegenwärtigen Vorstellungen, sie befänden sich im Blickfeld des Bewusstseins, so kann man denjenigen Theil des letzteren, dem die Aufmerksamkeit zugekehrt ist, als den inneren Blickpunkt bezeichnen. . . . Der innere Blickpunkt kann sich nun successiv den verschiedenen Theilen des inneren Blickfeldes zuwenden. Zugleich kann er sich jedoch, verschieden von dem Blickpunkt des äusseren Auges, verengern und erweitern, wobei immer seine Helligkeit abwechselnd zu- und abnimmt. . . . Je enger und heller hierbei der Blickpunkt ist, in um so grösserem Dunkel befindet sich das übrige Blickfeld." This is familiar teaching. It must be taken in connection with Wundt's refusal to grant any psychological place to the subconscious or the unconscious. He freely admits the influence of feeling on the course of ideational association, but he

will not allow the feeling to stand alone in consciousness, the counterpart of an 'unconscious'
idea. The fact is rather "dass die betreffende
Vorstellung im Bewusstsein vorhanden sei, dass
sie aber zu jenen *dunkleren* Inhalten desselben
gehörte, die überhaupt mehr durch ihre Wirkung-
en auf andere Bewusstseinsvorgänge als durch
ihre eigenen Bestandtheile erkennbar werden." [22]
Hamilton's doctrine of 'mediate association' —
"one idea mediately suggests another into consciousness, the suggestion passing through one
or more ideas which do not themselves rise into
consciousness" — is treated in the same way.
"Man hat wohl ein Recht von 'unbemerkten'
oder von 'dunkler bewussten' Mittelgliedern
solcher Associationen zu sprechen, nimmermehr
aber von 'unbewussten.'" [23]   And Herbart fares
in like manner: "es gibt keine 'frei aufsteigende'
Vorstellungen." [24]

Morgan, as we all know, gives a prominent
place in his psychology to the distinction between 'focus' and 'margin' of consciousness.
"In any moment, . . . there are, in addition to
and alongside the dominant elements constituting
the summit of full clear consciousness, dimly felt
elements which may have little or no direct connection with those dominant elements. These
we will speak of as *subconscious*," [25] — a quite

unnecessary term, since for Morgan the processes in question are all conscious. "Directly we begin to examine and measure any part of the margin," he says, "it thereby ceases to be marginal and becomes focal;" but we cannot examine and measure the subconscious. You will have been wondering, too, why I have not mentioned James' chapter on the *Stream of Thought*.[26] I have omitted it, because I think that it belongs to another part of our subject, to which I come in a moment.

I do not know, now, how the 'law of the two levels' is to be put to any conclusive test. If Baldwin and Angell find their three degrees of consciousness below the apperceptive level, and if Marshall finds his *aura* below the second level, of obscure consciousness, I can only fall back upon Stumpf's 'individual differences' and envy those whose minds are richer than my own. I find nothing of the sort. Working from the other end, from the level of clear apprehension, I am accustomed to use the following illustration. Take one of the familiar puzzle pictures, a picture which represents, we will say, a house and garden, and somewhere in which is concealed the outline of a human face. As you search for the face, the contents of the whole picture are at the conscious focus. Suddenly you find it:

and what happens? Why, as you do so, the picture drops clean away from the focus; the face stands out with all imaginable clearness, and the house and garden are no clearer than the feel of the paper between your fingers. The experience is very striking, as I have described it; it is more striking still if the face baffles you, and you go off on false scents. For every time that you think you have found the hidden outline, the picture slips from you, — slips, to come back with a mental jerk as you realise your failure. There is no poising of the picture, after the riddle has been read, midway between crest and base of the wave of consciousness.

Suppose, however, that we accept the law; suppose that we agree upon the dual clearness of consciousness. The duality will range from maximal to minimal difference, according to the degree of 'concentration' of attention. When we are totally absorbed, we are also absent-minded; the upper level is admirably clear, the lower is exceedingly obscure. When we are less fixedly attentive, there will be a less marked difference between the two conscious levels. Now, then, the question arises: Do all the part-contents, within the two divisions of consciousness, show one and the same degree of clearness? The main division, we will assume, is plain enough; consciousness is arranged step-fashion. But is the surface of consciousness, at the two levels, smooth and unwrinkled, or are there differences of emphasis both over the area of relative clearness and over the area of relative obscurity?

We will begin at the bottom. Morgan makes his 'subconscious' elements "subconscious in different degrees"; he speaks of "a short rising slope of dawning consciousness and a longer falling slope of waning consciousness." [27] I am not sure, however, how far this purports to be matter of observation, and how far it is merely a diagrammatic representation, due to the 'wave' metaphor. Angell, you will remember, speaks of a 'gradual' fading away into 'vaguer and vaguer consciousness'; and if he had not accepted Baldwin's fourfold arrangement, we might, perhaps, interpret these words to indicate simply relative difference of obscurity within a single general obscurity. Wundt seems, at first reading, to be quite definite. "[Es] lässt sich experimentell mit Sicherheit nachweisen, dass [die dunklen,] mit dem appercipirten Inhalt meist nur in einem losen und äusseren Zusammenhang stehenden begleitenden Vorstellungen die allerverschiedensten Grade der Klarheit darbieten können, von einer oberen

Grenze an, wo sie noch als zwar undeutliche, jedoch in ihren allgemeinen Eigenschaften noch einigermassen erkennbare Objecte erfasst werden, bis zu einer unteren, wo nur festzustellen ist, dass überhaupt in einem bestimmten Sinnesgebiet irgend etwas vorhanden war, das im Bewusstsein wirksam wurde, aber schon im Moment, nachdem der Eindruck vorübergegangen, nicht mehr zur Apperception gebracht werden kann." [28] I say that this seems definite; and I think there can be no doubt as to Wundt's general opinion, — that, within the total obscurity of marginal consciousness, differences of relative position may be made out. At the same time, he speaks of the 'passage of *the* impression,' and a footnote refers us to his discussion of tachistoscopic experiments. I am, then, after all not sure that Wundt is not illustrating one thing by another, illustrating marginal differences of clearness by reference to differences within the upper level of consciousness.

For myself, I find the issue very difficult to decide. Since the relative clearness of any particular process depends upon conditions, — the conditions that we listed in the last Lecture, — and since our nervous system is an extraordinarily complex mechanism, and may be very variously affected at any given time, I see no

reason *a priori* why there may not be differences of obscurity in the lower level as there
undoubtedly are differences of·clearness in the
upper.   Nevertheless, I am by no means sure
that I discover these differences.   Observation
in the large is practically impossible; one must
catch favourable moments as they occur in the
course of experimentation.   And I mean by
'favourable' moments occasions when the difference between the two main levels is not
overgreat, — when, for one reason or another,
the observer's attention is less fixed and concentrated than the experiment properly requires.
I have caught myself, time and again, slipping
from the prescribed object of attention to some
secondary circumstance or obtruding idea; but
when I ask whether, a few seconds earlier, that
circumstance or idea was clearer amidst obscurity than the look of my surroundings or
the organic background of consciousness, I am
unable to give a definite answer.   The problem
might, perhaps, be attacked indirectly by an
inversion of the method of distraction.   If, *e.g.*,
we could show that very various degrees of
reinforcement were needed to shift the focus of
attention to contents that were known to be in
the conscious margin, then we might argue that
these contents themselves were originally pres-

ent at different degrees of clearness or, rather, of obscurity. It is further possible that the experiments would give opportunity for the introspective verification of the differences thus objectively determined.

We have better evidence to go upon when we look at the contents of the upper level, the apperceived contents; for we may appeal to the results of all the experiments upon the 'span of consciousness' or the 'range of attention.' I begin with Dietze's determination of what Wundt still terms the 'Umfang des Bewusstseins.'[29] The observer in these experiments listened to series of metronome beats, which were separated into groups by the sound of a bell; the problem was to discover the upper limit at which two successive series might be discriminated, without counting, as of different lengths. We are interested just now, not in the numerical results, but in the state of consciousness. Dietze writes on this topic as follows: "Bedingung der Zusammenfassung einer gegebenen Anzahl von Vorstellungen in eine Reihe ist, . . . dass, wenn nach Ablauf der Reihe eine neue, in gleichem Zeitintervall folgende . . . Vorstellung appercipirt wird, in diesem Moment die erste Vorstellung eben erst auf der Schwelle des Bewusstseins angelangt ist.

. . . Der Grad der Klarheit der gleichzeitig anwesenden Vorstellungen wird nun einmal abhängen von der jeweiligen Entfernung der Vorstellungen vom Blickpunkt des Bewusstseins und zweitens von der Energie, mit welcher die Vorstellungen appercipirt worden sind;" [30] the ideas show a gradation of clearness, which in part is a simple function of time elapsed, in part depends on the emphasis of subjective accentuation. Wundt writes to the same effect, though less cautiously, in the *Physiologische Psychologie*. "In dem Moment, wo ein neuer Reiz . . . in den Blickpunkt des Bewusstseins tritt, werden stets die vorangegangenen noch in abgestufter Klarheit vorhanden sein." "Die unmittelbar vorangegangenen Eindrücke sind . . . keineswegs aus dem Bewusstsein, ja die nächsten nicht einmal ganz aus dem engeren Focus der Aufmerksamkeit verschwunden, sondern sie treten nur allmählich in den dunkleren Umkreis des inneren Blickfeldes zurück. Hier verdunkeln sie sich dann um so mehr, je weiter sie durch die inzwischen abgelaufene Reihe von dem momentan appercipirten Eindruck getrennt sind, bis sie endlich bei einem bestimmten Punkte aus dem Bewusstsein verschwinden." [31]

I shall not discuss the general question, how far or in what sense these experiments serve to measure the span of consciousness. But I must take issue with Wundt's introspective interpretation. We are to suppose that the metronome beats march out of consciousness, in single file, each one growing dimmer and dimmer until it finally crosses the conscious limen and disappears. Now look at that statement logically. You remember that the sounds are not all equally clear; some of them are subjectively accentuated. Suppose, then, that an eight-membered rhythmical unit is passing out of consciousness. The first member is relatively very clear; the second member is relatively obscure. Will the first pass out before the second? It ought not to do this; it is only one place ahead in the order of time, while it is three places ahead in the order of clearness, of rhythmical accent. Logically, the prior but clear term should remain after the later but obscure term has disappeared.

I know that logic is not psychology; but then psychology is not, either, illogical. You may, however, urge that the unit in the present instance is the complete rhythmical form, not the single metronome stroke; and that the rhythmical units may tail off in consciousness in the way that Wundt describes. Wundt speaks, definitely, of the individual *Schallreiz;* but I will accept the amendment. The appeal then lies to introspection : do we actually find the gradations of clearness, as between unit and unit, incoming and outgoing ideas ? Schumann, who engaged Wundt in a controversy on this matter, finds no trace of them. "So oft ich auch bei den obigen Experimenten versucht habe, etwas von den in den dunklen Umkreis des inneren Blickfeldes zurücktretenden Vor-stellungen zu bemerken, so ist es mir doch nie gelungen und ebensowenig den Versuchsperso-nen [among whom was Müller], welche ich darauf aufmerksam machte." Schumann's own explanation is couched in terms of sensory and motor *Einstellung*, feelings of fulfilled or dis-appointed expectation.[32]

On the negative side, my own introspection agrees with that of Schumann and his observers; I cannot put my finger on the train of vanishing ideas. On the positive side, I think that Schu-mann's account holds under certain conditions, — not under all. But even if we accept the theory of a 'simultane Gesammtvorstellung,' there is no need to assume Wundt's series of graded ideas; all sorts of surrogates are possible.

I am sorry to have led you so far afield; but there was no alternative. If Wundt's analysis were correct, we should have not only to give up our law of the two levels, but also, I believe, to recast a good portion of his own systematic teaching. I do not propose to do either, but to utilise Dietze's results in another direction. The important thing for our present purpose is this: that the experiments show, without any question, the coexistence of different degrees of clearness at the higher level of consciousness. While a rhythmical unit may be clear as a whole, its constituent elements vary in clearness-degree.

The same thing holds of simultaneously presented visual impressions, all of which fall within the area of distinct vision. "Man bemerkt," says Wundt, "ausser den deutlich appercipirten Eindrücken zunächst eine Anzahl anderer, die sich als 'halbdunkel' bezeichnen lassen: hier ist man im stande, einzelne nachträglich durch angestrengte Aufmerksamkeit auf das reproducirte Bild des Gesammteindrucks zu erkennen. Daneben existirt aber immer noch ein weiteres, 'ganz dunkles' Feld, bei dem man nur überhaupt feststellen kann, dass irgend etwas da war." [33] This last, the 'wholly obscure' field, belongs unquestionably — if I may trust my own observation — to the lower level of consciousness; the 'something there' is a something of precisely the same kind as the look of the tachistoscope itself, or of the black walls of the observing tube.   But the other two grades, the 'clear' and the 'half obscure,' belong, as certainly, to the upper level.   Let us see precisely what the distinction means.

When a tachistoscopic field is exposed for the first time to an unpractised observer, he will very probably fail to 'make out' anything at all; the lines or letters or geometrical figures are seen as a general impression, without discrimination of detail.   Was, then, the field obscure?   Surely not!   The observer was 'attending' with all the concentration he could summon; the field was the clearest thing in his consciousness.   What he failed to do was to *cognise*.   Cognition is not clearness; it is an associative process of the assimilative kind. Apperception and cognition are so usually conjoined, in our adult experience, that we may sometimes forget to separate them; but psychologically they are different things.   When, then, the practised observer tells us that some of the details in the exposure-field are 'clear' and others 'half obscure,' he means that he has cognised the former and failed to cognise the latter; all alike were clear, but the clearness did not, in all cases, suffice for cognition.   The fact that the half-obscure elements are recoverable in the 'image of reproduction' shows that they

were well within the field of clearness; the fact
that they were not directly cognised shows that
this field is not uniformly illuminated, that parts
of it are more strongly accented than others, —
just as, in the temporal field, there are degrees
of clearness among the members of a rhythmical
unit.[34]

We must conclude, therefore, that — whatever
is the case at the lower level — there are noticeable differences of clearness in the processes at
the upper level of consciousness. It would be
strange if there were not! And one of the most
interesting new departures in experimental psychology, to my mind, is the work now in progress
in the Leipsic laboratory upon this very point.
Attempts are being made to measure the differences of clearness in focal contents, whether
by determining the limen of change at various
parts of a spatial field or by comparing the times
of reaction obtained with varying distribution
of attention.[35] Here is the beginning of a new
chapter in scientific psychology; and here is
Wundt handling the problems of attention as
masterfully as when he first began to experiment
nearly fifty years ago.

We are now, I think, at the point where it is
fitting to refer to James and his conscious
'fringes.' Ordinarily, the distinction which

James draws is taken to be the same as that
drawn by Morgan in the terms 'focal' and
'marginal.' "The margin of mental processes,"
says Angell, "outside the focal point of attention, constitutes what James calls the 'fringe of
consciousness.'" [36]   No doubt there are plenty
of passages in which this use may be found.
But if we turn to the *locus classicus*, the chapter
on the 'Stream of Thought,' I think it is clear
that James is dealing throughout with the upper
level of consciousness, the field of attention.
He comes to his "psychic overtone, suffusion,
or fringe" by way of 'transitive states,' 'feelings
of relation,' 'feelings of tendency.' And his
point is that "every definite image in the mind
is steeped and dyed in the free water that flows
round it." I do not understand that the 'free
water' is flowing at a lower level, but simply
that — within the area of attention — it is less
stable and therefore less clear than the 'definite
image.' "The fringe . . . is part of the *object
cognised*, — substantive *qualities* and *things* ap-
pearing to the mind in a *fringe of relations*.
Some parts — the transitive parts — of our
stream of thought cognise the relations rather
than the things." James is considering the
'cognitive function of different states of mind.'
"Knowledge *about* a thing is knowledge of its

relations. . . . Of most of its relations we are
only aware in the penumbral nascent way of a
'fringe' of unarticulated affinities about it."
This penumbra is surely the analogue of the
marginal impressions in tachistoscopic experiments, the impressions that are apperceived but
not cognised. I do not want to labour clumsily
at a thing that James has treated with all his
accustomed lightness and freshness of touch, —
but I think it is pretty obvious that, in this part
of his psychology of cognition, James is primarily
concerned with the upper conscious level. He
is distinguishing degrees of clearness within the
clear, not distinguishing clearness from obscurity. That distinction he discusses in the
following section, in its relation to interest and
attention, accentuation and emphasis.[37] —

In fine, then, a diagram of consciousness
would show, in terms of the foregoing analysis,
a two-level formation, broader below and narrower above, — the relative width and height
of the two stages differing at different times.
The surfaces are not smooth; the upper certainly, the lower probably, is creased or wrinkled.
The number and depth of the wrinkles will
depend upon circumstances: upon the conditions of clearness as an attribute of sensation,
and upon the more complicated conditions

R

which govern the degree of clearness of the part-
contents of ideas. So much we can, perhaps,
say. with a fair amount of confidence.[38]   But the
really hopeful thing, for experimental psychology, is the programme of further work, the
long array of definite problems that our review,
ever so hasty as it is, has already brought to
light. We can hardly be on a wrong track if
perspectives open as they are opening to-day to
the students of attention.

We may look, in the third place, (3) at the
temporal relations of attention, as expressed in
the laws of *accommodation* and of *inertia*. "Die
Aufmerksamkeit," says Stumpf, "braucht eine
gewisse Zeit, um sich dem Eindruck s. z. s.
zu accommodiren, um ihr Maximum zu er-
reichen." [39]   The fact here alluded to is familiar
to all of us in connection with the reaction experiment; for the simple reaction, the optimal
accommodation-time — the optimal interval between signal and stimulus—is about 1.5 seconds,
while for transit-observations it is apparently a
little shorter, about 1 second.   Attention is,
however, flexible, labile; we are able, as Wundt
points out, to adapt ourselves, within certain
limits, to rhythms of different period, just as we
can adapt ourselves to different intensities and
qualities of stimulus.[40]

It would be quite wrong, however, to identify this 'accommodation' of attention with the rise of a particular sensation to maximal clearness. We have a number of determinations, beginning in the early sixties and extending down to the present day, of the *Ansteigen* of sensations; [41] and as they were all made in the state of concentrated attention, the times which they furnish may be taken as the times required for a stimulus, acting under the most favourable conditions, to produce its full conscious effect. These, therefore, are the times that a psychology of clearness must analyse and interpret. The accommodation-time is rather the time required for peripheral or central *Einstellung*, — for the accommodation of a sense-organ, or for the establishment of a psychophysical disposition; it gives us the temporal limen, not of clearness, but of certain conditions of clearness.

Let me quote you an observation of Pillsbury's. "Si, tandis qu'on lit, vient un désir soudain de savoir l'heure, les images de la pendule rappelées à la conscience se présentent avant que le mouvement ne commence, et il y a un intervalle considérable entre l'instant ou les yeux sont fixés sur la pendule sans adaptation complète et celui ou l'image est assez nette pour que l'on ait connaissance de l'heure." [42]   Pillsbury is arguing that peripheral adaptation is subsequent to attention itself. If, however, we read 'clearness' for 'attention,' the facts wear a little different appearance. I want to know the time, and I look across the room at the clock. The clock is, at once, the clearest thing in consciousness; but it is not yet maximally clear, clear enough for cognition. To see the position of the hands, I must wait for the 'accommodation of attention,' *i.e.* for the adjustment of the mechanism of visual accommodation. This peripheral adjustment is one of the conditions of maximal clearness. Before accommodation is effected, I am in much the same position as one who is listening to a lecturer whose voice is too weak to carry across the room. The sounds heard are, again, the clearest things in consciousness; but they, too, fall short of the degree of clearness necessary to cognition, because intensity — one of the conditions of maximal clearness — is lacking to them.

The law of 'accommodation of attention' is a real law; it covers a large number of facts of observation. But it is a law of the conditions of clearness, or, if you like, a law of the total attentive consciousness, rather than of clearness itself; and in an elementary psychology of attention we shall do well to pass it over, and to limit

ourselves to the interpretation of the *Anstieg*.
Very much the same thing, I think, holds of the
law of inertia, to which I now turn.

The law is formulated by Fechner as follows:
"es behagt uns bis zu gewissen Grenzen mehr,
in einer einmal eingehaltenen Richtung und
hiemit Beschäftigung der Aufmerksamkeit zu
verharren, als sie zu verlassen, die Beschäftigung
zu unterbrechen"; and by Stumpf, in similar
terms, as follows: "die Aufmerksamkeit hält
leichter etwas bereits Gegebenes fest, als sie
etwas zu Suchendes findet."[43] It covers a wide
range of experience: that you can follow the
movement of a single instrument in the orches-
tra better, when there has been solo-playing
before, than when the whole number of instruments begin together; that you can finish a
conversation, once begun, at a distance which
would render the words of an unexpected question altogether inaudible; that you can trace the
upward course of a fire-balloon to a point at
which it would otherwise be quite invisible.
These are matters of perception; but there are
analogies in plenty in the realm of ideas. It is
difficult to break away from a current train of
thought, and to give your full attention to a
letter or a visitor; it is difficult to come back to
your scientific work when you have been bothered
by details of business or administration.

These are important facts; and they have been taken account of, in various ways, by experimental psychology. But they seem to me to be facts which, on the psychophysical side, relate to the conditions of clearness, — peripheral adaptation, psychophysical disposition, *Perseverationstendenz*,[44] — and, on the psychological, to the time relations of the total attentive consciousness. They are therefore beyond the range of our present consideration. An elementary psychology will deal with the sensation, under its aspect of clearness; it will determine the least time interval between two maximal clearnesses in the same and disparate senses; and it will measure the carrying power of clearness, the amount of fluctuation which may be introduced into a continuous stimulus without impairment of sensible continuity. Here, again, there are methods ready for our use, and a body of experimental results awaiting our interpretation.[45] And the law of inertia offers us problems of ever increasing complexity. For, since inertia is the opposite of motility, and the carrying power of clearness is the opposite of our liability to distraction, the determinations which I have just mentioned must be made under all sorts of conditions, and we shall be led on, as it were, by force of circumstance, from sensation to the simpler complexes, and from these to consciousness itself.

So far, I think that my proposal of a simplified psychology of attention has been justified, — although I realise to the full the schematic character of this treatment of the subject. In the next Lecture we shall see how it fares with still other laws of attention.

VII

THE LAWS OF ATTENTION: II

LECTURE VII

THE LAWS OF ATTENTION: II

I HAVE suggested that an elementary psychology of attention will deal, not with the
facts of attentional accommodation, but rather
with the 'rise' of the single sensation; that it will
begin, not with the gross facts of attentional
inertia, but rather with the absolute temporal
limen and the carrying power of clearness under
simple conditions. I have been careful to say
that the results of experiment in these fields must
be 'interpreted' by a psychology of attention;
the factors that make for clearness must be
separated from the other conditions involved,
and must if possible be separately estimated or
'weighted.' We get a hint towards this analysis
in the fourth law that I shall mention, — (4) the
law of prior entry. The stimulus for which we
are predisposed requires less time than a like
stimulus, for which we are unprepared, to produce its full conscious effect. Or, in popular
terms, the object of attention comes to consciousness more quickly than the objects that we are
not attending to.

We have rough-and-ready illustrations of this law in various features of the reaction experiment.[1]   Many of the effects that we ascribe to 'practice,' in the most diverse kinds of experimental work, also fall under the same heading. A strict test, of the elementary sort, would consist in the comparative measurement of the *Anstieg* and of the absolute temporal limen, first with complete predisposition, and secondly under measurable distraction.[2]   Unfortunately, as we shall see later, measurable distraction is still a problem for the future.

In the meantime, we have a qualitative demonstration of the law of prior entry in Stevens' inversion of the complication experiment.[3]   The arrangement is very simple.   We take a bell metronome, and a cardboard arc whose radius is the length of the metronome pendulum. Scale divisions of 5° are laid off upon the circumference, and the arc — with the zero-point of the scale corresponding to the position of equilibrium of the pendulum — is impaled upon the eye which serves to lock the lid of the metronome.   The white cardboard thus forms a background, in front of which the pendulum oscillates.   A piece of red paper, cut to the shape of an arrow-head, is spitted upon the end of the pendulum.   The metronome is set to the

rate of, say, 72 in the one minute, and the bell
rings at every complete oscillation. The position of objective coincidence of bell-stroke and
arrow-head may be found, approximately, by
slowly moving the pendulum with the hand
until the bell sounds; in our instrument, it
comes at about 22°. The experiment is then
performed in two ways. First, the observer

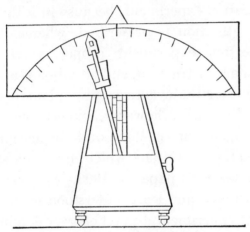

Fig. 6. Simple Complication Pendulum.

attends to the moving pointer; the sound of the
bell is secondary, — it floats, so to say, upon
the main current of visual change. Under these
conditions, the pointer carries the bell out; an
average determination of subjective coincidence
is 30°. Secondly, the observer attends to the
bell; the movement of the pendulum is now
secondary, — the expected bell-strokes stand

out upon an indifferent shifting field. Under these conditions the temporal displacement of the sound is negative, not positive; the point of subjective coincidence lies, on the average, between 10° and 15°. It is very clear that the stimulus for which we are predisposed has the advantage over its rival.

I call this observation the 'inversion' of the complication experiment, because in it the direction of attention is prescribed, whereas, in the complication experiment proper, there is no preliminary instruction, and attention is appealed to only after the event, as an explanatory principle. You will, however, expect me to say something about the temporal displacement in complications, — a fact which, until the appearance of Geiger's paper in 1903,[4] was one of the most disputed and least understood in the whole range of experimental psychology. I think that Geiger's introspective analyses give us a definitive insight into the mechanism of the 'complicated' consciousness, although, doubtless, there is work of detail still to be done.

You remember the circumstances. A pointer revolves at uniform rate before a scaled clockface. At some moment of its revolution, unknown to the observer, a bell is sounded. The observer is to report the point of subjective coin-

cidence of sight and sound, the moment of formation of an Herbartian 'complication.' [5] Introspection varies very considerably with variation
of conditions; but the important and curious
result is that, under certain conditions, the bell-
stroke suffers a negative displacement; it is
conjoined, in consciousness, with a division of
the scale which the pointer has already passed
when the objective sound is introduced. The
sound is 'thrown back'; it is heard 'too early.'
What is the explanation?

Very different explanations have been suggested. One of the first investigators, von
Tchisch, sought an analogy in the premature
reaction.[6] Theoretically, he says, two things are
possible: the visual perception may be delayed,
or the auditory anticipated. Now there is no
assignable reason for delay. "Es ist dagegen
leicht zu erklären, dass momentane Reize vor
ihrem Erscheinen appercipirt werden." In reaction experiments with a constant interval between signal and stimulus you find a gradual
reduction of the reaction time; the values become very small, and finally reach zero, — "die
Reactionszeit . . . wird negativ." Just the
same thing happens in the complication experiment; each recurring bell-stroke is the 'signal'
for the next following, the 'stimulus.'   "Durch

dieses Wiederholen wird die Apperception nicht
nur vorbereitet, sondern dieselbe reproducirt
unmittelbar den Eindruck.   Mithin sind das die
Bedingungen unter welchen wir hören, fühlen,
ehe der Reiz thatsächlich zustandekommt."

Ideas of this sort were natural enough in 1885,
when the psychology of the simple reaction was
still crude, — though von Tchisch might, perhaps, have learned better from the *Physiologische
Psychologie* of 1880.[7]   But, whether natural or
not, they are psychologically impossible.   "The
explanation," says James, "requires us to believe that an observer . . . shall steadily and
without exception get an hallucination of a bell-
stroke before the latter occurs, and *not hear the
real bell-stroke afterwards.*   I doubt whether this
is possible, and I can think of no analogue to it
in the rest of our experience." [8]   We may all
subscribe to this criticism.   Indeed, the explanation satisfied nobody; every later psychologist who has discussed the complication experiment has sought to improve upon it.   Sometimes,
recourse has been had to physiological factors,
the quick rise of auditory and the slow rise of
visual sensations; sometimes to psychological,
the interruption of the visual perception of
movement and the substitution therefor of a
perception of position; sometimes the explana-

tion has gone still further afield, to the observer's desire to make a good showing, to do as well in observation as his fellows.[9] All unnecessary labour! Wundt had given the right cue, in his doctrine of the "Spannungswachsthum der Aufmerksamkeit"[10]; it was only needful to follow up the cue into the labyrinth of observational detail.

Suppose that a naïve observer takes his place before the complication clock; and suppose that the rate of revolution is moderate, so that the bell-stroke sounds once in every 1.5 seconds. The observer follows the pointer with his eye, and in the very first revolution refers the sound to some region of the circle. Notice that it is a *region;* the sound seems to spread over, to be coincident with, a fairly wide range of scale marks. The second revolution narrows this region; the third narrows it still more, — and so on, until finally there are only a few scale divisions, one or two on either side of the objectively correct position, with which the bell appears to coincide. In the meantime, attention has been sharpening to the sound; and, more than that, an accommodation of attention has taken place; the observer is predisposed to hear the bell at a certain instant. The instant arrives; the sound is apperceived, rises to maximal

s

clearness, in a minimum of time; and the result
is that scale marks which the pointer had traversed before the hammer struck are themselves
apperceived, come to the focus of attention, only
along with the objectively later complicating
stimulus. "[Der Schall] überholt gleichsam [die
Theilstriche] auf dem Wege zur Apperception." [11]
It is all a matter of prior entry, due to definite
predisposition of the attention; and the puzzle
arises simply from the continuity of the visual
movement. Had there been one sound and one
sight, and had the sound come to consciousness
before the (objectively simultaneous) sight, no one
would have wondered. It is the backthrow of
the sound which surprises us; and yet that backthrow is, under the conditions, the inevitable
result of attentional accommodation.

I need not go into this question at greater
length; you will find a full and clear discussion
in Geiger's article. I quote only a few sentences
from the *Physiologische Psychologie* of the same
year. "[Die negativen Zeitverschiebungen] sind
natürlich nicht so aufzufassen, als wenn man
einen Reiz wahrnehme, noch ehe er wirklich
stattfindet; sondern in eine Reihe von Gesichts-
eindrücken, die im Bewusstsein die *simultane*,
aber stetig fliessende Vorstellung eines Zeitver-
laufs bilden, tritt ein momentaner Schall- oder

Tasteindruck ein, der als solcher nur mit irgend
einem einzelnen Punkt dieser Zeitvorstellung
associirt werden kann : mit welchem, dies hängt
lediglich von den Bedingungen theils des Eindrucks selbst, theils seiner Apperception ab.
Je mehr die Aufmerksamkeit auf ihn gespannt
ist, um so mehr wird er an den Anfang der ihm
zugeordneten Zeitstrecke des Gesichtssinnes ver-
schoben, je mehr jene Spannung erschwert ist
oder aus irgend einen Ursachen abnimmt, um
so mehr rückt er gegen das Ende derselben. . . .
Es wird *stets gleichzeitig gehört und gesehen;*
aber der Umfang, in dem die beiden nebeneinander hergehenden Vorstellungsreihen zusammen im Bewusstsein anwesend sind, lässt der
Verbindung beider einen Spielraum, innerhalb
dessen nun theils den äusseren Bedingungen
theils und vornehmlich der Aufmerksamkeit der
entscheidende Einfluss zukommt." [12]

Unless, then, I am unduly optimistic, the
negative displacement of the bell-stroke, in
complication experiments, need give psychologists no further trouble. I pass to a brief consideration of (5) the *law of limited range.*

You recall the facts. If a group of objects,
all of which lie within the scope of clear vision,
is momentarily exposed by means of some

tachistoscopic arrangement, a practised observer
is able to cognise from four to six of them 'by
a single act of attention.'   It makes no difference
whether the objects are lines, or geometrical
figures, or numbers, or letters, or short words;
under all these conditions, the range of clearness
is approximately the same.   Hence you find, in
the current text-books of psychology, the statement that the grasp of visual attention covers
from four to six simultaneously presented simple
impressions.[13]

Ebbinghaus takes issue with this statement.
"Die so erhaltenen Werte . . . sind als Um-
fangsbestimmungen der Aufmerksamkeit zweifellos zu hoch." He points out that "das
gleichzeitig aufgefasste immer nur . . . als ein
Ganzes mit mehreren Teilen erkannt wird";
we are dealing, not with four to six separate
objects, but with separately distinguished parts
of an unitary whole.   He argues, however, from
the results of the complication experiment, "dass
[die Seele] auf zwei voneinander ganz unab-
hängige Reihen einfacher Eindrücke längere
Zeit hindurch gleichzeitig aufmerksam bleiben
kann, ja daneben noch imstande ist . . . mancherlei Ueberlegungen zur besseren Lösung der
Aufgabe anzustellen." In simple cases, then,
"kann die Aufmerksamkeit ohne Schwierigkeit

zwei, äussersten Falls vielleicht drei, voneinander ganz unabhängigen Dingen zugewandt werden."[14]

If we accept this discussion as it stands, the number of objects simultaneously apprehensible by the attention reduces from four or six to two or three. But I think that Ebbinghaus has misread his authorities. One would hardly gather, from his text, that Wundt, in the *Physiologische Psychologie*, had laid equal stress upon the unitary character of the tachistoscopic field. Yet Wundt says, definitely: "immer bildet dieses Feld der Apperception eine *einheitliche* Vorstellung, indem wir die einzelnen Theile desselben zu einem Ganzen verbinden. So verbindet die Apperception eine Mehrheit von Schalleindrücken zu *einer* Klang- oder Geräuschvorstellung, eine Mehrzahl von Sehobjecten zu *einem* Gesichtsbild." And again: "man bemerkt übrigens leicht, dass sich die Eindrücke auch dann, wenn sie nicht Bestandtheile einer schon geläufigen Vorstellung sind, doch zu *einem* zusammengehörigen Bilde vereinigen."[15] Can anything be plainer? Ebbinghaus' "reichhaltige und gegliederte Einheit," which is apprehended as a whole while certain divisions or subdivisions stand out in clear isolation, — "mehr oder minder deutlich gesondert,"[16] — is no new discovery, but a transcript of the Wundtian doctrine.

The other side of Ebbinghaus' exposition is similarly open to criticism. The bell-stroke and the visual impressions of the complication experiment are, as stimuli, disparate, addressed to different sense-departments. But psychologically they are by no means "voneinander ganz unabhängig." On the contrary, the sound, after a very few observations, becomes organically related to the movement of the pointer; the two things seem to go together naturally, to belong to each other; there is no disparateness in idea. There remain the 'mancherlei Ueberlegungen'; but so far as my experience goes — and Geiger bears me out [17] — these reflections exist only in Ebbinghaus' imagination.

The case stands, therefore, as follows. Whenever in the state of attention two stimuli are given simultaneously or in immediate succession, they form a connected whole; that is the most general law of association, in Ebbinghaus' phrasing.[18] From this point of view, then, the field of attention is limited always to one complex, a single associated whole. The question of the range of attention thus becomes the question of the conscious articulation of the unitary complex. In psychological terms it runs: How many part-contents are, under the most favourable conditions, distinguishable within the whole? In psychophysical terms: How many stimuli may become clear in consciousness at one and the same time? And the current answers, although they are liable to experimental revision, may be taken as valid for their day and generation.

We are on much more difficult ground when we turn (6) to the *law of temporal instability*. This law, also, may be approached from the side either of descriptive psychology and the attentive consciousness, or of experimental psychology and the attribute of clearness.

According to Wundt, attention is discontinuous from force of circumstances and intermittent by its very nature. It is discontinuous because ideas come and go in consciousness, and attention grasps but one idea at a time: "zwischen der Apperception je zweier auf einander folgender Vorstellungen wird immer eine Zwischenzeit liegen, in der die eine schon zu weit gesunken, die andere noch nicht zureichend gehoben ist, um klar appercipirt zu werden." It is also intrinsically intermittent. "*Dauernd* eine Vorstellung mit der Aufmerksamkeit festzuhalten ist, wie die Erfahrung lehrt, schlechthin unmöglich: . . . ein dauernder Eindruck kann nur festgehalten werden, indem Momente der Spannung und der Abspannung derselben mit einander

wechseln. Auf diese Weise ist die Aufmerksamkeit ihrem Wesen nach eine *intermittirende*
Function." [19]

In his remarks on discontinuity, I think that
Wundt has in mind what he himself elsewhere
terms a limiting case, the typical associative
consciousness of the English school.[20] For, so
far as introspection goes, we may attend, con-
tinuously and unremittingly, for very considerable periods: we read a novel or a scientific
monograph at a sitting, we follow a whole act of
grand opera, we work at our special subject for
two or three or four hours at a time, without
sensible interruption of attention. There are
objective interruptions, of course: we stop reading to pursue a train of thought, to work out a
difficulty, to cut the pages of the book; we look
away from the stage to exchange a remark with
our neighbour; we get up to verify a reference,
or we pause to slip a fresh sheet of paper into the
typewriter. And these interruptions illustrate,
often enough, the labile, instable character of
attention; we drop from our high level of
concentration to 'take things easily,' to 'let
our mind wander' for a while. But instability
is not discontinuity; and, in the experiences now
under consideration, instability itself is not the
universal rule. We may very possibly give our

full attention, without lapse of any sort, to the question asked of us, or to the accurate adjustment of the new sheet; or, contrariwise, we may hold firmly to our original topic, and speak and act automatically. All these cases demand closer analysis; but on the whole James' statement — that "thought is sensibly continuous" [21] — seems to me to be nearer the facts, and nearer also to Wundt's general psychological doctrine, than the counter-assertion that attention is discontinuous. I should question the appearance of discontinuity even in extreme instances of successive association. "Dauernde Aufmerksamkeit," says Ebbinghaus, "gibt es nur bei einem stetigen Wechsel der Inhalte, in deren Hervortreten das Aufmerksamsein besteht." [22] The 'nur' we have still to discuss; but we may surely agree that attention can be sustained, and that the shift of ideas is continuous.

What, then, of the *Apperceptionswellen?* Is attention intrinsically intermittent, and is it impossible to hold a single, simple content steadily in the focus of consciousness?

We must not demand too much. Consciousness is always in flux, and 'dauernd' is a relative term. Sensible quality, for instance, cannot maintain itself in consciousness for any length of time; wherever there is sensory adaptation —

in pressure, in temperature, in sight, in smell, to some extent in taste — there is also gradual change or disappearance of quality. The conditions of clearness, central predisposition and peripheral accommodation, may be given; but the quality will still fade out. Yet we do not speak of quality as an intrinsically intermittent attribute of sensation! What is the evidence, then, in the case of attention, of clearness itself?

It is necessary, at this point, to change the *venue* to the laboratory, because descriptive psychology cannot distinguish between discontinuity, due to the come-and-go of ideas, and intrinsic intermittence. The chief and obvious reason that we are unable, under the conditions of everyday life, to hold fast to a single idea is that other, invading and competing ideas oust it from the conscious focus. Only experiment, therefore, can decide regarding the 'fluctuation' of attention. And experiment, as you know, has been at work with ever increasing frequency since 1875. Investigations have been made by the help of 'minimal' stimuli, — stimuli that are so small or so weak or so little different from their surroundings that the least slip of attention, the slightest loss of clearness, will mean their complete disappearance from consciousness; it is far easier to say that we do or do not hear or see something than it is to be sure that what we see or hear has grown more or less clear. Visual, auditory, and cutaneous stimuli have been employed: light and colour, tone and noise, mechanical pressure and the interrupted current. The questions at issue may be formulated, in logical order, as follows: Does fluctuation occur in all sense-departments? Are the conditions of fluctuation, where it occurs, central or peripheral? And, if they are central, are they the conditions of 'attention'? We begin with the question of sense-departments.

Lange, who was the first systematically to investigate the subject, found fluctuation in all three, — sight (Masson disc), hearing (watch-tick) and touch (induction current). Let us confine ourselves for the moment to touch. Fluctuations of electro-cutaneous sensations were later observed by Lehmann; and fluctuations of areal pressure by Wiersma. On the other hand, Ferree and Geissler, working recently in my own laboratory, have been unable to confirm these results. Ferree reports briefly that "liminal pressure stimuli [very smooth cork wafers supporting minimal weights] were applied to several observers, but no fluctuations were experienced"; and that with liminal electro-cutaneous stimulation at the tip of the tongue "no fluctuations of intensity could be detected, although repeated attempts were made on a number of observers." Geissler, who repeated and extended the experiments of Wiersma and Ferree, comes to the same conclusion. "Under favourable circumstances, attention focussed upon liminal and supraliminal cutaneous sensations remains approximately constant for at least two to three minutes, provided that physiological adaptation of the sense-organ and violently obtruding distractions can be avoided for this length of time." The 'two to three minutes' is a conservative estimate; the time was often exceeded, and on one occasion a trained observer reported no fluctuation for ten minutes! How much longer he might have attended we do not know; at the end of the ten minutes his observation was interrupted by the experimenter, who thought that something was the matter.

This absence of fluctuation in the sphere of touch — if we may accept it as fact — strongly suggests that the conditions of fluctuation at large are not central but peripheral. For the skin has no special mechanism of accommodation, and possesses but a poor substitute in the 'Tastzuckungen' that Czermak noticed in his blind observers. Involuntary tremors in the hand were a minor source of disturbance in Geissler's ex-

periments. We might argue, therefore, that
fluctuation will appear only where there is a
peripheral apparatus for accommodation, and
that the appeal to central conditions is unnecessary. Unfortunately, as we shall see, the issue
is more complicated.[23] —

Aside from touch, we have a reported failure
of fluctuation in the case of auditory stimuli.
The experimental results are, however, contra-
dictory; Heinrich, whose observations upon tones
were in part confirmed in the Cornell laboratory,
finds no fluctuation, while Dunlap declares that
"the fluctuations were unmistakably observed
by each of the five subjects employed." The
difference is, apparently, a matter of conditions,
which must be further studied. I return to the
point presently.[24]

Our second question was that of the peripheral
or central seat of the fluctuations; and, in turning
to it, we shall naturally think, first of all, of the
mechanisms of accommodation. There can,
however, be no doubt that their presence is not
essential. Visual fluctuations have been observed
by Pace during temporary paralysis of the muscles
of accommodation, and by Slaughter and Ferree
in the case of aphacic subjects; auditory fluctuations occur, according to Urbantschitsch and
Eckener, despite the lack of a tympanic mem-

brane. At the same time, the occurrence of fluctuation when the mechanisms are absent does not prove that shift of accommodation has nothing to do with fluctuation in the normal organ, where they are present and in working order. And Heinrich maintains, as a matter of fact, that the fluctuation of visual point-areas corresponds with variation in the curvature of the lens, and that the fluctuation of minimal noises is due to "pulsatorische Aenderungen des tensor tympani in seinem Erregungszustande." [25]

It is impossible, in the present state of our problem, to take a definite stand for or against Heinrich's explanations. The peripheral theory which he represents obviously requires a central supplement; but that is not a decisive argument. What compels us to a suspension of judgment — perhaps even to a negative attitude, at least so far as vision is concerned — is the appearance of new observations and a new theory. Ferree has published two elaborate investigations, in which he seeks to show "that the intermittences of sensation resulting from minimal visual stimuli . . . are, in reality, simply adaptation-phenomena somewhat obscured by the special conditions." "Adaptation is, in itself, a continuous phenomenon, but its continuity is interfered with by eye-movement, blinking, etc. Through these influences, probably essentially through that of eye-movement alone, it becomes an intermittent process, whether the stimulus be liminal or intensive, provided that proper areas be used. The conditions are especially favourable for short periods of intermittence when the stimuli are liminal and of small area." The central idea of this theory, the combination of local adaptation and eye-movement, goes back at least as far as 1894; but the theory itself, as fitted to the phenomena of visual fluctuation, may justly be described as new. Ferree has worked it out for adaptation and for the converse of adaptation, the negative after-image; he has taken account both of voluntary and of involuntary eye-movement; he has made observations in direct and in indirect vision; he has determined the conditions under which fluctuation does and does not occur. In particular, he has been venturesome enough to announce a new discovery in physiological optics: "eye-movement . . . determines or influences the washing or streaming over the retina of some material capable of directly affecting the visual processes." His chain of evidence is not yet complete, and I may be prejudiced in favour of an investigation which was begun and largely carried out in my laboratory; but it seems to me that Ferree's principles are likely

to give us a definitive solution of the problem
of fluctuation in the sphere of vision.

Hammer, like Ferree, appeals to local adaptation and slipping of fixation : "doch ist es wohl
überdies nicht unmöglich," he says, "dass der
Adaptationsprozess gleichwie der negativen Nach-
bilder seiner Natur nach intermittierend ist."
Ferree finds, however, that adaptation is 'a continuous phenomenon,' and that "fluctuation is
not grounded in the nature of the after-image
process." Hammer then proceeds to report
experiments on sound, and concludes — this is
the point to which I said just now that I should
recur — that there is no such thing as auditory
fluctuation. "Auf dem Gebiete des Gehörs-
sinns existieren überhaupt keine Aufmerksam-
keitsfluktuationen." If that conclusion could
be accepted, our path would be smooth indeed !
— no fluctuations in touch; no fluctuations in
hearing, — the whole question of the rôle of the
tensor in fluctuation shelved for ever; fluctuations
in sight alone, and due in the case of sight to
very special conditions residing in the function
of the peripheral organ. But too many observers
have recorded auditory fluctuation for us lightly
to disregard the positive testimony; all that we
may do, again, is to suspend judgment.[26] —

We are not even yet out of the wood. For

peripheral — or at least subcortical — conditions of fluctuation may be found, not only in the organs of sense themselves, but also in those systemic changes that are studied by the method of expression. The influence of the pulse, for instance, is attested by Stumpf, Mach, and Preyer for tones, and by Stumpf for visual stimuli.[27] The influence of respiration is mentioned by Helmholtz: "ich erinnere daran, dass selbst die Athembewegungen auf das Eigenlicht der Netzhaut einwirken"; it has been traced also by Lehmann and Slaughter.[28] And within the last few years a series of investigations, carried out in Pillsbury's laboratory, has emphasised the correspondence of sensible fluctuation with the Traube-Hering wave of blood pressure.[29] Exner had said, in 1894: "es liegt nahe, als Erklärungsgrund aller dieser Erscheinungen vasomotorische Ursachen anzunehmen"; and Pillsbury, in 1903, would explain the 'fluctuations of attention' as "a resultant of two physiological processes, of the degree of efficiency of the cortical cells, on the one hand, and of the state of excitation of the vasomotor centre on the other."[30]

In estimating this position, I feel a strong inclination to shelter myself behind Pace, and to say simply: "the results thus obtained are obviously of great importance; and they are certainly open

T

to various interpretations." [31]   For indeed criticism at this time and in this place is impossible; it must be criticism of detail, — of the interpretation of records, of the differential value of control experiments, of the probability of rival theories. Slaughter uses the vasomotor phenomena in one way; but Fechner, and Fick and Gürber, and Lehmann, and now Ferree suggest other ways in which they may be turned to theoretical account.[32]   I am by no means convinced that Slaughter's hypothesis is the best.—

Until we know more about these peripheral conditions it is, I think, useless to appeal to the centre. In particular, it is useless to raise our third question, and to attempt any characterisation of possible central conditions. There are many psychologists who have a predilection for the cortex; my own leaning is towards the sense-organ. But apart from that — or, if you like, because of that! — I believe that experimental psychology has always made most progress when it has worked from without inwards: "It is a healthy instinct," I have said elsewhere, "that sends us back and back again to the channels of sense, as we seek an appreciation of the fulness and richness of the mental life." I do not deny that the cortex is concerned in the 'fluctuations of attention'; no one at the present time

can make such denial.   But I look for explanation from the behaviour of the sense-organs.[33]

At this level of 'minimal stimuli,' then, the law
of temporal instability will mean that the peripheral conditions of clearness are intermittent.
Whether the central predisposition persists or
itself oscillates, during peripheral intermittence,
is an open question.   I think that the predisposition is sustained.   Geissler is of the same
opinion.   Even Pace writes in similar vein.
The attention, he says, "must undergo a change
of some kind when the stimulus disappears. . . .
When the gray ring or band of light vanishes, the
attention is divided between the memory-image
of that which has just disappeared and the impression actually received from the general field.
Again, while it may be said that the attitude of
the attention in both phases of each fluctuation
is one of expectancy, it is also true that the term
of this expectation varies: in one phase, the observer awaits the disappearance of the stimulus,
in the other, he looks for the reappearance of the
stimulus."   This 'change' of attention, 'division' of attention, shift of expectant attitude, —
all this is very different from a fluctuation of
attention, a more or less periodic rise and fall of
attentional energy.   There is nothing in Pace's

language to bear out the Wundtian statement: "die Aufmerksamkeit ist ihrem Wesen nach eine *intermittirende* Function." [34]

Let me add, for the avoidance of misunderstanding, that the law of temporal instability holds, without any question, for central predisposition in the large. The instances of continued attention that I gave some pages back were extreme instances; and even they, as I said, "illustrate often enough the labile, instable character of attention."* But these fluctuations of the total attentive consciousness lie beyond our present horizon.

There should, now, be a final law (7) of *degree of clearness*, — a law that would stand to clearness as Weber's Law stands to intensity of sensation, and as the various discriminative constancies stand to the qualitative, temporal and spatial attributes. "The discovery of a reliable measure of the attention," Külpe says, "would appear to be one of the most important problems that await solution by the experimental psychology of the future." [35]   The discovery has not yet been made; but we may devote a little space to methods.

There seem to be two possible ways, a direct

* P. 264.

and an indirect, of 'measuring attention,' form-
ing a scale of clearness-degrees, by appeal to the
attentive consciousness. The first or direct way
is to utilise the observer's introspections of clearness itself. Suppose that an observer has attained to maximal practice in some field, let us
say, of discriminative sensitivity. Maximal practice may, for experimental purposes, be considered a constant. Suppose, again, that we have
arranged a series of distracting stimuli, homogeneous in kind but graded in complexity, such
that we are able to reduce the observer's percentage of right cases from 100 to 95, 90, 85 . . .
according to the distraction employed. It is
necessary that the action of the distractors be
constant; and it is necessary that they be of the
same kind, and therefore exert an influence which
differs only, and differs measurably, in degree.
Having secured these conditions, we should let
the observer decide whether the clearness of
conscious contents was distinguishably different
under a 5 per cent. and a 10 per cent. distraction,
or under a 5 per cent. and a 15 per cent. distraction, or again under an 80 per cent. and an 85 per
cent. distraction, and so on, all through the series.
We should thus finally obtain a scale of notice-
ably different clearnesses paralleled by a scale of
measured amounts of distracting stimulus; we

should have the materials for formulating our law; we should have solved the problem of measurement of attention.

With this idea in mind, I set a number of my advanced students to work, years ago, upon the preliminary question of the distractor. We discovered some interesting things: that distraction may spur instead of distracting; that intermittent distractions, the ordinary 'intellectual operations,' are unreliable; that odours are admirably constant distracting material, — if only they could be measured! and so forth. But we got no farther; and no one else has got any farther by that road. Nevertheless, I am not yet persuaded that the road is altogether impracticable, and we are now making a renewed attempt to open it up.[36]

The other, indirect way of measuring attention is to measure the concomitant sensations of strain, the 'effort' of attention. "Wir besitzen an gewissen begleitenden Gefühlen einer grösseren oder geringeren Anstrengung . . . ein Mittel, uns zu vergewissern, ob unsere Disposition in zwei Fällen annähernd dieselbe sei"; that is a suggestion of Stumpf's. May we not generalise it, and argue that different degrees of effort run parallel to the distinguishable degrees of clearness? Unfortunately, no! In the first place, the concomitant effort is an indication, not of degree of attention, but rather of inertia of attention; strained attention is attention under difficulties; we attend best when effort is small. May we, then, reverse the parallelism, and make degree of effort an inverse measure of degree of clearness? No, not that either! For, secondly, experiment has shown that under certain circumstances attention is maximal when we are slightly 'distracted'; a modicum of effort is favourable to clearness. In a word, the relation of effort to degree of attention is equivocal; even if we could accurately measure effort, we should have no measurement of clearness.[37]

It does not follow, however, because we are as yet unable to measure attention, that we may not devise objective tests which shall inform us, on the one hand, of gross differences in attentional degree or attentional capacity as between observer and observer, and on the other hand of approximate constancy or marked fluctuation of attention in the same observer. Four kinds of test offer themselves at once. We may determine the 'range of attention, simultaneous or successive; we may have recourse to tests of sensitivity and sensible discrimination; we may determine associability, the rate and stability of association and reproduction; and we may measure the promptness of voluntary action, the time of simple reaction. The application of such tests is by no means easy, and I imagine that it can rarely be direct. The test will rather appear as an incidental feature of some more general investigation; or it will be made an end in itself, and its result then carried over by analogy to investigations whose main purpose is of a different nature.

A good deal of work has already been done. Binet subjected two groups of school children, classed by their teachers as intelligent and unintelligent, to a long series of tests: the children were required to discriminate æsthesiometric impressions, to count dots by eye and sounds by ear, to memorise letters, to read a word exposed by the movement of an instantaneous shutter, to perform simultaneous additions, to correct proofs, to make reactions, etc. I think that, on the whole, the outcome of the inquiry justified the time and care devoted to it; but the results, as is only natural, leave us in doubt as to the permanent value of the individual tests and their precise relation to the attention. Janet, taking the cue from his experience with hysterical subjects, proposes a perimetrical test of the degree of attention. Of a somewhat different order are the proposals of Oehrn and Henri, to measure attention by reference to mean variation, and of Wiersma and Pillsbury, to utilise for the same end the duration of noticeability (or the ratio of the periods of noticeability and unnoticeability) in experiments on fluctuation. Oehrn's suggestion, in particular, may very well prove to be of value, though it is clear that detailed analysis of conditions, a careful sifting out of contributory factors, must precede its application.[38]

The number of possible tests is thus very great. And since all psychological observation is done in the state of attention, and distracting stimuli may always be 'thrown in,' there is no single form of experimental procedure that cannot be made to afford a rough gauge of concentration. It would be strange if, out of this multitude of possibilities, there should be no positive gain for psychology. There will be, — if analysis is pushed far enough, and if recourse is had to the observer's introspection; otherwise, we shall remain upon the plane of the roughly practical. I gave, at the beginning of this discussion, a schematic outline of a psychological distraction-method. I remark, in conclusion, that it will be wise to combine such a method with the technique of the method of expression. I have no faith in the power of the expression-instruments to tell us of the nature and number of the affective qualities. But they may help — one never knows! — towards an objective differentiation of the conscious degrees of clearness.[39]

I am at the end of my review. I have done my best to make the review complete, on our elementary level, and to disentangle the really elementary problems from the problems of the total attentive consciousness. In the next Lecture we must try to gather up the critical threads and to weave them into a pattern; we must consider the status and the relations of affection and attention within a systematic psychology.

VIII

AFFECTION AND ATTENTION

LECTURE VIII

AFFECTION AND ATTENTION

THROUGHOUT our discussion of attention, I have been urging that it is advisable, in an elementary psychology, to shift the emphasis from total attentive state to sensation and the attribute of clearness; the discussion has centred about that suggestion. Our treatment of the affective processes, on the other hand, was almost wholly critical. Construction is always more difficult than criticism, — even when it takes the very modest form of making up one's mind in the face of rival theories. But you have the right to look here also for some positive suggestion; and, although I have nothing original to say, I shall accordingly begin this final Lecture with a brief outline of an elementary psychology of feeling. Let me assure you again, as I have assured you before, that my position is tentative, provisional, not fixed and dogmatic.

We find, in the history of psychology, two opposed views of feeling, views that I shall distinguish as the intellectual and the affectional.

The intellectual view considers feeling as a form
of cognition; the affectional gives it an independent place among the mental faculties.   On
the score of formal expression, the intellectual
view is undoubtedly the older; human thought,
in the early stages of its activity, is prone to
rationalise, and for a long time — for a time,
indeed, that extends well into the modern period
— it was also dominant.   But the affectional
view crosses it at many points; and when we
come to Kant, the traditional status of the two
theories has completely changed, and the affectional has gained the day.   The faculty of feeling is added, as intermediary, to the faculties
of knowledge and of desire.

Kant's authority was, of course, very great;
and the affectional view of feeling held its place
in the writings of those later psychologists who
escaped the influence of Herbart.   Fortunately
or unfortunately, however, the main current of
modern psychology takes its source from the
intellectualism of Herbart and the sensationalism
of contemporary physiology.   Hence — if I may
change the figure — experimental psychology
had, from the outset, a strong intellectual bias,
a definite leaning towards *Gefühlsempfindungen*
or a *Gefühlston der Empfindung*.   We saw, in
an earlier Lecture, that Wundt at first resisted

the pressure of this tendency, but later for a while succumbed to it.*

In a word, then, the intellectual view of feeling has been favoured in two ways: by the inertia of a settled philosophical tradition, and by the nature of the sources from which modern psychology derives.[1] But the tradition, after all, merely illustrates an inherent onesidedness of reflective thought; and we must remember that it was successfully overcome by the psychology of the eighteenth century. As for Herbart and the physiologists, it is — for our immediate purpose — nothing more than an historical accident that the succession of the faculty-systems should have devolved upon a rigorous intellectualism. What is significant, again, is this: that modern psychology, just like the psychology of the eighteenth century, has finally revolted against intellectualism, so that the majority of present-day psychologists recognise the independence of the affective processes, and the doctrine of the 'affective tone' has well-nigh disappeared.

But, you may ask, has this second movement for affective independence really accomplished anything? Have we not ourselves admitted and emphasised the unsettled state of the psychology of feeling? Are not the opposed camps, of

* P. 133.

majority and of minority alike, split into num-
berless factions? — I will try to answer these
questions: premising only that ground once
gained, in the history of a science, is never wholly
lost, and that our modern movement could not
have culminated so quickly, had we not had the
example of the eighteenth century before our
eyes.   And my answer will be twofold.

Do not let us forget, in the first place, that the
physiological tradition is unbroken.   The theories of Bourdon and von Frey can trace their
descent, in the spirit if not in the letter, from a
long line of workers in 'physiological psychology';
and the *Gefühlsempfindungen*, whatever may be
thought of them by the descriptive psychologist,
will. not easily yield their claim on the side of
explanation.   Sensational theories of feeling we
shall have always with us.   But let us reflect,
secondly, that a period which is sterile in observation is, invariably, fruitful in speculation.
When, a few years ago, I was classifying the contents of the leading psychological journals, I was
amazed at the small number of the experimental
studies of feeling.[2]   I had known, as we all
know, that a marked interest in feeling is of quite
recent growth; I had not realised how profound
was the lack of interest that preceded.   No wonder, then, that every psychologist has his own

hypothesis; no wonder that no two psychologists can agree upon 'the definition of feeling'![3] We have a fairly exact parallel in the history of psychophysics. There was a time, in that too, when all the world was writing theory and nobody was doing work, — the time when Merkel prayed aloud that his own experiments might lead, not to "weitere theoretische Discussionen von Seiten der vielen Gegner,"[4] but to more accurate tests, made by better men. We have come out of this sterile period in psychophysics, and we shall come out of it also in the psychology of feeling. For a while yet we shall go on wrangling about opinions; but every experimental study helps to clear the air, and as observations multiply, theory will reshape itself to accord with fact.

My personal opinion is, as I have shown plainly enough, that affection must be given elemental rank in consciousness, as a process coördinate with sensation. I rely, primarily, upon the lack of the attribute of clearness; all sensations may become clear, while an affection — however prolonged or intensive — is never clear, never comes to the focus of attention. I rely also upon the criterion of 'movement between opposites'; it seems to me that conscious opposition is always a matter of affection, never of sensation.

U

And I rely, to some extent, upon the concurrence of these distinguishing characters, and upon their implication — or, at least, suggestion — of certain other differences between the two modes of conscious process. On the whole, I am convinced that a generic difference can be made out, in the adult human mind, between sensation and affection. I therefore believe that Stumpf's proposal, to treat affective processes as if they were sensations, to bring all the machinery of sensation-method to bear upon the feelings, is a mistaken proposal; I do not think that it is worth while to assume after-images and memory-images, and contrasts and inductions, in the sphere of feeling. What do you gain by the assumption, if you cannot find the facts?

On the question of the number of the affective qualities, I have no choice but to abide by my experimental results. The situation has its humorous side; for I have tried, I suppose, as hard as any one to discover the pluralists' variety — with 'vorgefasste Meinung' and 'leere Schablone' and 'Dogma der Lust- Unlusttheorie' and 'völlig haltlose Behauptung' all the while buzzing about my ears. I do not know why Wundt should be so severe upon those who differ from him, seeing that his own opinion has more than once changed, and that what he himself terms the

"erste, vorläufige Darstellung des dreidimension-
alen Systems der Gefühle" [5] was not given to the
world until 1896. I do not think, either, that the
'Lust-Unlusttheorie' is a dogma. It has been a
dogma; it was allowed to become a dogma by
the supineness, not of the dualists (for we were all
dualists together), but of the experimentalists in
general; and, as I have pointed out, this dogmatic slumber of experimental psychology is responsible for the current hypertrophy of theory.
But to charge the dualist with dogmatism, in the
year 1908, is simply to charge him with acceptance, in a modern version, of the traditional doctrine of pleasure-pain. Is a man dogmatic every
time that his experiments lead him into agreement with Aristotle?

I will now venture to sketch a theory of feeling which seems to me to be sufficiently plausible,
and which serves to round out, by explanation,
the remarks of the preceding paragraphs.[6] It
is natural to suppose that the material of consciousness, the stuff out of which mind is made,
is ultimately homogeneous, all of a piece. Let
us make that supposition. The affections then
appear — I do not like to say, as 'undeveloped
sensations,' for an undeveloped sensation is still
a sensation; but at any rate as mental processes
of the same general kind as sensations, and as

mental processes that might, under favourable
conditions, have developed into sensations. I
hazard the guess that the 'peripheral organs'
of feeling are the free afferent nerve-endings dis-
tributed to the various tissues of the body; *
and I take these free endings to represent a
lower level of development than the specialised
receptive organ. Hence we have peripheral
organs of sense, but no 'organs,' in the strict
meaning of the term, for affective processes.
Had mental development been carried farther,
pleasantness and unpleasantness might have
become sensations, — in all likelihood would
have been differentiated, each of them, into a
large number of sensations. Had our physical
development been carried farther, we might have
had a corresponding increase in the number of
internal sense-organs.

What does this theory explain? It explains,
first, the obscurity of feeling, the absence of the
attribute of clearness. Affective processes are
processes whose development has been arrested;
they have not attained, and now they never can
attain, to clear consciousness. Affective experience is the obscure, indiscriminable correlate
of a medley of widely diffused excitatory pro-

* We must, of course, except the free nerve-endings at the
periphery of the body, which are probably the 'organs' of pain.
I do not think that the exception hurts the theory.

cesses.[7] The theory explains, secondly, the
movement of affective process between opposites,
and the relation of this movement to the health
and harm, the weal and woe of the organism.[8]
For the excitatory processes will report the 'tone'
of the bodily systems from which they proceed,
and the report will vary, and can only vary, between 'good' and 'bad.'   At this point, of course,
the theory takes account of 'mixed feelings.'
It explains, thirdly, the lack of qualitative differentiation within pleasantness-unpleasantness.
The report of 'good' or 'bad' may show variation in degree, but cannot change in kind.   And,
lastly, the theory explains the introspective resemblance between affections and organic sensations.
Genetically, the two sets of processes are near
akin; and it is natural that they should be intimately blended in experience.

I shall not attempt further details.   If the
theory appeals to you, you will work out details,
applications and corollaries, for yourselves.   If
it does not, you will pursue some other path, —
and we shall see presently who has made the wiser
choice. A distinguished physicist remarked the
other day that theories are matters, not of creed,
but of policy; [9] and it seems to·me that it is
better policy to look at the affective processes
in the manner here outlined than to think of

them as apperceptive reactions, or as centrally
aroused concomitant sensations, or as indices of
the state of nutrition of the cerebral cortex, or as
symptoms of the readiness of central discharge.
But every one cannot be right; and where our
positive knowledge is practically *nil*, there is no
disgrace in being wrong.

I pass on, then, to another question. Let us
take it as agreed that affection is an independent
mental process, inherently obscure, and evincing
a qualitative duality. What, now, is the relation of affection to attention ?

When I read Ebbinghaus' chapter on Attention in 1902, I was greatly surprised at the mention, among the 'Bedingungen der Aufmerksamkeit,' of the affective value of impressions.
"Diejenigen Ursachen, die einen stark lustbe-
tonten oder unlustbetonten Bewusstseinsinhalt
zur Folge haben, setzen diesen Inhalt leichter
durch als andere Ursachen ihre indifferenten
Wirkungen." I had supposed that 'interest'
still figured as a condition of attention only in
quite popular psychologies; yet Ebbinghaus
said in 1902, and repeats in 1905, that "Interesse
. . . besonders häufig ein stärkeres Hervortreten [eines] Eindrucks in der Seele bewirkt."
This doctrine implies, first, that feeling precedes

attention, that sensory clearness follows in the train of pleasantness-unpleasantness. Indeed, the point is explicit; for interest *bewirkt*, effects or induces clearness, and interest (Ebbinghaus is properly careful to define it) is itself "[eine] Lust, die hervorgebracht wird durch das harmonische Zusammengehen eines gegenwärtig der Seele nahegelegten Eindrucks mit früher erworbenen, jetzt durch ihn geweckten Vorstellungen."[10] Pleasure, then, comes first, and attention afterwards. The doctrine implies, secondly, that certain of the conditions of attention are non-affective, that sensory clearness may be established in the absence of pleasantness-unpleasantness. On the former issue, Ebbinghaus comes into direct conflict with Stout. "The assumption that attention *depends* on pleasure-pain seems to have no sufficient basis. . . . Interest and attention do not seem to be related as antecedent and consequent, but rather as different aspects of the same concrete fact. . . . Feelings of pleasure and pain . . . do not determine attention as antecedent conditions."[11] On the latter, he comes into conflict with Wundt's well-known definition of feeling as "the reaction of apperception upon sensations."[12]

Ebbinghaus supports his assertion, that attention is conditioned upon feeling, by reference to incidents of everyday life: the attraction of a pretty face or a bad accident, the fascination of anything connected with a man's particular hobby, etc.; he offers no experimental evidence. Now Stout and Pillsbury have analysed a number of precisely such instances, and have been led to precisely the opposite conclusion. Stout I have already quoted. Pillsbury declares, in the same sense: "les choses ne sont intéressantes que parce que nous portons sur elles notre attention, et nous ne portons pas sur elles notre attention parce qu'elles sont intéressantes."[13] Unless, then, there are outstanding facts, which refuse to be analysed in this way, we must, I think, decide against Ebbinghaus. Personally, I confess that, after the discussion as before, I find it difficult to take his position seriously.

The second question that he raises for us is, on the contrary, of very great systematic importance. Do we ever attend without feeling? Or is it rather true that whenever we attend we feel, and whenever we feel we attend?

In so far as Ebbinghaus' treatment implies that we may attend without feeling, I am in agreement with it. I am afraid, however, that that bare statement is misleading; and I shall accordingly try to give it a systematic setting. Consider the attentive consciousness in the large:

what is its place in a psychological system? Wundt, of course, places it under the heading of 'will.' "Die Apperception ist gleichzeitig elementarer Willensact und constituirender Bestandtheil aller Willensvorgänge." [14] Stumpf takes a similar view, though he seems to have felt a difficulty (as Wundt does not) in bringing involuntary and voluntary attention under a single heading.[15] Ebbinghaus finds that, in voluntary attention, "der Gesammtzustand durchaus gleich dem . . . als Wollen beschriebenen ist;" but he distinguishes involuntary from voluntary attention, as he distinguishes *Trieb* from *Wille*. Since, however, will is a development from impulse, — "der Wille ist der vorausschauend gewordene Trieb," — the distinction is merely terminological.[16]

Other psychologists have held other opinions. I cannot here discuss them; I can only say that, so far as I see, the term 'will' affords the best general title for two great groups of psychological facts: the facts of attention and the facts of action. There can, I think, be no doubt that these two groups are intimately related, that action is simply a special case of attention. But, if that is the case, we may use our knowledge of either one to throw light upon the other. Thus, psychologists and moralists alike have long dis-

puted whether 'pleasure and pain' are the sole
conditions of action. I do not consider that
they can be numbered at all among the conditions of action; I believe that the conditions
of action are to be learned from a study of the
conditions of attention; and I should analyse
the alleged positive instances on the lines of
Stout's and Pillsbury's analyses in the sphere of
attention. On the other side, our immediate
question — 'Do we ever attend without feeling?' — is answered as soon as we appeal to
action. Do we ever act without feeling? Very
certainly we do! Actions may be classified in
various ways, and I shall not try to impose upon
you a classification of my own; but we shall
agree that there are many types of action, reflex
and automatic and ideomotor and what not,
that are performed without the arousal of pleasantness-unpleasantness in consciousness. In just
the same way, as it seems to me, may we have an
automatic or instinctive or mechanised attention
that is altogether free of feeling. No one will
deny that pleasantness and unpleasantness appear often and often again — 'besonders häufig,'
as Ebbinghaus says [17] — as the accompaniments
of attention; it would be strange if our experience
were otherwise, since all the conditions of attention are at the same time conditions of a powerful

impression of the nervous system. The connection is, indeed, so obvious and so widespread that it is only natural to regard it as universal; I have myself for many years subscribed to this belief, and have taught that affection and attention are simply back and front, obverse and reverse, of the same consciousness. But, after all, views must give way before observations; and though I have, for clearness' sake, thrown our discussion into systematic form, my reliance throughout is, as you will have understood, upon observed instances of feelingless attention. Now that I have once noticed such cases, they prove to be of fairly common occurrence; and I am sure that you will have no especial difficulty in discovering their like: — only you must not look for them in the professional spirit, but keep your eyes open to mark them as they come.

You may, perhaps, demur to my proposal that all these phenomena of attention and action be brought under the heading of 'will.' Reflex actions and instinctive attentions are, indeed, from one point of view, the antipodes of will. If, however, I adopt the term, it is because I accept the genetic theory of Wundt and Ward. I believe, with Wundt, that "die zweckmässigen Reflexbewegungen stabil und mechanisch gewordene Willenshandlungen sind"; [18] I believe, with Ward, that "volition or something analogous to it" has, in the race as in the individual, invariably "preceded habit"; [19] and I believe, with Cope, that even "the automatic 'involuntary' movements of the heart, intestines, reproductive systems, etc., were organised in successive states of consciousness." [20] Argument, on so large a subject, is here out of the question; but I am glad of the opportunity to recite my *credo*. And the more strongly you react against it, the more earnestly do I beg you to give it a fair examination.[21] —

So far, then, the relation between affection and attention is hardly more than external. Affection reports the tone of the great bodily systems that lack organs of sense; attention means the clarifying of sensory contents under the influence of powerful nervous stimuli. The organism may, with time, become adapted to these attentional stimuli, — so that, while the corresponding sensations appear, at least momentarily, at the conscious focus, there is no felt shock or tilt of the whole living body, no concomitant pleasantness or unpleasantness. We may attend without feeling. May we, on the other hand, feel without attending? Can there be a change in general organic tone, sufficiently marked to reveal itself as feeling, while the

sensory contents of consciousness are still obscure? Wundt answers this question with a
decided affirmative. "[Die Gefühle] können
auch dann, wenn ihre Vorstellungsgrundlage
ausserordentlich dunkel bleibt, eine relativ grosse
Intensität gewinnen." [22] And again: "erhebt
sich irgendein psychischer Vorgang über die
Schwelle des Bewusstseins, so pflegen die Gefühlselemente desselben, sobald sie die hinreich-
ende Stärke besitzen, zuerst merkbar zu werden,
so dass sie sich bereits energisch in den Blickpunkt des Bewusstseins drängen, ehe noch von
den Vorstellungselementen irgend etwas wahrgenommen wird." [23] Here, I think, Wundt is
working with 'feelings' where he should be
working with organic sensations and pleasantness-unpleasantness; and, in so far forth, his
statements are unconvincing. But this objection does not fully meet the issue; we have to
consider the question on its psychological merits.

Notice, then, that the question itself takes two
forms, a popular and a scientific. I gave them
just now as if they were interchangeable; but
a very little reflection brings out their difference.
The popular form of the question is: 'May we
feel without attending?' And the implication
here is that attention, the attentive consciousness,
is something sporadic and occasional; that the

two-level consciousness alternates with a one-level, wholly 'inattentive' consciousness. Now it is possible that this state of inattention exists, though I confess myself sceptical in the matter; I doubt whether inattention, in the waking life, is not always 'attention to something else.' [24] But, at all events, I do not think it likely that any one will argue for the affective character of inattention; the very word suggests a state of indifference.

In its second and scientific form the question asks whether the obscure contents of a two-level consciousness may be as strongly 'toned' as the clear. Wundt declares that they may; my own analysis leads me to the opposite conclusion. I grant that we attend without feeling; and this admission seems to me to bring with it a very welcome 'loosening up' of systematic psychology. But I cannot grant that — in the sense of this paragraph — we feel without attending. I incline rather to find a fairly close parallel between degree of clearness and degree of pleasantness-unpleasantness, and thus to regard the relation between affection and attention, on this side, not as external, but as intrinsic. Wundt has missed the organic sensations altogether; and we, who emphasise them, must ourselves be careful not to confuse the clearness of a sensory fusion either with qualitative articulation or with definiteness of localisation. Bearing this caution in mind, you will surely agree that, whenever we are moved and stirred to feeling, the sensible factors in the total process are relatively clear.[25]

It is now necessary to go back a little way, in order to remove a possible misapprehension. I said that the list of conditions of attention, in Ebbinghaus' *Grundzüge*, implies that we may attend without feeling. And I said that that implication is in conflict with Wundt's familiar definition of feeling as the reaction of apperception upon the sensory contents of consciousness. How can we attend without feeling, if feeling is generated in the act of attention? But I have just now quoted from Wundt sentences which affirm that feeling may be present, at a relatively high intensity, while its sensory substrate is still 'extraordinarily obscure.' Do not these sentences suggest that feeling may be generated without attention? And is not Wundt, therefore, inconsistent?

When Wundt wrote, in 1893, that feeling is "die Reactionsweise der Apperception auf die sinnliche Erregung," he meant that statement to be understood in its obvious and literal sense.

"Der Gefühlston" — we are in 1893 ! —"kommt
überhaupt nur zu Stande, insofern wir die
Empfindungen *appercipiren*, und er kann daher
als die *subjective oder psychische Seite jenes cen-
traleren Voranges der Apperception* angesehen
werden, der zu der centralen Sinneserregung
hinzukommt, wenn sich die Thätigkeit des
Bewusstseins ihr zuwendet." [26]   In 1902 he has
kept the phrase, — feeling is still the "Reaction
der Apperception auf das einzelne Bewusstseinserlebniss"; it is of the essence of feeling "Reactionsweise der Apperception auf den Bewusstseinsinhalt zu sein," [27] — but he has changed its
meaning. Feeling is no longer confined to those
sensory contents that are the 'object' of attention; on the contrary it may accompany any
contents, clear or obscure. "[Die] centrale
Function der Apperception ist in jedem Augen-
blick auch für den ganzen übrigen Bewusstseinsinhalt bestimmend, indem dessen sämmtliche
Elemente nach ihrem Verhältniss zu den appercipirten Elementen geordnet werden. So erscheinen denn auch die an die einzelnen Bewusstseinsinhalte gebundenen Gefühle durchaus als
subjective Bestimmungen, die jedes einzelne Bewusstseinserlebniss durch seine Einwirkung auf
die Function der Apperception empfängt. In
diesem Sinne" — in this new and modified sense

— "ist jedes Gefühl . . . Reaction der Apperception auf das einzelne Bewusstseinserlebniss." I do not understand how conscious contents can be reacted upon by apperception without thereby becoming clear. But, however that may be, this reaction, which evokes feeling over the whole of the obscure background of consciousness,[28] is something entirely different from the direct reaction of attention upon its object. The tridimensional theory of feeling has compelled Wundt to change his exposition; and he has changed it in such a way that, so far as the phrases go, he is not inconsistent. At the same time, his revised doctrine is, I am sure, only transitional, and I hope that we may presently have an essay in which it is fully worked out.

That was a digression. We have next, picking up again the main thread of the discussion, to attempt a rough characterisation of the attentive consciousness. Its central feature, the two-level formation, has already been described.* But besides the "Klarheitszunahme einer bestimmten Vorstellung oder Vorstellungsgruppe" and the "Hemmung anderer disponibler Eindrücke oder Erinnerungsbilder," — besides, that is, the appearance of the two levels, — Wundt

* P. 241.

x

finds an essential constituent of every process of
apperception in the concomitant *Thätigkeitsgefühl*.[29]   What are we to say with regard to the
feeling of activity?

Wundt has often been charged with circularity
of statement.   Feeling is the reaction of apperception upon sensation; yet apperception itself
comes to consciousness as a feeling.   Or again:
apperception is the primitive act of will; acts
of will are feelings; yet feeling presupposes the
direction of an act of will upon sensation.[30]
I have been accustomed to meet this charge by
the reply that the feeling of activity is the discovery of introspection.   Let me quote a parallel
case.   James has told us that "the acts of attending, assenting, negating, making an effort are
felt" by him "as movements of something in the
head."   "Whenever my introspective glance
succeeds in turning round quickly enough to
catch one of these manifestations of spontaneity
in the act, all it can ever feel distinctly is some
bodily process, for the most part taking place
within the head."[31]   Kohn objects to this description that "if the feelings were present while
the attention is directed upon some other object,
there would be no need at all of the 'turning
round' or the 'introspective glance.'   We should
be conscious of them without this."[32]   To which

the obvious rejoinder is that we are conscious of
them 'without this'; otherwise there would be
no cue for introspection. We do not attempt to
introspect the non-existent. But, when we are
giving a psychological account of any contents,
we examine it in the state of attention.*

Apply that, now, to Wundt. The typical form
of attention, if one induces it for purposes of
introspection, is voluntary attention. Consciousness in the state of voluntary attention is composed, in part, of 'muskuläre Spannungsemp-
findungen.' When, then, one seeks to introspect
the attentive consciousness, one comes naturally
upon these sensations of strain; they are made
focal; and, in the process of their focalisation, a
'feeling of activity' must, on Wundt's view, be
struck out. Hence it is impossible to introspect
the state of voluntary attention without discovering a *Thätigkeitsgefühl*.

I think that this explanation heads off the
charge of circularity; and it seemed worth while
to lay it before you because, as I said, the charge
has often been made. It must, however, be
pointed out that the independent status of the
feelings in Wundt's recent writings changes the
whole situation. The *Thätigkeitsgefühl* has now

---

* It must be remembered that James and Kohn use 'feel' and
'feeling' where we should employ 'perceive' and 'perception.'

to stand on its own feet, without aid from introspection; we either experience it — as feeling —
in every instance of attention, or we do not.   My
own opinion is that we do not.[33]   In frequent
cases of what I have called reflex or instinctive or
mechanised attention I find no trace of feeling at
all.   The depressing *Gefühl des Erleidens* and
the subsequent exciting *Gefühl der Thätigkeit*
are both, in my experience, conspicuous by their
absence.   Wundt's schema for voluntary attention is expectation, followed by a very brief feeling of satisfaction or fulfilment, followed again
by the feeling of activity.[34]   But everything depends, surely, upon what you mean by voluntary
attention.   Wundt is thinking of reaction experiments;[35] and there are, I admit, — though
with a reservation to be made in a moment, —
certain forms of compound reaction in which
that sequence of feelings is realised.   On the
other hand, I have noted many instances of what
would pass, in ordinary psychological usage, for
voluntary attention, in which one or two or all
three of the feelings were lacking.

My reservation is not serious; it concerns
merely the naming of the processes in question.
Expectation and effort are not, in my view,
necessarily affective, though both of them may,
under certain circumstances, be accompanied by

pleasantness-unpleasantness. It is more important, however, to examine the part that effort actually plays in the attentive consciousness. Such an examination brings us face to face with two large questions: the 'motor' interpretation of attention, and the distinction of attentive states as active and passive, voluntary and involuntary.

On these two questions I can only repeat what I have said elsewhere. I have always regarded, and I probably shall always regard, the motor interpretation of attention as one-sided. We have already seen, on the plane of descriptive psychology, that kinæsthetic sensations stand in an equivocal relation to 'degree' of attention.* And it may be seriously doubted whether they are a necessary and integral part of the attentive consciousness. Kinæsthesis is, I suppose, always present in the obscure background of consciousness; but I question if, in states of what I term 'secondary passive attention,' these kinæsthetic processes are necessarily intensified, or new kinæsthetic sensations introduced. Wundt remarks that the 'muskulären Spannungsemp-findungen,' which are a frequent partial contents of apperception, may "fehlen oder von sehr geringer Stärke sein." [36] What we need, in this matter, is less theory and more observations of

* P. 279.

fact. On the side of explanation, I suggest that a like one-sidedness is shown in the constant insistence on the reflex arc as the functional unit of the nervous system. It seems to be forgotten that, from another point of view, the office of the cortex may properly be described as the disjunction of the reflex arc, the interposition of resistance between sensory stimulus and motor response. The result of this disjunction is that the attitude of the organism may be typically receptive, typically elaborative, or typically executive. In sensible discrimination, the attitude is mainly receptive; there are no known muscular adjustments that can keep pace with the just noticeable differences of colour and tone. In concentrated thought the attitude is mainly elaborative; and where is the evidence of motor outflow here? I am not disputing the neurone theory; but I argue that the longer a principal path is made, the more synapses there are in its course, and the more numerous the bypaths become, the more difficult will it be for an excitatory process to find its way out in the straightforward sensorimotor fashion. McDougall writes, to the same effect, that the "physiological basis of the 'Lebhaftigkeit' of the presentation" is to be found in "the complexity of the upper levels" of the nervous system; [37] and Ebbing-

haus, too, lays great stress upon the 'Querver-
bindungen' in his theory of attention.[38]

Whether, then, we consider it psychologically
or physiologically, the motor interpretation of
attention appears to be one-sided. How does
it gain acceptance? Pillsbury gives a reason;
he suggests that all the motor theories derive, in
the last resort, from "la tendance populaire à
regarder l'activité accompagnant le processus de
l'attention comme sa cause."[39] If, however,
this is correct reasoning, the theories are doubly
suspect: they stand committed, from the outset, to a partial view of the facts. We may
cheerfully grant that, for this very reason, they
have done psychological service; where the
problem is complex, exaggeration in one quarter
may be necessary to prevent neglect in another.
But this does not mean that exaggeration is itself laudable; and I can see nothing but a
palpable exaggeration in the definition of attention as a motor reaction.[40]

I must hurry on to our second question, —
the question of the distinction between passive
and active, involuntary and voluntary attention.
"La distinction entre l'attention passive et l'attention active est basée," Pillsbury says, "sur
l'absence ou la présence de sensations d'effort.
. . . Mais comme les sensations d'effort sont

des accompagnements fortuits, ne correspondant ni aux conditions, ni au degré de l'attention, il semble impossible de retenir une partie de cette classification sans compliquer considérablement la terminologie, et cela sans grand profit." [41] On the historical issue, Pillsbury is undoubtedly right; and I have already expressed my agreement with the view which he takes of sensations of strain.   But I doubt very much whether we can afford to discard altogether the use of the terms active-passive or voluntary-involuntary. Better a poor terminology than the slurring of an observed difference!   And, at any rate, it is interesting to note that neither Wundt nor Ebbinghaus relies for the distinction — which both draw, though in characteristically different ways — upon strain sensations.   According to Ebbinghaus, 'sensations of activity' are marks of attention in general. [42]   Wundt, on the other hand, is so largely occupied with the feelings that sensations of strain play a very minor part in his account.

How, then, are the two forms of attention distinguished?   For Wundt there is, first of all, the difference of feeling.   Further: "die active Apperception ist im allgemeinen eine durch die Gesammtlage des Bewusstseins *vorbereitete*, die passive ist in der Regel eine *unvorbereitete*."

And this means, again, that passive attention is "im allgemeinen eine Willenshandlung unter der Wirkung *eines* Motivs, oder . . . eine *Triebhandlung*." Active attention, on the contrary, is equivocally conditioned; it is a *Willkürhandlung*, subject to the interplay of primary with secondary motives, or a *Wahlhandlung*, the resultant of a conflict of primary motives. The two criteria (prepared, unprepared; univocally conditioned, equivocally conditioned) are coördinate, — or rather represent two aspects, the descriptive and the causal, of one and the same general difference.[43]

I think that these distinctions hold; and I think that, if we have recourse to our general law of the rise and fall, the expansion and reduction of conscious formations,[44] and classify attentions accordingly as primary passive, active, and secondary passive, we are able to do rough and ready justice to the facts. This classification is, in the first instance, genetic. We may assume that attention, in its beginnings, was a definitely determined reaction — sensory and motor both — upon a single stimulus. As sense-organs multiplied, two or more disparate stimuli might, each one in its own right, claim the organism's attention; here, in sense-rivalry and the conflict of motor attitudes, we should have the birth of ac-

tive attention. When, later on, image super-
vened upon sensation, conflict and rivalry were
largely transferred to the field of ideas, and we
find in consequence that separation of the receptive, elaborative, and executive attitudes of which
I spoke just now. So far, there has been a pro-
gressive increase in the complexity of the attentive consciousness. At this point reduction sets
in; choice and deliberation give way to secondary impulses, and active gives way to secondary
passive attention. The ground is thus cleared
for further growth; new formations appear in the
state of active attention, to be simplified in their
turn, — and the cycle recurs, with constant alternation of habit and acquisition, so long as the
organism retains its flexibility. This account
shows, in barest outline, my own systematic use
of the distinction; and you see that the whole
schema is implicit in Wundt's doctrine, and follows naturally from it.[45]

Genetic psychology lends itself to a summary
exposition of this kind; to its wider view the
principle stands out, clear of confusing details.
But Wundt himself is writing descriptive psychology; and descriptive psychology is always
in the grip of details. This is a fact that we
must bear in mind when we seek to appraise the
distinction of voluntary and involuntary atten-

tion in Ebbinghaus' system. "Die willkürliche
Aufmerksamkeit," he says, "ist die vorausschauend gewordene unwillkürliche. . . . Sie verhalten sich also zueinander wie Trieb und Wille."[46]
I remarked, a little while ago, that the difference
between Wundt and Ebbinghaus, in regard to
the will, is at bottom no more than a difference
of terminology. Very much the same thing
may be said here, except that Ebbinghaus con-
fines himself wholly to description, and rejects
the coördinate causal explanation, while at the
same time his descriptive distinction is cleaner
cut, more dogmatic, than that of Wundt. I
should give the preference, on both counts, to
Wundt's exposition.[47] It must be remembered
that we are dealing with formations of bewilder-
ing complexity, with total consciousnesses; and
that we have little more to guide us than psychological tradition and the casual observations
made in the course of experimental work or in
everyday life. Under these conditions, we ought
to follow up every clue that offers, and we
ought also to leave room in the system for doubtful cases, intermediate forms, transitional modes.
No doubt, the hostile critic will at once raise the
cry of inconsistency. Comfort yourselves with
the reflection that the hostile critic is generally
superficial! It is the sympathetic critic who dis-

covers your real weaknesses, and helps you by showing where they lie; and the sympathetic critic is less likely to charge inconsistency than to probe for its underlying reasons.

I am now at an end. I finished writing the last paragraph with a feeling compounded, in Wundtian terms, of pleasantness, relaxation, and tranquillisation. We set out from uncertainty and chaos; and we have at least achieved a fairly definite point of view, and have laid out a programme of experimental work for the future. Unfortunately, affective processes move between opposites: and that first feeling — which in my own poverty-stricken terminology would be merely a feeling of relief — soon gave way to a feeling of unpleasantness, tension, and depression. We know so very little of the subject of these Lectures, and the work that we have found to do will take so long in the doing! But feelings, again, are subject to *Abstumpfung*, show the phenomena of adaptation; and the feeling of depression passed as the feeling of relief had passed before it. The professional attitude came to its rights. And that attitude, in the case of the experimental psychologist, is — how shall I describe it? — an attitude of patient confidence. We must be patient, because of all the objects of human inquiry mind is the most baffling and the most complex; we must expect that the systems of to-day may have only an historical interest for the next generation. But we may have absolute confidence in our method, because the method has proved itself in the past; it has done far more for psychology than is generally acknowledged, far more even than is recognised in the ordinary text-book of psychology: for the law of attentional inertia holds in science as it holds in ordinary life. There is not the slightest doubt that the patient application of the experimental method will presently solve the problems of feeling and attention.

NOTES

NOTES TO LECTURE I

[1] It is, of course, an open question whether the sensation and the image may be bracketed under a single heading (Külpe) or must be treated as distinct elements (Ebbinghaus). I am not here prejudging this question. Whichever view one holds, the combined doctrine of sensation and image is set off, in systematic regard, from the doctrines of affection and attention.

[2] W. Wundt, *Grundzüge der physiologischen Psychologie*, i., 1902, xiv.; ii., 1902, v. Cf. also i., 353. — H. Ebbinghaus, *Grundzüge der Psychologie*, i., 1905, 183 f., 432.

The difference might, no doubt, be moderated. Thus Wundt wrote as early as 1896: "Kommt daher auch die Grösseneigenschaft als solche, und zwar im allgemeinen in verschiedenen Formen, nämlich als Intensität, als Qualität, als extensiver (räumlicher oder zeitlicher) Werth, und eventuell, nämlich wenn die verschiedenen Bewusstseinszustände berücksichtigt werden, als Klarheitsgrad, jedem psychischen Element und jedem psychischen Gebilde an und für sich schon zu, u.s.w." (*Grundriss der Psychologie*, 1896, 296 f.; 1905, 312 [Engl., 1897, 252; 1907, 288 f.]). And Ebbinghaus declares that the general attributes appear "in ᕁder Regel je mit mehreren einer bestimmten Klasse von [den spezifischen Empfindungen] auf einmal"; difference and multiplicity, for instance, presuppose at least two sensations (*op. cit.*, 433 f.). At the same time, the two systems cannot be brought into accord.

[3] *Völkerpsychologie, eine Untersuchung der Entwick-*

lungsgesetze von Sprache, Mythus und Sitte. I. *Die Sprache,* i., 1900, 37 ff.   Also 1904, 43 ff.

It may be urged that, for Wundt's constructive purposes, it matters little whether the dimensions of strain-relaxation and excitement-depression represent "einfache Gefühls-formen" or simple syntheses of affective process with organic sensation.   The reply is twofold.   If such a change of standpoint is immaterial, then the system cannot be very closely articulated; the superstructure (to change the figure) must sit rather loosely upon its foundations.   And again, if the change of standpoint is psychologically necessary, then it also becomes necessary to inquire whether there are not other, fundamental and typical syntheses, over and above strain-relaxation and excitement-depression, which have an equal claim to recognition.

[4] W. B. Pillsbury, *L'attention,* 1906, v.   "Dans l'état chaotique où se trouvent les théories contemporaines de l'attention," etc.   *Attention,* 1908, ix.

[5] E. Mach, *Beiträge zur Analyse der Empfindungen,* 1886, 121 f., 134; *Die Analyse der Empfindungen und das Verhältniss des Physischen zum Psychischen,* 1900, 180 f., 193.

[6] See, *e.g.,* the discussion of the Method of Limits in my *Experimental Psychology,* II., ii., 1905, 99 ff.

On the general topic of elements and attributes it may suffice here to refer the reader to A. Meinong, Ueber Begriff und Eigenschaften der Empfindung, *Vjs. f. wiss. Philos.,* xii., 1888, 324 ff., 477 ff.; xiii., 1889, 1 ff.; Bemerkungen über den Farbenkörper und das Mischungsgesetz, *Zeits. f. Psychol. u. Physiol. d. Sinnesorgane,* xxxiii., 1903, 1 ff., esp. § 6; E. B. Talbot, The Doctrine of Conscious Elements, *Philosophical Review,* iv., 1895, 154;

I. M. Bentley, The Simplicity of Colour Tones, *American Journal of Psychology*, xiv., 1903, 92; M. Meyer, On the Attributes of the Sensations, *Psychological Review*, xi., 1904, 83. Of the systematic treatises I mention only C. Stumpf, *Tonpsychologie*, i., 1883, 108. The departure from psychological tradition in H. Münsterberg's *Grundzüge der Psychologie*, i., 1900, is noteworthy; but its discussion would take us too far afield. See M. F. Washburn, Some Examples of the Use of Psychological Analysis in System-Making, *Philos. Review*, xi., 1902, 445 ff. — Further references are given in later Notes.

[7] G. E. Müller, Zur Psychophysik der Gesichtsempfindungen, *Zeits. f. Psychol. u. Physiol. d. Sinnesorgane*, x., 1896, 2 f., 25 ff.

[8] G. T. Fechner, *Elemente der Psychophysik*, i. (1860) 1889, 15.

[9] W. James, *The Principles of Psychology*, ii., 1890, 136.

[10] See, *e.g.*, the discussion in Wundt, *Physiologische Psychologie*, i., 1902, 14 f. (*Principles*, i., 1904, 12 ff.), 339 ff., 350 ff. It is needless to multiply references, as the usage of the experimentalists is now strict and consistent. James himself often employs the term 'sensation' very loosely (cf. the discussion in *Principles*, ii., 1), though he offers two definitions. On the one hand, (1) sensation is a limiting form of cognition, the form in which "the object cognised" comes nearest "to being a simple quality like 'hot,' 'cold,' 'red,' 'noise,' 'pain,' apprehended irrelatively to other things" (*loc. cit.*). Sensation is realised only in the earliest days of life; it is impossible, or all but impossible, to adults whose cognitive function has passed from acquaintance-with to knowledge-about (*ibid.*, 3, 7 f.; cf. i., 221 ff., 478 f.; *Text-*

book, 1892, 12 ff.). On the other hand, (2) sensation is "the object cognised" in this limiting form of cognition, "namely, simple *qualities* or *attributes* like *hard, hot, pain*" themselves. In this sense, too, a pure sensation is known to the adult only by way of abstraction (*Principles*, ii., 3; cf. i., 195, 224, 478 f.; *Text-book*, 40 ff., etc.). It is clear, I think, that on either of these definitions the statement of the text is valid.

[11] With this whole discussion, cf. C. Stumpf, *Tonpsychologie*, i., 1883, 207 ff.; ii., 1890, 56 ff., 535 ff. Ebbinghaus regards volume merely as a 'characterisation' of pitch, and thus endows tonal sensations with but a single qualitative attribute: *Grundzüge*, i., 1905, 294 f., 445.

[12] The preceding paragraphs are the outcome of personal observations, taken especially during the year 1906–1907. The views which they embody are stated in more detail in the forthcoming edition of my *Outline of Psychology*. On the question of itch and its relation to pain I may also refer to L. Török, Ueber das Wesen der Juckempfindung, *Zeits. f. Psychol.*, xlvi., 1907, 23 ff.

[13] E. Hering, *Zur Lehre vom Lichtsinne*, 1878, 55 f.; *Grundzüge der Lehre vom Lichtsinn*, 1907, 111. F. Hillebrand, Ueber die specifische Helligkeit der Farben, *Sitzungsber. d. kais. Akad. d. Wiss. in Wien, mathem.-naturw. Classe*, xcviii., 3, 1889, 89. O. Külpe, *Outlines of Psychology*, 1895, 30, 114, 119; Ueber die Objectivirung und Subjectivirung von Sinneseindrücken, *Philos. Studien*, xix., 1902, 509. E. B. Titchener, *An Outline of Psychology*, 1896, 68, 71, 77. G. E. Müller, Zur Psychophysik der Gesichtsempfindungen, *Zeits. f. Psychol. u. Physiol. d. Sinnesorgane*, x., 1896, 30 ff., 411 f.; xiv., 1897, 40 ff., 60 ff.

The psychophysical argument which Müller urges against Hillebrand (*Zeits.*, x., 33) is, I suppose, implied in one form or another by the taper of the colour pyramid. I do not see, however, how it can be translated into psychological terms, as an introspective argument for the intensity of visual sensation. Wundt constructs the colour pyramid from hue, chroma, and intensity (*Physiol. Psychol.*, ii., 1902, 159 ff.); but this procedure necessarily leads to confusion.

[14] Duration has been discussed by M. W. Calkins, Attributes of Sensation, *Psychological Review*, vi., 1899, 506 ff. (cf. xi., 1904, 221 f.), and M. F. Washburn, Notes on Duration as an Attribute of Sensations, *ibid.*, x., 1903, 416 ff.

A few additional words may, perhaps, prevent misunderstanding of the text. When I say that extension and duration are the attributes to which we attend when we are asked certain questions, I do not mean that extension, as such, is or has a definite form or a definite magnitude or a definite local arrangement of parts, or that duration, as such, is or has a definite length or a definite serial arrangement of parts. I mean only that there are questions which direct us to the fundamental spreading-out character of the sensation, and that there are other questions which direct us to its fundamental going-on character; and that we are able to attend, by abstraction, to these attributes and to neglect the rest. I have never believed, in particular, that locality and order, place in space and position in time, are attributes of sensation.

A discussion with which I am in essential agreement will be found in H. Ebbinghaus, *Grundzüge der Psychologie*, i., 1905, 445 ff., 480 ff.

[15] Külpe says, in *Outlines*, 30, that " extension belongs only to the visual and cutaneous sensations (Hautsinn) " ; and, in *Outlines*, 335, that it belongs to " the visual and ' tactual,' — the latter term embracing both cutaneous sensations proper and the articular sensations set up in the motile parts of the body (sowohl die Hautempfindungen als auch die Gelenkempfindungen)." Ebbinghaus (*Grundzüge*, i., 445 f.) predicates extension only of visual and cutaneous sensations.

[16] Cf. my Postulates of a Structural Psychology, *Philosoph. Review*, vii., 1898, 461 f. ; I. M. Bentley, The Psychological Meaning of Clearness, *Mind*, N. S., xiii., 1904, 242 ff.

[17] C. Stumpf, *Tonpsychologie*, i., 1883, 202 f. ; ii., 1890, 524 ff. According to the footnote, *ibid.*, ii., 525, the attribute of tone-tint was recognised independently in 1885 by Stumpf and by G. Engel ; I have not seen Engel's paper.

J. Passy distinguishes between the 'pouvoir odorant' and the intensity of odours. The former is inversely proportional to the *RL*. "Tout le monde sent," he says, "que le camphre, le citron, la benzine sont des odeurs fortes, la vanille, l'iris des odeurs faibles," although the 'pouvoir odorant' of vanilla is at least a thousand times as great as that of camphor: *Comptes rendus de la Société de Biologie*, [19 Mars] 1892, 240. It is clear that the 'pouvoir odorant' belongs to psychophysics, not to psychology; but it is clear also that we must distinguish, psychologically, between the intensity and the penetratingness of an olfactory sensation.

G. E. Müller insists on *Eindringlichkeit*, as distinct from *Intensität*, in his Psychophysik der Gesichtsempfindungen, *Zeits. f. Psychol.*, x., 1896, 26 ff. Cf. also *Die Gesichts-*

punkte und die Tatsachen der psychophysischen Methodik,
1904, 123; J. Fröbes, *Zeits. f. Psychol.*, xxxvi., 1904,
368 ff.; and see Lecture V., note 33.

On the *Eindringlichkeit* of certain pains, see W. James,
Psychol. Review, i., 1894, 523 note; M. von Frey, *Die
Gefühle und ihr Verhältnis zu den Empfindungen*, 1894, 15.

[18] Ebbinghaus, *Grundzüge*, i., 1905, 195; H. Aubert,
Grundzüge der physiologischen Optik, 1876, 532. Ebbinghaus is speaking in general terms; it is difficult to see the
basis of Aubert's statement. Cf. also Külpe, *Outlines*,
106 f., 122, 127; Helmholtz, *Physiol. Optik*, 1896, 325.
I owe to Professor Bentley the suggestion that tonal
volume may vary without variation of pitch; the point is
well worth investigation. Preliminary experiments of my
own have, so far, yielded a positive result.

[19] R. H. Lotze, *Metaphysik*, 1879, § 258; 1884, 511 ff.;
Outlines of Psych., (1881) 1886, 17; cf. *Medicinische
Psychologie*, 1852, 208, and my *Exper. Psychol.*, II., ii.,
1905, xlviii. ff. M. W. Calkins recognises 'sensational
elements' of brightness or visual intensity, of loudness,
etc.: *An Introduction to Psychology*, 1901, 42, 53, 59, 61,
67, 75, 77. Ebbinghaus writes (*Grundzüge*, i., 444):
"Gesehene und getastete Ausdehnung sind ohne weiteres
miteinander vergleichbar, ebenso die Dauer eines Tones
mit der eines Schmerzes. Dagegen hell, laut und heiss,
. . . oder . . . violett, sauer, hart, haben schlechterdings
gar nichts miteinander gemeinsam."

NOTES TO LECTURE II

[1] Brentano is vouched for by Stumpf, *Zeits. f. Psychol.*, xliv., 1906, 4.

[2] The doctrine of continuity is pithily expressed by J. Rehmke in the sentence: "es lässt sich doch garnicht leugnen, dass der sogenannte 'Ton der Sinnesempfindung' im 'physischen Schmerze' oder in der 'Wollust' und das durch einen Todesfall oder eine Siegesnachricht bedingte 'Gefühl' *wesentlich gleiche* Bewusstseinsbestimmtheiten sind." *Lehrbuch der allgemeinen Psychologie*, 1894, 317. For my own view, I can refer only to chap. ix. of my *Outline of Psychology*, which unfortunately is both schematic and, to some extent, out of date. Stumpf's view is given in his paper, Ueber den Begriff der Gemüthsbewegung, *Zeits. f. Psychol.*, xxi., 1899, 47 ff., which has full references to the literature. I add only G. F. Stout, *A Manual of Psychology*, 1899, 63. The phrase quoted from Stumpf will be found in *Zeits.*, xliv., 7. — A pathological case, in which the same conditions were apparently responsible for the loss both of feeling and of emotion, is reported by G. R. d'Allonnes, *Rev. Philos.*, Déc., 1905, 592 ff.; I confess, however, that I attach no great weight to observations of this sort. Cf. P. Sollier, *Le mécanisme des émotions*, 1905, 126 ff.

[3] *Tonpsychologie*, i., vi.; ii., vii.; *Zeits.*, xliv., 1 ff.

In the article of 1899 (*Zeits.*, xxi., 63) Stumpf writes: "Macht man bei diesen Organempfindungen noch einen Unterschied zwischen der Empfindung selbst und ihrem

'Gefühlston,' z. B. der Hungerempfindung und der Unannehmlichkeit dieser Empfindung, so versteht es sich wohl von selbst und ist von James zuletzt auch noch besonders hervorgehoben, dass für die Natur des Affects der Gefühlston das Ausschlaggebende ist." The 'zuletzt' refers to James' discussion of the Physical Basis of Emotion, *Psychol. Review*, i., 1894, 516 ff. I am altogether unable to read Stumpf's interpretation into this paper. James says, when discussing the 'tone of feeling,' 'pleasantness or unpleasantness of the sensible quality,' that "in addition to this pleasantness or painfulness of the content, we may also feel a general seizure of excitement, . . . which is what I have all along meant by an emotion. Now whenever I myself have sought to discover the mind-stuff of which such seizures consist, it has always seemed to me to be additional sensations . . . localized in divers portions of my organism" (523). That is, the *Gefühlston* is precisely not the important or decisive feature of the emotion. Again (524): "I am even willing to admit that the primary *Gefühlston* may vary enormously in distinctness in different men. But speaking for myself, I am compelled to say that the only feelings which I cannot more or less well localize in my body are very mild and, so to speak, platonic affairs. I allow them hypothetically to exist, however, . . . where no obvious organic excitement is aroused." This is very different from making them *das Ausschlaggebende* where organic excitement, the 'emotional seizure,' is the very thing to be explained.

[4] With the foregoing paragraphs (criterion of subjectivity) cf. M. F. Washburn, Some Examples of the Use of Psychological Analysis in System-Making, *Philos. Review*, xi., 1902, 445 ff.; E. H. Hollands, Wundt's Doctrine of

Psychical Analysis and the Psychical Elements, and Some Recent Criticism: i. The Criteria of the Elements and Attributes, *Amer. Journ. Psychol.*, xvi., 1905, 499 ff.; ii. Feeling and Feeling-Analysis, *ibid.*, xvii., 1906, 206 ff. (esp. 221, 226); J. Orth, *Gefühl und Bewusstseinslage, eine kritisch-experimentelle Studie*, 1903, 20 ff.; Stumpf, *Zeits.*, xliv., 8 ff., 34; R. Saxinger, Dispositionspsychologisches über Gefühlskomplexionen, *Zeits.*, xxx., 1902, 399; Külpe, *Outlines*, 227 f.; Wundt, *Physiol. Psychol.*, iii., 1903, 110 ff., 514 f., 552 ff.; G. T. Ladd, *Psychology, Descriptive and Explanatory: a Treatise of the Phenomena, Laws, and Development of Human Mental Life* 1894, 181; J. Ward, Psychology, *Encyc. Britan.*, xx., 1886, 67; W. B. Pillsbury, *Attention*, 1908, 191.

I say, on p. 38, that nobody confuses organic sensations with properties of external things. This seems to be true of all the more specific organic sensations, — hunger, thirst, nausea, lust, etc. I am not sure, however, that certain organic sensations or organic complexes, of a diffuse and general character, are not projected *along with the accompanying affection* into the outer world. What do we mean when we speak of 'a pleasant day,' 'very unpleasant weather,' 'a comfortable chair,' 'an uncomfortable waiting room'? I do not find the analysis easy; but I think that these adjectives are applied as objectively, at least in many instances, as the adjectives 'green' or 'hot.' Von Frey points out (*Die Gefühle und ihr Verhältnis zu den Empfindungen*, 1894, 14) that cutting and stabbing weapons, instruments of torture, etc. are directly apprehended as 'schmerzhaft'*; we speak in English of a

* Cf. M. Dessoir, Arch. f. [Anat. u.] Physiol., 1892, 230; W. Nagel, *Handbuch d. Physiol. d. Menschen*, iii., 1905, 731.

'painful-looking' instrument. Against the illustration of p. 37 we might cite such expressions as: "How pleasant your wood fire is!"

The appeal to language is always dangerous, because a given phrase may mean very different things. Unless I am mistaken, however, we do at times objectify our feelings (diffuse organic sensations and affection) * just as we objectify the 'secondary qualities.' It is needless to say that this amendment of the text does not at all invalidate, but rather supplements, the argument of the paragraph. Some sensations, I there say, are subjective. Affection, I here add, is sometimes objective.

⁵ On the second criterion, of non-localisableness, see M. von Frey, *Die Gefühle*, 1894, 12; W. Nagel, *Handbuch der Physiologie des Menschen*, iii., 1905, 617; J. R. Angell and W. Fite, *Psychol. Review*, viii., 1901, 245, 451, 455, 458; J. R. Angell, *ibid.*, x., 1903, 5, 14; A. H. Pierce, *Studies in Auditory and Visual Space Perception*, 1901, 191 f.; Orth, *Gefühl und Bewusstseinslage*, 1903, 29 ff., † 117 ff.; Stumpf, *Zeits.*, xliv., 1906, 12 ff.; R. Lagerborg, Zur Abgrenzung des Gefühlsbegriffs, *Arch. f. d. ges. Psychol.*, ix., 1907, 460; Külpe, *Outlines*, 1895, 264 f., 274; Ebbinghaus, *Grundzüge*, i., 1905, 564 f.; Wundt, *Physiol. Psychol.*, ii., 1902, 341; J. Sully, *The Human Mind: a Text-book of Psychology*, ii., 1892, 43; W. McDougall, *Physiological Psychology*, 1905, 80; Ladd, *Psychology, Descriptive and Explanatory*, 1894, 182, 201, 536 f., 554; Rehmke, *Lehrbuch*, 1894, 323 ff.; T. Lipps,

* In the same way, we objectify the pleasantness and unpleasantness of tastes and smells. Cf. the discussion of *Gefühlsbetonung* by E. Freiherr von Gebsattel, *Arch. f. d. ges. Psychol.*, x., 1907, 145 ff.

† Cf. E. Meumann, *Arch. f. d. ges. Psychol.*, ix., 1907, 57 f.

Komik und Humor: eine psychologisch-ästhetische Unter-suchung, 1898, 114 f.; E. Kraepelin, Zur Psychologie des Komischen, *Philos. Studien*, ii., 1885, 329, 351; A. Lehmann, *Die Hauptgesetze des menschlichen Gefuhls-lebens*, 1892, 177, 201, 214, 216, 258, 267; G. Störring, *Arch. f. d. ges. Psychol.*, vi., 1905, 318 f.; P. Sollier, *Le mécanisme des émotions*, 1905, 81 ff. (cf. 75 ff.); N. Alech-sieff, Die Grundformen der Gefühle, *Psychol. Studien*, iii., 1907, 259 ff.; C. H. Johnston, The Combination of Feelings, *Harvard Psychological Studies*, ii., 1906, 159 ff. (esp. 175–179); cf. *Journ. Phil. Psychol. Sci. Meth.*, iv., 1907, 215; *Psychol. Bulletin*, ii., 1905, 163, 166; iv., 1907, 363 ff. On methodical difficulties and the attitude of observation, see F. E. O. Schultze, *Arch. f. d. ges. Psychol.*, viii., 1906, 372 ff.; xi., 1908, 151 ff.

M. Geiger's Bemerkungen zur Psychologie der Gefühls-elemente und Gefühlsverbindungen (*Arch. f. d. ges. Psychol.*, iv., 1904, esp. 262 ff.), and the paper by Saxinger quoted in the previous Note, published under the auspices of Lipps and of Meinong respectively, rest upon elaborate theoretical foundations, and are beyond the range of the present discussion.

[6] With this discussion of the third criterion cf. Wundt, *Grundriss der Psychologie*, 1896, 40; 1905, 40 (Engl., 1897, 33; 1907, 36); *Vorlesungen über die Menschen-und Thierseele*, 1897, 240; *Physiol. Psychol.*, i., 1902, 353; and many other passages. Rehmke, *Lehrbuch*, 1894, 295 ff. Stumpf, *Zeits.*, xliv., 1906, 7 note, 17, 22. Orth, *Gefühl und Bewusstseinslage*, 1903, 28 f. Külpe, *Outlines*, 1895, 93, 242. Ebbinghaus, *Grundzüge*, i., 1905, 564. T. Lipps, *Grundtatsachen des Seelenlebens*, 1883, 273 ff. W. Wirth, Vorstellungs- und Gefühlscontrast, *Zeits. f.*

Psychol., xviii., 1898, 49 ff.   P. Sollier, *Le mécanisme des émotions*, 1905, 244 ff., esp. 253.

Lipps, if I understand him aright, has recently changed his opinion with regard to 'mixed feelings'; see *Leitfaden der Psychologie*, 1906, 297 f.

[7] On Külpe's criterion see Külpe, *Outlines*, 1895, 185 f., 225 f., 238; Ladd, *Psychology, Descriptive and Explanatory*, 1894, 196, 199; Stumpf, *Zeits.*, xliv., 1906, 23 ff.; Pillsbury, *Attention*, 1908, 190 f.

On the difference between 'zufällige innere Wahrnehmung' and 'planmässige Selbstbeobachtung,' see Wundt, *Essays*, 1885, 127 ff.; 1906, 187 ff.; *Philos. Studien*, iv., 1888, 292 ff. (esp. 301); etc., etc.

On the phrase 'centrally excited sensations,' see E. Meumann, *Vorlesungen zur Einführung in die experimentelle Pädagogik und ihre psychologischen Grundlagen*, i., 1907, 205.   It might be objected to Külpe that the experiments of H. Münsterberg (*Beitr. z. experiment. Psychol.*, iv., 1892, 17 ff.), A. Goldscheider and R. F. Müller (*Zeits. f. klin. Medizin*, xxiii., 1893, 156 ff.), and W. B. Pillsbury (*Amer. Journ. Psychol.*, viii., 1897, 355 ff.) indicate, under certain conditions, an intensive equivalence of peripherally excited and centrally excited sensations. Külpe has, however, forestalled the objection in *Outlines*, 183.

[8] On habituation, see James, *Principles*, ii., 475 f.; Stumpf, *Zeits.*, xliv., 1906, 7 note; *Bericht über d. II. Kongress f. exper. Psychologie*, 1907, 213; Külpe, *Outlines*, 261; Ebbinghaus, *Grundzüge*, i., 1905, 574 ff.; A. Lehmann, *Die Hauptgesetze des menschlichen Gefühlslebens*, 1892, 182 ff.; Wundt, *Physiol. Psychol.*, ii., 1902, 332 (with continuous stimulation, initial pleasantness may

pass directly, through indifference, into unpleasantness);
Sollier, *Le mécanisme des émotions*, 1905, 97 ff. "Use
blunts feeling and favours intellection," says Ward:
Encyc. Britan., xx., 1886, 40.

[9] On the relation of affection to attention, see Külpe,
Outlines, 1895, 258 ff., 430; Titchener, *Philos. Review*,
iii., 1894, 429 ff. (the systematic setting of this paper is
crude, but I think that the observations are reliable);
Psychol. Review, ix., 1902, 481 ff.; P. Zoneff and E. Meumann, *Philos. Studien*, xviii., 1903, 4 f., 67 ff. (cf. Lecture III., note 43); W. B. Pillsbury, *Psychol. Review*, ix.,
1902, 405; Meumann, *Experimentelle Pädagogik*, i., 1907,
82; W. Hamilton, *Lectures on Metaphysics*, 1859, i., 236;
ii., 432; J. Ward, Psychology, *Encyc. Britan.*, xx., 1886,
40 ff.; Hollands, *Amer. Journ. Psychol.*, xvii., 1906, 211;
Wundt, *Physiol. Psychol.*, ii., 1902, 357; iii., 1903, 114,
348; Saxinger, *Zeits.*, xxx., 1902, 400, 412; A. Lehmann,
Die körperlichen Aeusserungen psychischer Zustände, i.,
1899, 140 ff.; W. H. Burnham, *Amer. Journ. Psychol.*,
xix., 1908, 16; F. E. O. Schultze, *Arch. f. d. ges. Psychol.*,
viii., 1906, 373.

Sully says definitely (*Human Mind*, i., 1892, 77) that
"we can intensify a pain or pleasure by attending to it as
such," — as definitely as he says (*ibid.*, 143) that "objects
of attention are either sensations, and their combinations,
sensation-complexes, or what we call ideas or representa-
tions." But he counts 'bodily pain,' 'the pain of indiges-
tion' as an 'affective state,' and admits that "in attending
to the feeling we necessarily embrace [the presentative
element] to some extent." It is true, as he remarks, that
"to listen to a musical sound so as to note its pitch, etc.,
and to listen to it solely for the sake of enjoying it, illustrate

two different directions of the attention"; but there is here no evidence of direction of the attention upon the enjoyment, and the latter's consequent intensification. Cf. also i., 67; ii., 12.

In his *Attention*, 1908, 187, Pillsbury writes: "as matters stand, the introspective evidence is universally favourable to the assertion that attention is antagonistic to the pleasantness-unpleasantness process as well as to the vague unanalysed processes of consciousness." The first part of this sentence, at any rate, confirms my own position. On another point, however, Pillsbury seems to disagree. "Of Wundt's three pairs," he says, "strain and relaxation would not be opposed to attending. . . . Of depression and exaltation it is difficult to speak, but it is by no means certain that attention to these processes would either oppose or favour their presence" (187 f.). I think that the disagreement is only apparent. Pillsbury is considering the Wundtian processes, so to speak, on their merits, as they occur in his experience; I am setting forth Wundt's own doctrine. I believe with Hollands that feeling, in Wundt's system, cannot be made the object of attention; and I find this teaching in his tridimensional theory as in the theory of affective tone. Nevertheless, I point out in Lecture VIII. that Wundt's present view of the relation of affection to attention is, in my judgment, transitional, and I therefore regard it as possible that his systematic position may be changed.

[10] The idea of this paragraph is that the criterion of movement between opposites may be coupled with that of coextension with consciousness, — opposition meaning, in fact, conscious incompatibility; and that the criterion of lack of clearness may be coupled with that of subjec-

tivity, — lack of clearness implying a textural difference between sensation and affection, which finds expression in the term 'subjective.' We thus reach a twofold characterisation of affection, to be explained and justified by psychophysical theory. I think that this bracketing "considerably strengthens the case for an elementary affection." We are led by it, *e.g.*, to mistrust the instances of localised affection, such as occur in Störring's experiments. Störring, it will be remembered, secured *Stimmungslust* and *Empfindungslust* by the following experimental procedure: "während man bei der Erzeugung von Lust, die an eine Geschmacksempfindung geknüpft ist, die Geschmackslösung während der Dauer des Versuchs im Munde behalten lässt, gab ich zum Zweck der Erzeugung von Stimmungslust der Vp. die Anweisung, die Lösung zu schlucken und dann von der Empfindung abzusehen, mit dem Schlucken den Geschmacksreiz als eine erledigte Tatsache zu betrachten" (*Arch. f. d. ges. Psychol.*, vi., 1905, 317). It is clear that the instructions are not parallel: so long as the fluid is in the mouth, the observer's attention is upon it, and the affection is localised along with its sensation (cf. Note 4, above); when the fluid has been swallowed, and the taste is past and done with, the affection is not localised. So much depends upon the conditions! But let the instructions be made parallel: let the observer be told, in the experiments on *Empfindungslust*, to consider the taste as past and done with so soon as it has come clearly to consciousness; let the retention in the mouth be merely a matter of convenience, of not interrupting the experiment. In this case, if I may trust my own introspection and that of three other observers, there is no localisation of the pleasantness; it is of precisely the same character as the pleasantness after swallowing. However, the subject needs renewed investigation of a systematic kind.

We have an analogy to the argument of the text in the position of those psychologists who make the image a distinct mental element, coördinate with sensation. 'You cannot distinguish sensation and image on the ground of quality alone, or of intensity, or of duration, or of extension, or of clearness. Can you not distinguish them in terms of the consensus of these attributes? Is there not a total textural difference between the two processes?' This, it seems to me, is the gist of the separatist argument, when it is couched in terms of content. No doubt, there is, in the case of the image, a further appeal to characteristic differences of context or background or setting.

NOTES TO LECTURE III

[1] B. Bourdon, La sensation de plaisir, *Rev. philos.*, Sept., 1893, 226 f.

[2] M. von Frey, *Die Gefühle*, 1894, 14 f., 17. — In this connection, mention should also be made, perhaps, of Sollier's recent theory of 'cénesthésie cérébrale': *Le mécanisme des émotions*, 1905, esp. 192 ff., 257 f.

[3] *Op. cit.*, 227 f.

[4] See, *e.g.*, *Rep.*, ix., 583 D; *Phaedo*, 60 A; *Phil.*, 51.

[5] *Bericht über den II. Kongress für experimentelle Psychologie*, 1907, 209 ff.; *Zeits.*, xliv., 1906, 1 ff. On p. 15, Stumpf makes the terminological suggestion that *Gefühlsempfindung* be rendered by 'emotional sensation.' This translation seems to me hardly possible; the English equivalent would be, I think, either 'affective sensation' or 'algedonic sensation.' The adjective 'algedonic' was coined by H. R. Marshall (*Pain, Pleasure and Æsthetics*, 1894, 9), not — as Stumpf and Lagerborg (*Arch. f. d. ges. Psychol.*, ix., 1907, 454) say — by Baldwin. In a systematic connection I should prefer the phrase 'algedonic sensation'; for the purposes of this Lecture its introduction appeared unnecessary.

[6] Pp. 1 ff.

[7] Pp. 2 ff.

[8] *Outlines*, 1895, 227 f.

[9] i., 282.

[10] T. Ziehen, *Leitfaden der physiologischen Psychologie in 15 Vorlesungen*, 1906, 162 note.

[11] P. 5 note.

[12] P. 4.

[13] H. R. Marshall, President's Address, American Psychological Association, Chicago Meeting, December, 1907: The Methods of the Naturalist and Psychologist, *Psychol. Rev.*, xv., 1908, 16 f. "If we could isolate psychic elements, . . . we would [sic] discover in connection with them elemental qualities . . . of the nature of pain and pleasure."

[14] T. Ziegler, *Das Gefühl: eine psychologische Untersuchung*, 1893, 100. Cf. Stumpf, p. 43 note.

[15] P. 6. — Under the theory which makes the affective processes "eine neue Gattung psychischer Elemente, Zustände oder Funktionen, die weder Empfindungen noch Eigenschaften von Empfindungen sind" (p. 3), falls the view which considers them as 'Gestaltqualitäten.' In *Bericht*, 213, Stumpf definitely rejects this view. I must say, however, that he seems to me to come very near it in his doctrine of the 'Reinheitsgefühl,' the feeling for the purity of consonant intervals: see F. Krueger, *Bericht*, 212; *Psychol. Studien*, ii., 1906, 371 f., 375 ff. (where full references are given). At any rate, we are here far removed from the positive rejection of mental chemistry, from the "Aus Nichts wird Nichts," of the *Tonpsychologie* (ii., 1890, 209, 525, etc.).

[16] Pp. 6 ff.

[17] Pp. 15 ff.

[18] P. 18.

[19] P. 21.

[20] P. 19.

[21] Pp. 16 f.

[22] A. Goldscheider, *Gesam. Abhandl.*, i., 1898, 411 f.; Stumpf, pp. 19 note, 21.

[23] P. 19.

[24] Pp. 16 f.

[25] Pp. 19 f.

[26] Pp. 2, 22.

[27] P. 21.

[28] See, *e.g.*, Külpe, *Outlines*, 124.

[29] H. Ebbinghaus, *Grundzüge*, i., 1905, 581; cf. R. Lagerborg, *Das Gefühlsproblem*, 1905, 95; P. Sollier, *Le mécanisme des émotions*, 1905, 244, 254 f.

[30] M. Kelchner, *Arch. f. d. ges. Psychol.*, v., 1905, 86.

[31] Pp. 21 f.

[32] P. 22.

[33] Pp. 22, 38 f.   In the latter passage Stumpf, while still leaving the question open, indicates his own belief in a plurality of affective qualities.

[34] Let it not be objected that these *Lustempfindungen* are sensations of pleasure for the reason that they "ein instinktives Annehmen und Begehren mit sich zu führen pflegen" (p. 22)!   For on p. 16 it is written: "die Annehmlichkeit ist nicht das Annehmen und der Schmerz nicht das Ablehnen."

[35] Pp. 26 ff.

[36] Pp. 27 f.

[37] P. 28.

[38] P. 29.

[39] P. 31; *Tonpsychologie*, ii., 1890, 209.

[40] Pp. 29 f.

[41] *E.g.*, pp. 18 note, 21, 22, 23, 26, 27, 29 f., 36, 39 f.

[42] P. 2; cf. p. 41.

[43] E. W. Scripture, Vorstellung und Gefühl, *Philos. Studien*, vi., 1891, 536 ff.; O. Vogt, Die directe psychologische Experimentalmethode in hypnotischen Bewusst-

seinszuständen, *Zeits. f. Hypnotismus*, v., 1897, 180 ff.;
F. Kiesow, Sul metodo di studiare i sentimenti semplici,
*Rendiconti della r. Accademia dei Lincei, Classe di scienze
fis., mat. e natur.*, (5) viii., 1, 1899, 469 ff.

Kiesow's experiments were made as follows. He first
determined two areas of the tongue that were equally
sensitive to sweet, and platted the curve of sensible discrimination. He then gave his observers preliminary
practice " a distrarre la loro attenzione dalla sensazione
e a concentrarla esclusivamente sul tono sentimentale
(Gefühlston) che accompagna ogni grado di sensazione."
The instruction is, evidently, ambiguous (cf. reference to
Zoneff and Meumann, Lecture II., note 9). Kiesow
naturally found, in consequence, that " in sulle prime
queste esperienze sono difficili e affaticanti: in alcune
persone mi pare di non essere potuto giungere a una
sufficiente concentrazione dell' attenzione sul tono sentimentale; esse erano sempre distratte passivamente dalla
sensazione. . . . In altri soggetti coll' esercizio si può
giungere al punto da poter astrarre dalla sensazione in
modo sufficiente." After practice, he began systematic
work upon pleasantness-unpleasantness, and platted an
affective curve, starting with the *RL* and employing the
DL as unit of abscissas. The curve shows, first, a stage
of indifference; next, a stage of slowly increasing pleasantness; thirdly, a second stage of indifference; and lastly
a stage of somewhat rapidly increasing unpleasantness.
Kiesow remarks that " nella curva cosi ottenuta le ordinate
non sono stabilite numericamente con una precisione
eguale a quella delle ascisse." He gives no further details,
and does not figure the curves.

⁴⁴ Affective Memory, *Philos. Rev.*, iv., 1895, 65 ff. See

T. Ribot, *The Psychology of the Emotions*, 1897, 140 ff.
A reference to the recent annual bibliographies will show
that the subject is still in debate. I find it discussed,
e.g., by W. Heinrich, La psychologie des sentiments
(*Bull. de l'Acad. des Sciences de Cracovie*, Jan., 1908, 36),
which reaches me as these pages are passing through the
press.

[45] Organic Images, *Journ. Phil. Psychol. Sci. Meth.*, i.,
1904, 36 ff.

[46] P. 23.

[47] P. 25. — The illustration is the more striking since
G. H. Meyer, a highly practised observer, declares his
inability to reproduce cutaneous sensations of intrinsically brief duration. "Auf der Haut gelingt es mir leicht,
an welcher Stelle ich will, subjective Empfindungen her-
vorzubringen. Weil aber längere Unterhaltung der Ans-
chauung dazu nothwendig ist, kann ich nur solche Empfindungen wecken, welche längere Zeit andauern, wie
Wärme, Kühle, Druck; schnell vorübergehende dagegen,
wie von einem Stich, Schnitt, Schlag, etc., vermag ich
nicht hervorzurufen, *weil es mir nicht gelingt, die entsprechenden Anschauungen so ex abrupto in der gehörigen Intensität zu wecken*" (*Untersuchungen über die Physiologie
der Nervenfaser*, 1843, 238: italics mine).* Personally,

* Meyer's work is not in the possession of any one of the four
university libraries to which I am accustomed to appeal. It may,
however, be procured from the Librarian of the Surgeon General's
Office, Washington, D.C. I may mention here — since I find that
the fact is less generally known than it deserves to be — that the
Surgeon General's Library is admirably supplied with the older
and scarcer books that bear upon experimental psychology. A
postcard from the librarian of any college or university library will
bring the required volumes, usually by return, and they may be
held for a fortnight.

I can image pressure and, I think, warmth; I cannot image pain, and I am very dubious as regards cold.   See my *Organic Images*, 38 f., and cf. F. E. O. Schultze, *Arch. f. d. ges. Psychol.*, xi., 1908, 157 f., 185 f.

[48] P. 26.

[49] See, however, pp. 35 note, 47.   I am not sure that I understand Stumpf's doctrine as regards rhythmical, formal, and harmonic feelings.

[50] Pp. 31 f.

[51] P. 32.

[52] G. T. Fechner, *Elemente der Psychophysik*, i., 1889, 75 (see also refs. given in my *Exper. Psychol.*, II., ii., 1905, lxviii.); Ebbinghaus, *Grundzüge*, i., 1905, 91.

[53] W. Nagel, *Handbuch d. Physiol. d. Menschen*, iii., 1905, 620.

[54] P. 36.

[55] Pp. 32 f.

[56] Pp. 33 ff.

[57] P. 36.

[58] Pp. 33, 37.

[59] Pp. 37 f.

[60] By the admission of instances from the field of emotion and of æsthetic and intellectual sentiment.   See, however, Note 49 above; and cf. Stumpf, pp. 33 ff.

[61] Pp. 38 f.

I may add that, so far as my experience goes, American libraries contain practically everything that is needed for historical research in experimental psychology.   In the preparation of my *Exper. Psychol.* I had to read a great many out-of-the-way things; but there were very few instances in which I was obliged to have final recourse to European collections.   As the great majority of the large libraries — there are a few bad exceptions! — are courtesy itself in the matter of lending, there is no excuse for 'ignorance of the literature' on the part of the American student.

[62] Pp. 39 f.

[63] *Grundzüge*, i., 1905, 566.

[64] Pp. 41 ff.

[65] Pp. 42, 48 f.

[66] Pp. 42 f., 44.

[67] Pp. 43 f.

[68] See, *e.g.*, R. H. Lotze, *Medicinische Psychologie oder Physiologie der Seele*, 1852, 254 f.; Stumpf, p. 32.

[69] P. 44; Ebbinghaus, *Grundzüge*, i., 1905, 582 f.

[70] *Outlines*, 1895, 228 ff.

[71] *Op. cit.*, 577.

[72] Pp. 44 f.

[73] P. 45.

[74] Pp. 45 ff.

[75] P. 46.

[76] P. 47.

[77] *Tonpsychologie*, ii., 1890, vii.   In Note 15 above I have expressed a certain misgiving as regards Stumpf's doctrine of the *Tongefühle*.

[78] P. 48.

NOTES TO LECTURE IV

[1] *Physiol. Psychol.*, i., 1893, 555 f., 561, 570 f.

[2] *Grundriss der Psychologie*, 1896, 33 f., 36, 39 ff., 97 f.,
100 (Engl., 1897, 28 f., 30, 33 ff., 82 f., 84 f.); cf. 1905,
34 f., 36, 39 ff., 99 f., 101 (Engl., 1907, 31 f., 32 f., 35 ff.,
91 f., 93).

[3] This is, I am convinced, the true version of a state of
affairs which James has unwittingly misrepresented in
Psychol. Review, i., 1894, 72 f.

[4] *Physiol. Psychol.*, 1874, 445. The passage which re-
lates to the æsthetic value of the higher senses is retained,
with some modification of context, in the edition of 1893
(i., 571); but the important thing is the insertion, in that
edition, of the new paragraph, i., 561.

[5] *Ibid.*, 1874, 426; i., 1893, 555.

[6] *Gefühl und Bewusstseinslage*, 1903, 49; Wundt, *Grundriss*, 1896, 97 ff. (Engl., 82 ff.); cf. 1905, 99 ff. (Engl.,
1907, 91 ff.).

[7] *Physiol. Psychol.*, 1874, 441, 721.

[8] *Ibid.*, ii., 1902, 284 ff.

[9] *Grundriss*, 1896, 100, 213 (Engl., 85, 181); cf. 1905,
101, 217 (Engl., 1907, 93, 202).

[10] *Zeits.*, xliv., 1906, 7 f. note.

[11] *Grundriss*, 1896, 103 (Engl., 88). Cf. 1905, 103 ff.
(Engl., 1907, 95 ff.).

[12] *Vorlesungen über die Menschen- und Thierseele*, 1897,
224 ff.

[13] *Philos. Studien*, xv., 1900, 151.

[14] This Lecture was not printed; but the material upon which it was based may be found in H. C. Stevens' A Plethysmographic Study of Attention, *Amer. Journ. Psychol.*, xvi., 1905, 482.

[15] *Grundriss*, 1896, 35 (Engl., 29); cf. 1905, 35 (Engl., 1907, 32).

[16] Cf. my note in *Psychol. Bulletin*, iv., 1907, 367 f.

[17] *Grundriss*, 1896, 99 f. (Engl., 84 f.). This § 9 is omitted in 1905.

[18] *Philos. Studien*, xv., 1900, 177.

[19] *Vorlesungen*, 1897, 238.

[20] *Ibid.*, 239.

[21] *Ibid.*, 239 f.

[22] *Physiol. Psychol.*, ii., 1902, 311 ff., 318 f., 326, 333, 336 f. The intensive reference of *Lust-Unlust* indicates a return to the teaching of 1874; see Note 4 above.

[23] *Ibid.*, 374.

[24] Cf. Wundt's own statement in *Grundriss*, 1896, 96 (Engl., 81); cf. 1905, 98 (Engl., 1907, 90).

[25] *Philos. Studien*, xv., 1900, 175.

[26] *Grundriss*, 1896, 98 (cf. 1905, 99); *Physiol. Psychol.*, ii., 1902, 286, 295.

[27] *Physiol. Psychol.*, 1874, 724; *Vorlesungen*, 1897, 238. In *Physiol. Psychol.*, iii., 1903, 253 f., 306 f. (cf. *Grundriss*, 1896, 256; 1905, 265), the *Erfüllungsgefühl* appears as a total feeling, based essentially upon relaxation and tranquillisation: cf., however, 347. *Befriedigung* (iii., 221) is a *Lustaffect*: the *Totalgefühl* will then be based upon pleasantness and relaxation.

[28] *Vorlesungen*, 1897, 228; *Grundriss*, 1905, 105.

[29] A. Gurewitsch, *Zur Geschichte des Achtungsbegriffes und zur Theorie der sittlichen Gefühle*, Würzburg dissert., 1897.

[30] O. Vogt, Normalpsychologische Einleitung in die Psychopathologie der Hysterie, *Zeits. f. Hypnotismus,* viii., 1899, 212.

[31] *Physiol. Psychol.,* iii., 1903, 249.

[32] J. Royce, *Outlines of Psychology,* 1903, 176 ff.

[33] *Philos. Studien,* xv., 1900, 172 f.

[34] J. Cohn, *Philos. Studien,* x., 1894, 562 ff.; xv., 1899, 279 ff. D. R. Major, *Amer. Journ. Psychol.,* vii., 1895, 57 ff.

[35] *Physiol. Psychol.,* ii., 1902, 285.

[36] *Locc. citt.*

[37] *Physiol. Psychol.,* ii., 1902, 333.

[38] *Ibid.,* 332.

[39] *Ibid.,* 335.

[40] *Ibid.,* 336 f.

[41] *Grundriss,* 1896, 96 (Engl., 81); cf. 1905, 98 (Engl., 1907, 90).

[42] *Ibid.,* 99 (Engl., 84); cf. 1905, 101 (Engl., 1907, 93).

[43] *Vorlesungen,* 1897, 235 ff.

[44] *Physiol. Psychol.,* ii., 1902, 290.

[45] *Ibid.,* 290 f.

[46] G. T. Ladd, *Psychology, Descr. and Explan.,* 1894, 167 ff.

[47] *Ibid.,* 537.

[48] *Psychol. Review,* i., 1894, 525.

[49] T. Lipps, *Vom Fühlen, Wollen und Denken,* 1902.

[50] *Zeits.,* xliv., 1906, 38 f.

[51] H. Höffding, *Psychologie in Umrissen,* 1887, 279; 1893, 305; Eng. tr., 1891, 222. Külpe, *Outlines,* 1895, 232 f. F. Jodl, *Lehrbuch d. Psychol.,* 1896, 378 f.; ii., 1903, 1 ff. Ebbinghaus, *Grundzüge,* i., 1905, 564 ff. A. Lehmann, *Hauptgesetze d. menschl. Gefühlslebens,* 1892, 32. J. Rehmke, *Zur Lehre vom Gemüt,* 1898, 47 ff.

[52] *Grundzüge*, i., 1905, 566.

[53] *Gefühl und Bewusstseinslage*, 1903, 39.

[54] *Psychol., Descr. and Explan.*, 183. "Nor is he who has felt that joy of scientific discovery which Niebuhr compared to the divine feeling in view of a new-made universe, likely to confuse it, as respects distinctive quality, with the sensuous thrill of gratified bodily appetite," etc.

[55] *Das Selbstbewusstsein, Empfindung und Gefühl*, 1901, 14.

[56] *Grundriss*, 1896, 188 f. (Engl., 160); cf. 1905, 192 f. (Engl., 1907, 178 f.); *Physiol. Psychol.*, ii., 1902, 344 f.

[57] *Grundriss*, 187 f. (Engl., 159 f.); cf. 1905, 191 f. (Engl., 1907, 177 f.); *Vorlesungen*, 234 ff.; *Physiol. Psychol.*, ii., 341 ff. The doctrine varies a little, from time to time, but is in principle as I state it in the text. It goes back as far as the essay on *Gefühl und Vorstellung* (*Essays*, 1885, 213; *Vjs. f. wiss. Philos.*, iii., 1879, 143), but appears clearly for the first time in the *Vorlesungen* of 1892.

[58] Wundt speaks, both in *Grundriss* and in *Physiol. Psychol.*, of the 'musical' tone, the 'musical' triad: my demonstration was made with tuning forks. I do not think that objection can be taken to the change, since musical reference, æsthetic association, must in any event be ruled out. Personally, I get the same result with harmonical or piano chords, except that the musical reference is, with them, much more difficult to exclude. The observation, to be strictly valid, should be varied as Wundt suggests.

[59] *Physiol. Psychol.*, ii., 1902, 42 ff. It is very interesting, in this connection, — and, indeed, in connection with the general subject of the present Lecture, — to read

Wundt's account of *Gemeingefühl*, in *Beiträge zur Theorie der Sinneswahrnehmung*, 1862, 376–400.

[60] *Arch. f. d. ges. Psychol.*, ix., 1907, Literaturbericht, 94. Meumann himself has recently published an extended article on the subject: *Arch.*, ix., 1907, 26 ff.

[61] *Amer. Journ. Psychol.*, xvi., 1905, 212. Cf. T. Lipps, *Das Selbstbewusstsein: Empfindung und Gefühl*, 1901, 24; M. Kelchner, *Arch. f. d. g. Psychol.*, v., 1905, 124.

[62] *Grundzüge*, i., 1905, 567.

[63] *Zeits.*, xliv., 1906, 2 note.

[64] Cf. Wundt's doctrine in *Physiol. Psychol.*, i., 1893, 561.

[65] O. Vogt, Zur Kenntnis des Wesens und der psychologischen Bedeutung des Hypnotismus, *Zeits. f. Hypnotismus*, iv., 1896, 127. Cf. *Grundriss*, 1905, 102 (Engl., 1907, 94).

[66] *Gefühl und Bewusstseinslage*, 1903, 129.

[67] G. Störring, *Arch. f. d. ges. Psychol.*, vi., 1905, 320 f. I am not even sure that the first of the phrases quoted refers to quality at all; the complete sentence runs: "Stimmungslust ist gleichartiger, die Lust erfüllt mehr das Bewusstsein." It may be that these two clauses express the same fact in different terms. Störring himself sums up in the words: "über Qualität der beiden Lustzustände machen alle drei Vp. die Angabe, es liege deutliche qualitative Differenz vor." Why does he not quote their words? He goes on: "ich lege aber auf diese Uebereinstimmung kein Gewicht, weil diese Aussage von . . . der Annahme der Realität qualitativer Differenzen . . . (die ich übrigens selbst akzeptiere), abhängig sein kann."

[68] Ein Versuch, die Methode der paarweisen Vergleichung auf die verschiedenen Gefühlsrichtungen anzuwenden, *Philos. Studien*, xx., 1902, 382 ff.; S. P. Hayes,

A Study of the Affective Qualities. i. The Tridimensional Theory of Feeling, *Amer. Journ. Psychol.*, xvii., 1906, 358 ff. I must refer the reader for details to these two articles, in both of which the 'curves' of the affective judgments are figured. Criticisms are met in the latter article (361 note), and also in my note on N. Alechsieff's Die Grundformen der Gefühle (*Psychol. Studien*, iii., 1907, 156 ff.), *Amer. Journ. Psychol.*, xix., 1908, 138 ff.

[69] *Physiol. Psychol.*, ii., 1902, 287. "So viel man auch mit der Eindrucksmethode hin und her experimentiren oder die unten zu erörternden Ergebnisse der Ausdrucksmethode zu Hülfe nehmen mag, immer kommt man bei der Analyse der concreten Gefuhlszustände oder der zusammengesetzteren Gemüthsbewegungen wieder auf diese [drei Gegensatzpaaren] zurück." I read this positive statement with surprise when it appeared; but, whatever grounds Wundt may have had for it in 1902, there is small evidence of it in 1908. Possibly for this reason Wundt, in his latest exposition (*ibid.*, i., 1908, 23 ff.), speaks very disparagingly of the *Reizmethode* as an affective method.

[70] M. Brahn, Experimentelle Beiträge zur Gefühlslehre, *Philos. Studien*, xviii., 1903, 127 ff.; W. Gent, Volumpulscurven bei Gefühlen und Affecten, *ibid.*, 715 ff. Wundt, *Physiol. Psychol.*, ii., 1902, 274, 291 ff. Orth, *Gefühl und Bewusstseinslage*, 1903, 58 ff.

[71] A first critique of Wundt's theory, under the title *Zur Kritik der Wundt'schen Gefühlslehre*, will be found in *Zeits.*, xix., 1899, 321 ff. A detailed *Kritik der modernen Gefühlslehre* (Lipps and Wundt) is given by Orth, *op. cit.*, 20 ff.

Lipps' doctrine of feeling may be studied in *Grundtat-*

sachen des Seelenlebens, 1883, 15 ff., 177 ff.; Bemerkungen zur Theorie der Gefühle, *Vjs. f. wiss. Philos.*, xiii., 1889, 160 ff.; *Göttingische gelehrte Anzeigen*, 1894, 85 ff.; *Komik und Humor*, 1898; *Das Selbstbewusstsein: Empfindung und Gefühl*, 1901; *Vom Fühlen, Wollen und Denken*, 1902; *Aesthetik: Psychologie des Schönen und der Kunst. I. Grundlegung der Aesthetik*, 1903, Abschn. i., vi.; *Psychologische Studien*, 1905; *Leitfaden der Psychologie*, 1906, 281 ff.; and numerous articles in psychological journals.

NOTES TO LECTURE V

[1] *Philos. Studien*, x., 1894, 124. Wundt gives illustrations, 123 f.

[2] As seen, *e.g.*, in Külpe, *Outlines*, 1895, 169 ff.; Wundt, *Physiol. Psychol.*, iii., 1903, 518 ff.; Ebbinghaus, *Grundzüge*, i., 1905, 633 ff.

[3] Meumann says (*Exper. Pädagogik*, i., 1907, 326 note): "wer den ganzen Fortschritt der experimentellen Psychologie gegenüber der früheren Psychologie der inneren Wahrnehmung deutlich vor Augen haben will, der vergleiche die in den folgenden Ausführungen dargestellten Methoden und Ergebnisse der experimentellen Forschung individueller Unterschiede mit dem, was ein so geistvoller Vertreter der älteren Psychologie wie Sigwart über unser Problem zu sagen wüsste. Vgl. Sigwart, Die Unterschiede der Individualitäten. Kleine Schriften, Bd. ii. [1889] S. 212 ff."

[4] Cf. my *Experimental Psychology*, I., ii., 1901, 186; W. James, *Princ. of Psychol.*, i., 1890, 402.

[5] W. Hamilton, *Lect. on Metaphysics*, i., 1859, 237 ff.

[6] J. Mill, *Analysis of the Phenomena of the Human Mind*, ii., 1869, 369 ff., with the notes by J. S. Mill and A. Bain.

[7] A. Bain, *The Emotions and the Will*, 1880, 370 ff., 540; *The Senses and the Intellect*, 1868, 558.

[8] D. Braunschweiger, *Die Lehre von der Aufmerksamkeit in der Psychologie des 18. Jahrhunderts*, 1899, 2.

[9] *Lectures on Human and Animal Psychology*, 1896, 270.

[10] Unfortunately, the knowledge often acts as a deterrent, — James, here as elsewhere, serving as excuse (*Psychol. Rev.*, i., 1894, 516 note). I had hoped a good deal from the publication of Wundt's *Grundriss:* but that, even in English translation, is too difficult for the average undergraduate. We sorely need a clear discussion, historical and critical, at the text-book level. —

I do not think that my statements with regard to attention are too strong, even in the light of what I said in Lecture I. of the threefold root of the psychological system. It seems to me that the doctrine of attention is of fundamental importance. And I believe that the strength of Wundt's system lies — and will lie, historically — in the fact of its being an attentional system, whether its special teaching is right or wrong. A system which makes little of attention is, in my judgment, foredoomed to failure.

I do not think, either, that I have entered too strong a claim for the modernity of the psychology of attention. Braunschweiger makes a great deal of the eighteenth century doctrine (*Die Lehre von der Aufmerksamkeit in der Psychologie des* 18. *Jahrhunderts*, 1899, 2 f., 38, 69, 95 f., 124, 150 ff.). But he is a special student within a special period, and the judgment of the special student is likely to lack perspective. A more impartial witness is M. Dessoir (*Geschichte der neueren deutschen Psychologie*, i., 1897–1902), and a cursory glance through Dessoir's index will show the approximate place that attention held in eighteenth century systems.

No doubt, the older psychologists were acute observers. Let me give an instance. I was looking up my *Light of Nature*, to verify the reference given in Note 20 of the following Lecture, — and I naturally read on, for a few

2 A

pages, as one is apt to do. I came upon the following:
"It has been generally remarked by schoolboys, that after
having laboured the whole evening before a repetition day
to get their lesson by heart, but to very little purpose, when
they rise in the morning, they shall have it current at their
tongue's end without any further trouble" (i., 1805, 248 f.).
Here is a direct anticipation of the modern psychophysics
of association! And a few pages further: "in a language
we are masters of what we read seems wholly to occupy
the imagination, yet, for all that, the mind can find room
for something of her own: how quick soever the eye may
pass along, the thought flies still quicker, and will make
little excursions between one word and the next, or pursue reflections of its own, at the same time it attends to
the reading" (*ibid.*, 253), — the very illustration that I
had myself chosen for my discussion of introspection! —
It will hardly be argued, now, that Tucker can compare,
as a student of association and memory, with Ebbinghaus
and Müller: and what holds here holds, so far as my
reading has extended, of attention as well. Everything
depends upon the context, upon the way the problem is
seen, upon the suggestion of method, upon the fruitfulness
of the idea for scientific purposes.

[11] *Grundzüge*, i., 1905, 611. So also Külpe, *Outlines*,
1895, 423.

[12] I. Kant, *Metaphysische Anfangsgründe der Naturwis-
senschaft*, 1786, x. f.; *Sämmtliche Werke*, ed. Rosenkranz
and Schubert, v., 1838–1842, 310. Cf. my *Exper. Psychol.*,
II., ii., 1905, cxlv.

[13] L. M. Solomons and G. Stein, Normal Motor Autom-
atism, *Psychol. Review*, iii., 1896, esp. 503 ff.

[14] The preceding paragraphs are taken, with some com-

pression, from the forthcoming edition of my *Outline of Psychology*. The position agrees, in the main, with that of W. B. Pillsbury, A Suggestion toward a Reinterpretation of Introspection, *Journ. Philos. Psychol. Sci. Meth.*, i., 1904, 225 ff. See also Külpe, *Outlines*, 1895, 8 ff.; Ebbinghaus, *Grundzüge*, i., 1905, 66 ff.; Wundt, *Physiol. Psychol.*, i., 1902, 4 ff. (Engl. 1904, 4 ff.), or i., 1908, 4 ff., 23 ff., with references there given.

It need hardly be said that the essential similarity of the methods of psychology and the natural sciences does not necessarily carry with it a corresponding similarity of subject-matter and problem.

[15] Külpe, The Problem of Attention, *The Monist*, xiii., 1902, 42.

[16] Cf. the remarks in *Amer. Journ. Psychol.*, xvi., 1905, 218 f.

[17] *Physiol. Psychol.*, iii., 1903, 341; 1874, 717 f.

[18] *L'attention*, 1906, 2.; *Attention*, 1908, 2.

[19] *Dict. of Philos. and Psychol.*, i., 1901, 86.

[20] T. Ribot, *Psychologie de l'attention*, 1889, 6, 9, 36, 95.

[21] G. T. Ladd, *Psychol., Descr. and Explan.*, 1894, 61, 66.

[22] Stumpf, *Tonpsychol.*, ii., 1890, 276 ff.; cf. i., 1883, 67 ff.

[23] G. F. Stout, *A Manual of Psychology*, 1899, 65 f. Cf. *Analytic Psychology*, i., 1896, 125 ff., 180 ff.

[24] J. M. Baldwin, *Handbook of Psychol.: Senses and Intellect*, 1890, 69 ff. Cf. *Feeling and Will*, 1891, 280 ff., 351 ff.; *Mental Devel. in the Child and the Race: Methods and Processes*, 1906, 428 ff.

[25] F. H. Bradley, Is there any Special Activity of Attention? *Mind*, O. S., xi., 1886, 306.

[26] D. Ferrier, *The Functions of the Brain*, 1886, 463.

[27] *Grundzüge*, i., 1905, 600, 612.

[28] J. R. Angell, *Psychology: an Introductory Study of the Structure and Function of Human Consciousness*, 1904, 65.

[29] C. H. Judd, *Psychology: General Introduction*, 1907, 191, 193.

[30] *Exper. Pädagogik*, i., 1907, 78 f.

[31] Cf. C. S. Squire, A Genetic Study of Rhythm, *Amer. Journ. Psychol.*, xii., 1901, 541 f.

[32] On intensity of stimulus, see Külpe, *Outlines*, 1895, 438; A. Pilzecker, *Die Lehre von der sinnlichen Aufmerksamkeit*, 1889, 19; Ebbinghaus, *Grundzüge*, i., 1905, 602; James, *Princ. of Psychol.*, i., 1890, 416 f.; Pillsbury, *L'attention*, 1906, 38 ff.; *Attention*, 1908, 28 ff.; Wundt, *Physiol. Psychol.*, iii., 1903, 336; G. E. Müller, *Zur Theorie der sinnlichen Aufmerksamkeit*, [1873] 110 ff. Müller refers to duration only as a condition of *Abstumpfung* of the attention: 126 ff.

[33] See James, *Princ. of Psychol.*, i., 1890, 417; ii., 383 ff. G. E. Müller, Zur Psychophysik der Gesichtsempfindungen, *Zeits.*, x., 1896, 27 f. Müller describes *Eindringlichkeit* as follows: "die Eindringlichkeit betrifft die mehr psychologische Seite der Empfindungen, sie scheint sich hauptsächlich nach der Macht zu bestimmen, mit welcher die Sinneseindrücke unsere Aufmerksamkeit auf sich ziehen, und könnte daher in sachlicher Hinsicht nicht unpassend auch als die Aufdringlichkeit der Sinneseindrücke bezeichnet werden. . . . [Sie] ist, wie es scheint, nicht bloss von der Intensität des psychophysischen Prozesses abhängig, sondern bestimmt sich zugleich auch nach der Häufigkeit der betreffenden Empfindung in unserer Erfahrung, nach dem Gefühlswerte derselben und nach anderen derartigen für die Erweckung unserer

Aufmerksamkeit wichtigen Faktoren." *Ibid.*, 26 f. Frequency is mentioned incidentally by Müller, in the *Sinnliche Aufmerksamkeit*, 135, as a condition of involuntary attention. — Ebbinghaus, *Grundzüge*, i., 1905, 602 f.

[34] Pillsbury, *L'attention*, 1906, 39 f.; *Attention*, 1908, 29 f.; Ebbinghaus, *Grundzüge*, i., 1905, 603 ff. The criticism of the text applies also to Ebbinghaus' treatment of expert disregard of irrelevant details (604 f.) and of habituation (712 ff.), in so far as these are made to depend upon mere repetition of stimulus. — Wundt, *Physiol. Psychol.*, iii., 1903, 340.

In Lecture VIII. I express my personal opinion that habit always implies foregone attention.

[35] Müller, *Sinnliche Aufmerksamkeit*, [1873] 125 f.; Pilzecker, *Sinnliche Aufmerksamkeit*, 1889, 20; Pillsbury, *L'attention*, 1906, 40; *Attention*, 1908, 30; James, *Princ. of Psychol.*, i., 1890, 416 f.; L. W. Stern, *Psychologie der Veränderungsauffassung*, 1898, 211 ff.

[36] Müller, *op. cit.*, 135; Pilzecker, *op. cit.*, 20; Külpe, *Outlines*, 1895, 300 f.; Stumpf, *Tonpsychol.*, ii., 1890, 337 ff. (with refs. to S. Exner); T. Heller, *Philos. Studien*, xi., 1895, 249; Stern, *Veränderungsauffassung*, 1898, 143, 181 ff., 201; James, *Princ. of Psychol.*, i., 1890, 417; ii., 173 f.; Pillsbury, *op. cit.*, 62 ff. (Engl., 48 f.).

[37] Müller, *op. cit.*, 135; Külpe, *op. cit.*, 438; James, *op. cit.*, i., 417; Ebbinghaus, *op. cit.*, 715; Pillsbury, *op. cit.*, 42, 64 f. (Engl., 31 f., 49); Wundt, *Physiol. Psychol.*, 336. Cf. the passage in T. Lipps, Suggestion und Hypnose, *Sitzungsber. der philos.-philol. u. der histor. Classe der k. bayer. Akad. d. Wiss.*, ii., 1897, 424: "der Reiz des Neuen und Ungewohnten ist nichts anderes als der Reiz d. h. die Fähigkeit der Inanspruchnahme

und der Festhaltung psychischer Kraft, die einem Vor-
stellungsinhalte oder Komplex von solchen zukommt,
ehe diese Fähigkeit durch die auf Erfahrungsassocia-
tionen beruhende Tendenz der Ausgleichung und des
Abflusses sich vermindert hat.   Der Reiz des Neuen
ist nichts als der unverminderte Reiz des Objektes."
At bottom, this doctrine agrees with that of Müller; the
stimulus of novelty is the stimulus of the object as such,
the claim that it has to attention in virtue of its intensity, quality, duration, etc.   While, however, I accept
Lipps' analysis, I still think that novelty has a special
place in our empirical classification.

[38] Müller, *op. cit.*, 40 ff., 123 ff.; Pilzecker, *op. cit.*, 19,
34 ff.; Pillsbury, *op. cit.*, 44 ff. (Engl., 32 ff.); Külpe, *Outlines*, 439 f.; *Monist*, xiii., 1902, 46 ff.; Ebbinghaus, *op.
cit.*, 603, 605 f.; Stumpf, *Tonpsychol.*, ii., 1890, 339; H.
Helmholtz, *Physiol. Optik*, 1896, 890 f.; *Popular Lectures
on Scientific Subjects*, [First Series] 1885, 294 f.; *On the
Sensations of Tone as a Physiological Basis for the Theory
of Music*, 1895, 50 f.; J. Jastrow, *Fact and Fable in
Psychol.*, 1900, 89; James, *op. cit.*, i., 437 f.   Relevant
observations are reported by B. B. Breese: *On Inhibition*,
1899, 18 ff.; W. McDougall, *Mind*, N. S., xii., 1903,
473 ff.; A. Brückner, *Zeits. f. Psychol.*, xxvi., 1901, 45, 53.

[39] Wundt, *Physiol. Psychol.*, iii., 1903, 336; Külpe,
Outlines, 1895, 437 f.; *Monist*, xiii., 1902, 44.

[40] Müller, *op. cit.*, 132 ff.; Ebbinghaus, *op. cit.*, 622,
714; Fechner, *Elemente d. Psychophysik*, ii., 1889, 446;
J. Delboeuf, *Examen critique de la loi psychophysique, sa
base et sa signification*, 1883, 166; Lehmann, *Hauptgesetze*, 1892, 194 ff.; Pillsbury, *op. cit.*, 38 f. (Engl., 29);
Münsterberg, *Grundzüge*, i., 1900, 228 f.

[41] This paragraph follows Müller, *Sinnl. Aufmerksamkeit*, 110 ff.

[42] Lotze, *Med. Psychol.*, 1852, 507 ff.; Wundt, *Physiol. Psychol.*, iii., 1903, 336 ff.; Külpe, *Outlines*, 436 ff.; *Monist*, xiii., 1902, 46 ff.; Pillsbury, *op. cit.*, 35 ff. (Engl., 26 ff.); James, *Princ. of Psychol.*, i., 1890, 434 ff.; J. von Kries, *Zeits. f. Psychol.*, viii., 1895, 12 ff.

Whence Lotze derived his list it would be difficult to say. The topic was a favourite one with the eighteenth century psychologists: see Braunschweiger, *Die Lehre von der Aufmerksamkeit*, etc., 1899, 50 ff.; Dessoir, *Geschichte*, i., 1902, 418. In i., 1894, 238, Dessoir exclaims, àpropos of E. Platner (1744–1818): "wäre es nicht vielleicht besser gewesen, Platner hätte uns gesagt, wodurch die Aufmerksamkeit *nicht* gereizt wird?" —

In *Die Lehre von der Aufmerksamkeit*, 1907, E. Dürr takes a view of attention (11 f.) which is practically the same as my own; he also reaches a like conclusion upon various special problems, though in certain cases (e.g., on the subject of fluctuation, 131 ff.) his position is different. Dürr, however, is writing of attention "mit besonderer Berücksichtigung pädagogischer Interessen" (4), so that the course and contents of his exposition are widely divergent from those of the present Lectures.

NOTES TO LECTURE VI

[1] Külpe, *Outlines*, 1895, 336 f., 379.

[2] Wundt, *Physiol. Psychol.*, iii., 1903, 339.

[3] Pillsbury, *L'attention*, 1906, 3 ff.; *Attention*, 1908, 2 ff.

[4] Külpe, *op. cit.*, 429, 441 f.

[5] Wundt, *op. cit.*, 339 f.

[6] Ebbinghaus, *Grundzüge*, i., 1905, 612 ff.

[7] Stumpf, *Tonpsychologie*, i., 1883, 72, 374; ii., 1890, 293.

[8] H. Münsterberg, *Grundzüge der Psychologie*, i., 1900, 227. — The mention of the lengthened line may, at first sight, appear gratuitous. The reference is, however, to experiments upon "the distances between visible points, the distances serving as measures for the intensity of the sensations produced by the movement of the eyes." See *Psych. Rev.*, i., 1894, 39; and cf. *Amer. Journ. Psych.*, viii., 1896, 50, 53.

[9] See Stumpf, *op. cit.*, ii., 293 f. Stumpf does not specify the instrument: he speaks only of a 'Zungenpfeifenaccord.'

It is, perhaps, worth while to add that, even when direct observations agree, their interpretation may be extremely difficult. Thus, Krueger writes of Stumpf's *Reinheitsgefühl:* "sicherlich ist die Theorie ausgegangen von wichtigen und genau festgestellten Tatsachen. Hochmusikalische Beobachter haben mit überraschender Feinheit und Konstanz kleine Verstimmungen der ihnen geläufigsten konsonanten Tonschritte als scharf, spannend, überreizt, beziehungsweise (die subjektiv verkleinerten

Intervalle) als matt, schal, stumpf bezeichnet. Dass es
sich dabei, wie weit und in welchem Sinne, um *Gefühle*
handle, ist natürlich nicht mehr zweifellos." — *Psychol.
Studien*, i., 1906, 381.

[10] See, *e.g.*, H. Münsterberg and N. Kozaki, The In-
tensifying Effect of Attention, *Psychol. Review*, i., 1894,
39 ff.; A. J. Hamlin, Attention and Distraction, *Amer.
Journ. Psychol.*, viii., 1896, 3 ff.; O. Külpe, Ueber den
Einfluss der Aufmerksamkeit auf die Empfindungsin-
tensität, *III. Internat. Congress f. Psychol.*, 1897, 180 ff.;
M. Tsukahara, *Problem of the Relation of Intensity of
Sensation to Attention*, 1907. — Cf., further, G. E. Müller,
Zur Theorie d. sinnlichen Aufmerksamkeit, [1873] 2 ff.;
Fechner, *Elemente d. Psychophysik*, ii., 1889, 452 f.; *Re-
vision*, 1882, 271; T. Lipps, *Suggestion u. Hypnose*, 1898,
398 ff.; A. Lehmann, *Die Hypnose*, 1890, 22; J. Geyser,
*Ueber den Einfluss der Aufmerksamkeit auf die Intensitat
der Empfindung*, 1897.

[11] Reported briefly in *Psychol. Bulletin*, iv., 1907, 212 f.
Professor Bentley allows me to quote here the full text
of his paper.

"I have to report, at this time, only a single group of
experiments, which deal with the intensity of noise; and
I shall reserve for some future occasion a full discussion
and interpretation of the results.

"Both my apparatus and my method are familiar. The
Leipsic type of gravity phonometer was used, and the
sound stimuli were given in pairs. To the one stimulus
the observer was attentive; from the other he was distracted. The distraction was made effective both by the
brevity of the sound and by the character of the distracting
stimuli (odours). The success or failure of distraction

was always checked (as were also the state and degree of attention and the conscious filling of the silent interval) by introspective control. Care was taken to eliminate constant and variable errors; and especially to keep the physical and organic conditions as unvarying as possible.

"The pairs of stimuli were given usually in series of ten, each pair occupying 13 sec., with an interval for rest between successive pairs. An equal number of Distraction-Attention $(D\text{-}A)$ and Attention-Distraction $(A\text{-}D)$ pairs were introduced in haphazard order in every series. The difference in height of fall within each pair was (with one exception noted below) 5 cm., and the absolute heights varied between 24.4 and 89.6 cm.

"Table I. gives the results for Set I. (100 pairs for each one of three observers) and Set II. (120 pairs for each observer). Set I. covers all intensities between 24.4 and 79.4 cm., while Set II. contains only two pairs of stimulus intensity, 24.4–29.4 and 74.4–79.4 cm. As a check upon these observations, a group of 'attention' experiments was added to Set II., where both sensations were received in maximal attention $(A\text{-}A$ order).

"As regards arrangement in the Tables, note the following points. The first horizontal line of figures contains the number of correct or 'true' judgments; the second line, the times that the 'attention' stimulus (R_a) was overestimated, i.e. judged too great; the third line, the underestimations of the 'attention' stimulus; and the fourth line, the cases thrown out on the basis of introspection (failure to attend or to distract). In the lower half of the Table, at the right, are given the $A\text{-}A$ series, which are self-explanatory.

"TABLE I

| No. of Set | I. (10 **A–D** and 10 **D–A** Series) | II. (8 **A–D**, 8 **D–A** and 4 **A–A** Series) |

Height of Fall					24.4–79.4 cm.					24.4–29.4 cm.					74.4–79.4 cm.		
Observer		B	G	M	Total	B	G	M	Total	B	G	M	Total	Total
Attention and Distraction	True	35	34	40	109	17	22	23	62	13	17	13	43	105
	R_a over-est'd	**52**	**42**	**42**	**136**	**11**	**11**	**12**	**34**	**19**	**17**	**13**	**49**	**83**
	R_a under-est'd	7	15	18	40	7	4	3	14	8	6	9	23	37
	Thrown out	6	9	0	15	5	3	2	10	0	0	5	5	15
	Total	100	100	100	300	40	40	40	120	40	40	40	120	240
Attention	Right × 2					12	28	24	64	14	12	12	38	102
	Wrong × 2					22	12	16	50	24	28	26	78	128
	Doubtful × 2					6	0	0	6	2	0	2	4	10
	Total × 2					40	40	40	120	40	40	40	120	240

"It is to be observed that, in nearly half (136) of the 300 experiments of Set I., the sound attended to is, for a wide range of intensities, overestimated. The number is somewhat greater than the number of 'true' cases (109) and is about three and one half times as great as the number of underestimated cases (40). Thus far, the results indicate, then, that a noise attended to is sensibly louder than the same objective sound received in distraction.

"But the problem demands more specific treatment. It demands, in the first place, the distribution of overestimated cases throughout the scale of intensity. Set I. furnishes too few judgments at any single intensity to meet this demand. But Set II. contains results from a single weak (24.4–29.4 cm.) and a single intensive pair (74.4–79.4 cm.). A comparison of the two pairs shows that the number of overestimated cases is uniformly increased, for all observers, with increase in physical intensity. That this relation does not obtain with weak and strong stimuli whose differences are *relatively* (not absolutely) the same, is shown by Table II.

"TABLE II

No. of Set   III and IV.* (14 A–D, 14 D–A, and 8 A–A Series)

HEIGHT OF FALL		24.4–29.4 cm.				74.4–79.4 cm.				
OBSERVER		B	G	M	Total	B	G	M	Total	Total
Attention and Distraction True		30	31	37	98	29	38	41	108	206
R_a overestimated .		**37**	**25**	**18**	**80**	**33**	**26**	**19**	**78**	**158**
R_a underestimated .		0	7	13	20	4	4	7	15	35
Thrown out		3	7	2	12	4	2	3	9	21
Total		70	70	70	210	70	70	70	210	420
Attention Right × 2 . . .		32	35	41	108	27	52	36	115	223
Wrong × 2 . . .		30	32	27	89	33	18	34	85	174
Doubtful × 2 . . .		8	3	2	13	10	0	0	10	23
Total × 2 . . .		70	70	70	210	70	70	70	210	420

"Table II. presents results from two pairs of stimulus intensities which may be supposed to measure (under Weber's Law) like sense-distances. Under the given conditions, the overestimations for weak and loud sounds are found to be almost identical (80 and 78); or, viewed from the negative side, distraction may be said to weaken, by a like amount, loud and weak auditory sensations.

"A comparison of the upper and lower halves of the Tables reveals the curious fact that the number of 'true'

* In Set IV. (4 distraction and 2 attention series), the position of *O*'s head was controlled by means of a biting board. The results were consistent with those of Set III.

cases with distraction is almost as great as the number of 'right' cases with continuous attention (*A-A* series), — namely, 206 and 223. It would seem, at first sight, as if the large constant error introduced by distraction must have materially damaged the function of judgment. But a moment's reflection will make it plain that this error would tend as often toward the increase as toward the decrease of the difference between sensations. Its effect appears, therefore, rather in the distribution (to under-estimations and overestimations) than in the number of incorrect judgments. The small difference in number obtained (17) is probably due to the more unfavourable conditions for judgment afforded by distraction from the one of the sounds compared. —

"It is plainly impracticable, at the present state of the problem, to attempt an explanation or even a full inter-pretation of the bare results. Granted that distraction lowers the intensity of certain sensations, we have still to ask what factor in the distracted consciousness is responsi-ble for the effect. Is loss of intensity due to loss of clear-ness? or to the affective colouring of the distracting odours? or to the impairment of memory through dis-traction? or, finally, are the conditions purely physio-logical, *i.e.* without conscious representation? We shall hope, by further work, to find satisfactory answers to these questions. At present we can make only preliminary observations. (1) Whatever relation obtains between clearness and intensity, the two things were distinct in the minds of the observers. Not only were the latter familiar with the difference between strength and clear-ness; they were also warned, during the experiments, against confusion of the terms. (2) As regards the possible influence of feeling, it may be noted that striking individual differences in depth and range of feeling did not, in our three observers, seem to run parallel with the overestimations in question. Finally, (3) against the indirect effect of memory upon intensity, we may bring the fact that overestimation through attention was independent of the interval separating the 'attention' and the 'distraction' stimuli. It obtained whatever the order: whether distraction came before or after the interval, and therefore whether judgment followed upon the heels of the distraction or only after the interpolation of another, attentive consciousness. —

"In conclusion: certain strong and weak sounds suffer an intensive reduction under distraction. Whether this reduction represents a general dependency of intensity upon attention, and whether the reduction rests upon physiological or psychophysical grounds, remain questions which demand further investigation."

This reference to the 'intensifying effect of attention' naturally brought out instances and opinions of a contrary tenor. So far as I see at present, the cases of the 'weakening' of an impression by direction of the attention upon it may be classified under the following heads.

(1) We prepare for the reception of a very intensive stimulus by protective adjustment of the sense-organ and by inhibition of the start of surprise. Cf. Müller in Pilzecker, *Sinnliche Aufmerksamkeit*, 1889, 80 f.

(2) Foregone accommodation of attention, sensory and motor *Einstellung*, may give a like result. If we are habituated to very heavy weights, a moderately intensive weight will seem light. — Cf. G. E. Müller and F. Schu-

mann, *Pflüger's Archiv*, xlv., 1889, 42 ff.; and references
in my *Exper. Psychol.*, II., ii., 1905, 366.

(3) Expectation may be 'worse than the reality.' The
expected impression may be weakened (*a*) by the fatigue
that follows from the strain of expectation itself, or (*b*) by
the conscious *Einstellung*, by expectation's overshooting
its mark and predisposing us for something more intensive
than we actually experience.

(4) Intensity may be affected in two ways by the concurrence of other stimuli. (*a*) An associated whole may
be stronger than any one of its constituents. Thus the
pain of a dental operation is enhanced by the odour of
the room, the sight of instruments, the uncomfortable position of the jaws and lips, etc., etc.: a resolute fixation of
attention on the pain itself will sometimes reveal a surprisingly low degree of intensity. Cf. Külpe, *Outlines*,
398. No doubt, a part is here played by (3) (*b*). —
(*b*) A sensation may be weakened by its fusion with other
sensations; thus an overtone, singled out by anticipatory
attention, may appear surprisingly weak. Cf. Müller,
Sinnliche Aufmerksamkeit, [1873] 21, 38 f., 71 ff.; Stumpf,
Tonpsychol., ii., 1890, 231.

(5) A simple case is that of the weakening of a sensation
by peripheral adaptation. The most sustained attention
cannot prevent adaptation; and, if sustained attention is
there, the adaptive weakening may appear, at first sight,
to be the direct result of attention itself. — Where the
stimulus is too strong for noticeable adaptation, or where
the phenomenon of adaptation is absent, sustained attention may, I think, result in a sort of hypnotic anæsthesia;
but I am not sure upon this point.

[12] J. M. Baldwin, *Senses and Intellect*, 1890, 63 ff., 68.

[13] J. R. Angell, *Psychology*, 1904, 65 f.

[14] *Monist*, xiii., 1902, 38 f., 57.

[15] *Zeits. f. Phil. u. philos. Kritik*, cx., 1896, 31 f., 35. Cf. H. E. Kohn, *Zur Theorie der Aufmerksamkeit*, 1894; F. Schumann, *Zeits.*, xxiii., 1900, 24.

[16] Art. Psychology, *Encyc. Britan.*, xx., 1886, 47.

[17] Fechner, *Elem. d. Psychophysik*, ii., 1889, 39. Cf. my *Exper. Psychol.*, II., ii., 1905, clxiii.

[18] H. R. Marshall, *Instinct and Reason*, 1898, 38 f.

[19] H. Helmholtz, *Zur Lehre von den Tonempfindungen*, 1877, 107; *Sensations of Tone*, 1895, 62.

[20] K. Fortlage, *System der Psychologie*, i., 1855, 102 ff.; Lotze, *Med. Psychol.*, 1852, 505; A. Tucker, *The Light of Nature Pursued*, 2d ed., i., 1805, 225. I have not found the metaphor, as I had expected to do, in I. H. Fichte's *Psychologie*, though the author indicates his familiarity with it in i., 1864, 161.

[21] Wundt, *Physiol. Psychol.*, 1874, 717; iii., 1903, 33 f. The change was made in the fourth edition of 1893.

[22] *Ibid.*, iii., 1903, 117 ff., 552, 557.

[23] W. Hamilton, *Lectures on Metaphysics*, i., 1859, 352 f.; Wundt, *ibid.*, 554 ff. with references.

[24] *Ibid.*, 595 f., 600 f.

[25] C. L. Morgan, *Introd. to Comparative Psychol.*, 1894, 14, 19.

[26] *Princ. of Psychol.*, i., 1890, 224 ff.

[27] *Op. cit.*, 13 f.

[28] *Op. cit.*, 119.

[29] G. Dietze, Untersuchungen über den Umfang des Bewusstseins bei regelmässig auf einander folgenden Schalleindrücken, *Philos. Studien*, ii., 1885, 362 ff.; Wundt, *op. cit.*, 351, 353.

[30] Dietze, *op. cit.*, 391.

[31] *Op. cit.*, 353, 356.

[32] F. Schumann, *Zeits.*, i., 1890, 77 f., 80; ii., 1891, 115 ff.; xvii., 1898, 121; Wundt, *Philos. Studien*, vi., 1891, 250 ff.; vii., 1892, 222 ff.; W. Wirth, *ibid.*, xx., 1902, 561 ff.; J. Quandt, *Psychol. Studien*, i., 1906, 137 ff. Külpe leaves the introspective question open: *Outlines*, 394. Münsterberg seems to accept Wundt's view, since he identifies the question of the range of consciousness with the question "wieviel Schallnachbilder bei regelmässig succedierenden Schalleindrücken gleichzeiting in unserem Bewusstsein bleiben": *Grundzüge*, i., 1900, 214. — Cf. also the discussion of the Psychische Präsenzzeit by L. W. Stern, *Zeits.*, xiii., 1897, 325 ff., and the references there given.

[33] Wundt, *Physiol. Psychol.*, iii., 1903, 353. These are the observations which I believe Wundt has in mind *ibid.*, 119.

[34] On cognition, see Wundt, *ibid.*, 535 ff. This explanation, which I have given in lectures since 1904, is also offered by K. Mittenzwey, *Psychol. Studien*, ii., 1907, 386.

[35] See W. Wirth, Die Klarheitsgrade der Regionen des Sehfeldes bei verschiedenen Verteilungen der Aufmerksamkeit, *Psychol. Studien*, ii., 1906, 30 ff.; K. Mittenzwey, Ueber abstrahierende Apperzeption, *ibid.*, 1907, 358 ff.; A. Kästner and W. Wirth, Die Bestimmung der Aufmerksamkeitsverteilung innerhalb des Sehfeldes mit Hilfe von Reaktionsversuchen, *ibid.*, iii., 1907, 361 ff.

[36] Angell, *Psychology*, 1904, 65.

[37] James, *Princ. of Psychol.*, i., 1890, 237 ff., 284 ff.; esp. 255, 258 f. In his last section James is dealing with clearness and obscurity. "We actually *ignore* most of

2 B

the things about us." "Attention, . . . out of all the sensations yielded, picks out certain ones as worthy of its notice and suppresses all the rest." Here, however, is no mention of 'fringes.'

[38] Certain of my hearers objected to this argument that I had worked out the 'law of the two levels' on the basis of the observation with the puzzle picture. This, they contended, represents an exceptional case: a consciousness may, in fact, show only a single level or may show a great variety of levels at a given moment.

The first part of the objection does not hold. I had worked out the 'law' long before I thought of the use of the puzzle-picture; it was in the course of an extended search for a suitable illustration of the law that the puzzle-picture occurred to me. I give the illustration because it seems to me to present, in clear and striking form, what is the normal state of affairs; but it is this latter, the normal conformation of consciousness, that I am concerned with. Continued observation of the conscious levels under very different circumstances, in the laboratory and in everyday life, led me to the law.

The second part of the objection raises the question of fact. So far, it is both legitimate and welcome. When, however, I pressed for instances, I found the following sources of error: (1) confusion of peripheral with attentional clearness; (2) confusion of attentional clearness with cognition; (3) confusion of a single consciousness with a series of consciousnesses, and therefore of a single 'act of attention' with several successive acts; and even (4) confusion of the question of the conscious 'levels' with the question of the 'range' of attention. I got no clear case either of a single-levelled or of a many-levelled consciousness.

In the abstract, the objection usually took this form. 'An idea or a presentation may pass very slowly from the background to the focus of consciousness; it does not always, does not ordinarily, jump from the one to the other. Hence a cross-section must show ideas or presentations in all sorts of intermediate positions between obscurity and maximal clearness; there are many levels.' I grant, of course, that we do not perceive anything of the nature of a jump, — but I cannot either find anything of the nature of the slow passage. *Now* a certain idea is obscure; *now*, without conscious transition, it is clear. I admit, also, that our response to an intruding stimulus, when the attention is already engaged, varies widely with variation of conditions; I discuss some instances in Lecture VII., under the 'law of temporal instability.' But I do not find, in this variation of response, any evidence of new levels. For the rest, observation of consciousness in the rough is always unsatisfactory; the appeal lies to experiment.

I may add — what my critics did not suggest — that in abnormal circumstances consciousness may conceivably show but one level; or, at any rate, that the normal relation of the two levels may be radically changed. The narrowed consciousness of profound hypnosis may, at moments, be wholly clear; the idiotic consciousness may be wholly obscure. Cf. my *Primer of Psychology*, 1902, 273.

[39] *Tonpsychol.*, i., 1883, 309.

[40] Wundt, *Physiol. Psychol.*, iii., 1903, 96 f., 337 f., 434, 439. Here we are already encroaching upon the field of inertia. — On accommodation-time in reaction experiments, cf. G. della Valle, *Psychol. Studien*, iii., 1907, 294 ff.

[41] See G. Kafka, *Psychol. Studien.*, ii., 1906, 256 ff.;
B. Berliner, *ibid.*, iii., 1907, 91 ff., with references.

In order to bring out my point clearly and sharply, I
have spoken in the text almost as if the *Anstieg*-determina-
tions might be transferred bodily from their present intensive context to that of clearness. I have, it is true,
safeguarded the proposal by insisting on the necessity of
'interpretation.' However, my idea may be expressed
more accurately — and more cautiously — as follows.
Clearness and intensity are both involved in the determinations; it is evidently wrong to ascribe everything to
intensity and nothing to clearness. Let us, then, take up
the *Anstieg*-question from the side of clearness, varying
our method in such a way as to secure varying degrees of
clearness. We shall then be able to give the earlier results
a setting in which due regard is paid to each one of the
two concurrent factors.

[42] *L'attention*, 1906, 17; *Attention*, 1908, 13.

[43] G. T. Fechner, *Revision der Hauptpuncte der Psychophysik*, 1882, 283; cf. Ueber einige Verhältnisse des
binocularen Sehens, *Abhandl. d. kgl. s. Ges. d. Wiss.*, vii.,
1860, 395: "bei der willkührlichen Richtung der Aufmerksamkeit selbst ist der bewusste Willensact, durch den
wir die Aufmerksamkeit richten, von dem Erfolge, d. i.
der gerichteten und fixirten Aufmerksamkeit, wohl zu
unterscheiden. Jener Act erfolgt ein- für allemal, und
dann bleibt die Aufmerksamkeit gerichtet, ohne dass wir
einen fortgesetzten oder neuen bewussten Willensact
nöthig haben, sie in dieser Richtung zu erhalten." —
Stumpf, *Tonpsychol.*, i., 1883, 386; cf. 244, 391; ii., 1890,
318, 358. F. Auerbach, in Wiedemann's *Annalen*, iv.,
1878, 509 f. F. Schumann, *Nachr. d. Ges. d. Wiss. zu*

Göttingen, 1889, 536 ff.; *Zeits.*, iv., 1893, 1 ff.; xxiii., 1900, 9; McDougall, *Mind*, N. S., xv., 1906, 349.

Here belong, at least in part, the experiments on word-exposure with previous suggestion; certain phenomena of sensory *Einstellung*, — absolute impression, etc.; and perhaps also certain optical illusions.

[44] On *Perseverationstendenz* see, provisionally, Ebbinghaus, *Grundzüge*, i., 691; Wundt, *Physiol. Psychol.*, iii., 600 f.

[45] See Wundt, *op. cit.*, 45 ff.

NOTES TO LECTURE VII

[1] James, *Princ. of Psychol.*, i., 1890, 427 ff.; Wundt, *Physiol. Psychol.*, iii., 1903, 410 ff.; Ebbinghaus, *Grundzüge*, i., 1905, 614 ff.

[2] Wundt, *op. cit.*, 64 ff.

[3] H. C. Stevens, A Simple Complication Pendulum for Qualitative Work, *Am. Journ. Psychol.*, xv., 1904, 581.

[4] M. Geiger, Neue Complicationsversuche, *Philos. Studien*, xviii., 1903, 347 ff. See also the references there given.

[5] Wundt, *op. cit.*, 67.

[6] W. von Tchisch, Ueber die Zeitverhältnisse der Apperception einfacher und zusammengesetzter Vorstellungen, untersucht mit Hülfe der Complicationsmethode, *Philos. Studien*, ii., 1885, 603 ff., esp. 621 f.

[7] *Physiol. Psychol.*, ii., 1880, 272 ff. Geiger (*op. cit.*, 400) says that Wundt's and von Tchisch's explanations are 'grundverschieden.' So they are! But I think that von Tchisch, if he believed that he was repeating Wundt, had some excuse for his mistake. He says (622): "die Apperception reproducirt unmittelbar den Eindruck." Wundt says (273): "es wird auch von der Apperception der Eindruck unmittelbar reproducirt." (Cf. also the passage in *Lehrbuch der Physiologie des Menschen*, 1878, 793: "das Centralorgan scheint auf einen erwarteten Eindruck so sich vorzubereiten, dass der Vorbereitungsact selbst, wenn er eine gewisse Intensität erreicht, zur Erregung wird.") All through the exposition of 1880

374

Wundt makes very incautious use of the 'Erinnerungsbild':
it is not difficult to read 'hallucination' into his pages.
In the edition of 1887 (ii., 339 f.) the 'reproduction'
and the 'memory image' have disappeared, and Wundt's
theory stands out in sharp contrast to von Tchisch's.
Since James had the edition of 1887 in his hands, when
preparing his chapter on Attention for the press, Geiger is
justified in charging him with an unwarranted confusion
of the two views.

[8] *Op. cit.*, 415 f.

[9] Geiger, *op. cit.*, 399 ff.   It is to be noted that the explanation offered by Ebbinghaus in *Grundzüge*, i., 1902,
593, does not appear *ibid.*, 1905, 615, save in the reference
to "allerlei Ueberlegungen."

[10] *Physiol. Psychologie*, 1874, 767.   The phrase appears
in all subsequent editions.

[11] Geiger, *op. cit.*, 409 ff.   I have, of course, taken the
simplest possible case.

[12] *Physiol. Psychol.*, iii., 1903, 75 f., 86.

[13] *Ibid.*, 352.

[14] *Grundzüge*, i., 618 ff.   Ebbinghaus is, perhaps, following James: *Princ.*, i., 409.

[15] *Op. cit.*, 334, 352.   The italics are in the original.

[16] *Op. cit.*, 621. — Both Ebbinghaus (620) and James
(408) refer here to the experiments of F. Paulhan (*Revue
scientifique*, 3 S., xiii., 1887, 684).   Neither these nor the
kindred experiments of A. Binet (*Rev. philos.*, xxix., 1890,
138) appear to me, however, to bear out the conclusions
derived from them.   I have myself repeated and extended
Paulhan's work, and have attained, with practice, to mark-
edly greater time-differences.   But the results belong to
the domain of habit, of 'normal motor automatisms,' —

where analysis is not difficult, but where we gain no knowledge of the range of attention.   Simultaneity of two psychologically disparate 'attentions' is, in my experience,
altogether impossible. — Cf. S. E. Sharp, *Amer. Journ.
Psychol.*, x., 1899, 356, 381.   It is noteworthy that, in the
case reported by R. d'Allonnes (*Rev. philos.*, Decr. 1905,
592 ff.), there was, apparently, no loss of attention with loss
of feeling: see pp. 611 f.   Cf., however, Lect. II., note 2.

[17] *Op. cit.*, 404.

[18] *Op. cit.*, 634.

[19] *Op. cit.*, 366.

[20] *Op. cit.*, 520; cf. 518 ff., 544 ff., 558 ff.

[21] *Principles*, i., 237.   The reader may be reminded that
the distinction between 'substantive' and 'transitive' parts
of the stream of thought, in James' exposition, is a distinction in terms of time alone; it does not imply discontinuity.
"The successive psychoses shade gradually into each other,
although their *rate* of change may be much faster at one
moment than at the next": *ibid.*, 243.

[22] *Op. cit.*, 624.

[23] References to the experiments on touch are given by
L. R. Geissler, Fluctuations of Attention to Cutaneous
Stimuli, *Amer. Journ. Psychol.*, xviii., 1907, 309 ff.   Cf. the
general account in my *Exper. Psychol.*, I., ii., 1901, 194 ff.;
and, for the 'Tastzuckungen,' J. Czermak, *Sitzungsber. d.
mathem.-naturw. Classe d. kais. Akademie d. Wissen-
schaften zu Wien*, xv., 1855, 486 f. (*Physiol. Studien*, ii.,
64 f.).

[24] References are given by K. Dunlap, The Fluctuation
of Diapason and Gas Flame Tones, *Psychol. Rev.*, xi., 1904,
314 ff.   See also W. Heinrich, *Zeits. f. Sinnesphysiologie*,
xli., 1906, 57.

[25] See my *Exper. Psychol.*, *loc. cit.;* C. E. Ferree, An Experimental Examination of the Phenomena usually attributed to Fluctuation of Attention, *Amer. Journ. Psychol.*, xvii., 1906, 84, 94 f. ; J. W. Slaughter, *ibid.*, xii., 1901, 331 ; W. Heinrich, Sur la fonction de la membrane du tympan, *Bull. de l'Académie des Sciences de Cracovie*, July, 1903, 536 ff. ; Ueber die Intensitätsänderungen schwacher Geräusche, *Zeits. f. Sinnesphysiologie*, xli., 1906, 57 f. ; Ueber das periodische Verschwinden kleiner Punkte, *ibid.*, 59 ff. Heinrich's view of auditory accommodation is that the drum-skin reacts to a given tone in very different states of tension, so that the pulsations of the tensor tympani have no effect upon tonal hearing. On the other hand, the adjustment of the membrane to noise is extremely delicate ("das Trommelfell ist äusserst fein auf Geräusche gestimmt; . . . man ist erstaunt zu sehen, wie indifferent das Trommelfell gegen Geräusche ist, bis man zu der richtigen für das Geräusch entsprechenden Spannung kommt "), so that after accommodation is effected the slight changes of tension due to the pulsating muscle make themselves apparent in sensation.

[26] C. E. Ferree, *Amer. Journ. Psychol.*, xvii., 1906, 81 ff., esp. 83 ; xix., 1908, 58 ff., esp. 129 ; C. Hess, *Arch. f. Ophthalmol.*, xl., Abth. 2, 1894, 274 ff. ; B. Hammer, *Zeits. f. Psychol. u. Physiol. d. Sinnesorgane*, xxxvii., 1905, 363 ff., esp. 365, 375. Hammer has the priority of extended publication; but I have given first place to Ferree in my text because his work was begun, and his theory already outlined, in 1903. A brief report will be found in *Journ. Philos. Psychol. Sci. Meth.*, i., 1904, 240 ; *Science*, N. S., xix., 1904, 659.

Hammer is criticised by C. E. Seashore in *Zeits.*, xxxix.,

1905, 448 ff. With the critique of the auditory experiments I am in general agreement. I do not understand, however, how Seashore can say of adaptation and eye-movement: "die wichtige Rolle der genannten und anderer physiologischer Momente ist wohlbekannt." I suppose that he refers to Pace, who had written in 1902: "for the eye, the 'peripheral' includes the retina; and, so far as I am aware, the retinal conditions as affected by the fluctuations have not been investigated" (*Philos. Studien*, xx., 234). Pace himself works in terms of retinal 'fatigue' (242), *i.e.* of local adaptation: but he brings peripheral fatigue into speculative connection with 'central changes' and the process of accommodation, and says nothing whatever of eye-movement (244). I know of no further reference before 1904, when G. E. Müller sets Hess' observations in the perspective of the experiments on attentional fluctuation (*Gesichtspunkte und Tatsachen*, 110), and the two notes on Ferree's work appear in Woodbridge's *Journal* and in *Science*. —

In a paper entitled The Fluctuation of Visual Stimuli of Point Area, read by title at the 5th Annual Meeting of Experimental Psychologists (Cambridge, Mass., April 15–17, 1908) and to be published in the *Amer. Journ. Psychol.*, Mr. Ferree reports a repetition and extension of the experiments of Heinrich, referred to in the foregoing Note, and concludes that "in so far as adaptation-tests can be applied, these stimuli follow the laws of adaptation and recovery, in the phase-relations of their fluctuations, as closely as do the areas commonly employed." Positive evidence is also adduced against Heinrich's theory of lenticular pulsation.

Mr. Ferree informs me, further, of the following results of unpublished experiments with auditory stimuli. (1) The tone of an electrically driven tuning-fork does not fluctuate at the limen, and objective interruptions of the sound are at once remarked. (2) Of three trained observers, tested at the same time with the watch-tick, two reported no fluctuations (90 sec.–2 min.), while the third gave fluctuations of the orthodox sort. Unfortunately, the positions of the observers were not interchanged.

Hammer has done good service in calling attention to the objective inconstancy of the watch-tick (*op. cit.*, 371 ff.). I am sure, however, that this observation must be supplemented, for explanatory purposes, by reference to sound-reflections or similar phenomena. We were accustomed, in the early nineties, to perform Sanford's experiment (58 *b*, *Amer. Journ. Psychol.*, iv., 1891, 307; 61 *b*, *Course in Exper. Psychol.*, 1898, 55) in the Cornell Laboratory with a number of students simultaneously. We found, as I remember, occasional instances of absence of fluctuation, and a good many cases of approximately coincident fluctuation; but we also found many cases of non-coincidence.

[27] See Stumpf, *Tonpsychol.*, i., 40 f., 360.

[28] Helmholtz, *Physiol. Optik*, 1896, 242, 510; so J. Müller, *Ueber die phantastischen Gesichtserscheinungen*, 1826, 15 f. ("diese Lichterscheinung war mit dem Ausathmen synchronisch"). Fechner, curiously enough, found no such oscillation: *Revision*, 1882, 32. — A. Lehmann, *Philos. Studien*, ix., 1894, 66 ff.; J. W. Slaughter, *Amer. Journ. Psychol.*, xii., 1901, 329 ff.

[29] The whole series of related articles is as follows: Slaughter, The Fluctuations of the Attention in Some of

their Psychological Relations, *Amer. Journ. Psychol.*, xii., 1901, 313 ff.; R. W. Taylor, The Effect of Certain Stimuli upon the Attention Wave, *ibid.*, 335 ff.; H. C. Stevens, The Relation of the Fluctuations of Judgments in the Estimation of Time Intervals to Vaso-motor Waves, *ibid.*, xiii., 1902, 1 ff.; W. B. Pillsbury, Attention Waves as a Means of Measuring Fatigue, *ibid.*, xiv., 1903, 541 ff.; C. E. Galloway, The Effect of Stimuli upon the Length of Traube-Hering Waves, *ibid.*, xv., 1904, 499 ff.; B. Killen, The Effects of Closing the Eyes upon the Fluctuations of the Attention, *ibid.*, 512 ff.; G. L. Jackson, The Telephone and Attention Waves, *Journ. Phil. Psychol. Sci. Meth.*, iii., 1906, 602 ff.

Cf. also Pillsbury's general account in *L'attention*, 1906, 90 ff.; *Attention*, 1908, 69 ff.; F. G. Bonser, A Study of the Relations between Mental Activity and the Circulation of the Blood, *Psychol. Rev.*, x., 1903, 120 ff. Ct. W. McDougall, *Mind*, N. S., xv., 1906, 356 f.; H. Berger, *Ueber die körp. Aeusserungen psych. Zustände*, ii., 1907, 153 ff.

[30] S. Exner, *Entwurf zu einer physiologischen Erklärung der psychischen Erscheinungen*, i., 1894, 302 f.; Pillsbury, *Amer. Journ. Psych.*, xiv., 552.

Exner writes (302): "nach meinen Selbstbeobachtungen dürfte die Dauer der gleichmässigen Lebhaftigkeit einer Vorstellung kaum eine Secunde sein." Even if we put the very strictest interpretation upon 'gleichmässig,' the statement seems curiously exaggerated.

[31] *Philos. Studien*, xx., 1902, 234.

[32] Lehmann, *op. cit.;* other references in Ferree, *Amer. Journ. Psychol.*, xix., 1908, 58 ff.

[33] Cf. The Problems of Experimental Psychology, *Amer. Journ. Psychol.*, xvi., 1905, 218.

In the first edition of his *Grundzüge* (i., 1897, 263) Ebbinghaus wrote as follows: "Nun sind aber doch die Licht- und Farbenempfindungen, wie wichtig sie auch immer als Material für weitere Verarbeitungen sein mögen, *an und für sich* noch relativ niedere und elementare Bethätigungen der Seele, das sie vermittelnde Organ ist ein Aussenwerk des eigentlichen Seelenorgans. Wenn also schon das vergleichsweise Einfache sich der eindringenden und intensiven Beschäftigung mit ihm als ein ungeahnt und fast verwirrend Reichhaltiges enthüllt, wie mag es erst mit dem höheren Seelenleben, das doch zweifellos etwas beträchtlich Verwickelteres ist, in Wahrheit bestellt sein?" I fear that there is here a 'trace,' as the analysts say, of an untenable genetic psychology. That apart, I am — as the above quotation shows — unable to see the force of Ebbinghaus' argument. The passage is not reprinted in 1905.

What are we to say, however, to the results of H. Berger (*Körp. Aeusserungen*, ii., 1907, 118 ff., 181 ff.), who was able, in Fechner's words, to look into the brain of another person, and who there saw the apperception waves with all desirable plainness? This, surely: that the introspective control which Berger finds lacking in his first series of experiments (139 f.) is equally necessary for the series made by 'Zoneff's method.' There is no evidence that the 'inattention' of his observers was not an 'attention to something else.' The same criticism holds of the experiments of Zoneff and Meumann, so far as their report has been published; we are not told anything in detail of the 'Nachlassen der Aufmerksamkeit' (*Philos. Studien*, xviii., 1903, 46). But, apart from this, it was a paradox of the older investigations that fluctuation of attention occurred *without* any subjective remission of attention.

[34] L. R. Geissler, *Amer. Journ. Psychol.*, xviii., 1907, 310 f.; E. A. Pace, *Philos. Studien*, xx., 1902, 244.

The fluctuation of two simultaneously presented stimuli offers no new difficulty. I have myself made preliminary experiments upon memory-images, without observing fluctuation. See, however, N. Lange, *Philos. Studien*, iv., 1888, 408 ff.; H. Eckener, *ibid.*, viii., 1893, 370, 379; H. Münsterberg, *Beitr. zur exper. Psychol.*, ii., 1889, 119 ff. The illusions of reversible perspective (Lange, 406), which still figure in Pillsbury's account (*L'attention*, 93; *Attention*, 1908, 71), have been ruled out of court by Wundt himself, who finds their primary conditions in the physiological processes of fixation and eye-movement (*Die geometrisch-optischen Täuschungen*, 1898, 23 [*Abh. d. mathem.-phys. Cl. d. kgl. sächs. Ges. d. Wiss.*, xxiv., 75]; *Phys. Psych.*, ii. 1902, 545 ff.).

[35] Külpe, *Outlines*, 429; Ebbinghaus, *Grundzüge*, 623 f.

[33] See A. J. Hamlin, *Amer. Journ. Psychol.*, viii., 1896, 3 ff.; F. E. Moyer, *ibid.*, 1897, 405; L. G. Birch, *ibid.*, ix., 1897, 45; L. Darlington and E. B. Talbot, *ibid.*, 1898, 332; E. B. Titchener, *ibid.*, 343. My outline of method is (as I say later in the text) entirely schematic; but I think that with time and patience and technical skill the method itself can be carried through. And I know of no other that will serve the same purpose.

It has often been proposed that the method of distraction should be applied objectively, without introspective control. See, *e.g.*, A. Bertels, Versuche über die Ablenkung der Aufmerksamkeit, 1889; E. J. Swift, *Amer. Journ. Psychol.*, v., 1892, 1 ff.; Külpe, *op. cit.*, 428 f.; E. Kräpelin, *Psychol. Arbeiten*, i., 1895, 57 ff.; R. Vogt, *ibid.*, iii., 1899, 62 ff.; W. McDougall, *Brit. Journ. Psychol.*, i., 1905, 435 ff.

Stumpf sees the difficulty, but does not suggest a way out: *Tonpsychol.*, i., 74 f. Pillsbury, in his new chapter in *Attention*, 89 ff., treats the method in this objective way, and thus naturally — but mistakenly — regards the work published from the Cornell Laboratory not as preliminary, but as done for its own sake. I have, however, never believed that the method of distraction, taken objectively, could furnish any psychological result, and I can therefore subscribe to Pillsbury's criticism. In 1898 I wrote as follows: "The three Studies . . . were undertaken with the view of discovering a means of distraction that should be capable of gradation, uniform in its working and applicable to normal subjects. With such a distraction it would be possible, on the qualitative side, *to describe the attributes of mental processes given in the state of inattention*, and, on the quantitative, to measure the magnitude and delicacy of sensitivity and sensible discrimination in the same state" (343 f.: the italics are not in the original). The 'state of inattention' is a clumsy expression, but it is evident that my psychological appeal was to lie to introspection.

[37] Stumpf, *Tonpsychol.*, i., 73 f.; H. Münsterberg, *Die Willenshandlung*, 1888, 72; *Beitr. z. exper. Psychol.*, ii., 1889, 24.

[38] See, *e.g.*, B. Bourdon, Observations comparatives sur la reconnaissance, la discrimination et l'association, *Rev. philos.*, xl., 1895, 166 ff.; E. Toulouse et N. Vaschide, Attention et distraction sensorielles, *Compt. rend. de la soc. de biol.*, 1899, 964 ff.; A. Binet, Attention et adaptation, *Année psychol.*, vi., 1900, 248 ff.; F. Consoni, La mesure de l'attention chez les enfants faibles d'esprit (phrénasthéniques), *Arch. de Psychol.*, ii., 1903, 209 ff.; W. Peters, Aufmerksamkeit und Reizschwelle: Versuche zur Mes-

sung der Aufmerksamkeitskonzentration, *Arch. f. d. ges. Psychol.*, viii., 1906, 385 ff.; P. Janet, *The Mental State of Hystericals*, 1901, 70 ff.; Münsterberg, Die Association successiver Vorstellungen, *Zeits. f. Psychol.*, i., 1890, 99 ff.; W. G. Smith, The Relation of Attention to Memory, *Mind*, N. S., iv., 1895, 47 ff.; T. Ziehen, Ein einfacher Apparat zur Messung der Aufmerksamkeit, *Monatsschr. f. Psychiat. u. Neurologie*, xiv., 1903, 231.

On the use of the *MV*, see A. Oehrn, Experimentelle Studien zur Individualpsychologie, *Psychol. Arbeiten*, i., 1895, 92 ff., esp. 128, 138; V. Henri, *Année psychol.*, ii., 1897, 245; J. J. van Biervliet, *Journ. de Psychol.*, i., 1904, 230; A. Binet, *Ann. psychol.*, xi., 1905, 71. On the use of the fluctuation-values, see E. Wiersma, *Zeits. f. Psychol.*, xxviii., 1902, 180 ff.; Pillsbury, *Amer. Journ. Psychol.*, xiv., 1903, 541 ff.

[39] For a list of the investigations of attention by the expressive method, see H. C. Stevens, *Amer. Journ. Psychol.*, xvi., 1905, table facing 469; and add E. A. McC. Gamble, *ibid.*, xvi., 261; M. Kelchner, *Arch. f. d. ges. Psychol.*, v., 1905, 7 ff.; H. Berger, *Körp. Aeusserungen*, i., 1904, 77 ff.; ii., 1907, 40 ff., 118 ff., 167 ff. Noteworthy is Binet's suggestion of immobility: *Année psychol.*, vi., 1900, 279.

NOTES TO LECTURE VIII

[1] With these paragraphs, cf. Wundt, *Physiol. Psychol.*, ii., 1902, 362 ff.; also the insertion from the fourth edition in *Princ. of Physiol. Psychol.*, i., 1904, 21 ff.; Orth, *Gefühl u. Bewusstseinslage*, 1903, 6 ff. (esp.the remarks on Tetens).

[2] *Amer. Journ. Psychol.*, xvi., 1905, 213.

[3] See the discussion in *Psychol. Bulletin*, iii., 1906, 52 ff.

[4] J. Merkel, *Philos. Studien*, iv., 1888, 594; v., 1889, 245.

[5] *Physiol. Psychol.*, ii., 1902, 369.

[6] The first idea of the theory here outlined came to me some years ago — in 1901 or 1902 — in the course of conversation with my then assistant, Professor G. M. Whipple. How much of it belongs to Dr. Whipple and how much to myself I cannot now say, and I imagine that Dr. Whipple is in the same case. In its general features, the theory seems to resemble that put forward by M. F. Washburn (*Journ. Philos. Psychol. Sci. Meth.*, iii., 1906, 62 f.). I do not agree, however, that mental processes may appear, in alternation, as feelings and as organic sensations or ideas. Another similar view is that of R. Lagerborg, *Das Gefühls-problem*, 1905, 36; *Arch. f. d. ges. Psychol.*, ix., 1907, 455 f.

[7] Cf. the terminological note in Orth, *Gefühl u. Bewusst-seinslage*, 1903, 5; and H. N. Gardiner, *Journ. Philos. Psychol. Sci. Meth.*, iii., 1906, 57 f.

[8] Ebbinghaus, *Grundzüge*, 568 ff.

[9] J. J. Thomson, *The Corpuscular Theory of Matter*, 1907, 1. "From the point of view of the physicist, a theory of matter is a policy rather than a creed; its object is to

2 c   385

connect or coördinate apparently diverse phenomena, and above all to suggest, stimulate, and direct experiment."

[10] *Op. cit.*, i., 1902, 577 f.; i., 1905, 602 f.

[11] G. F. Stout, *Analytic Psychol.*, i., 1896, 224 ff.; cf. *Manual of Psychol.*, 1899, 232 ff.

[12] Külpe, *Outlines*, 272.

[13] *L'attention*, 1906, 72; *Attention*, 1908, 55. "Things are interesting because we attend to them, or because we are likely to attend to them; we do not attend because they are interesting." — Cf. with this discussion F. Arnold, The Psychology of Interest, *Psychol. Rev.*, xiii., 1906, 221 ff., 291 ff.; Interest and Attention, *Psychol. Bulletin*, ii., 1905, 361 ff.; W. H. Burnham, Attention and Interest, *Amer. Journ. Psychol.*, xix., 1908, 14 ff.

[14] *Physiol. Psychol.*, iii., 1903, 342: the following pages give the distinction between active and passive apperception. Cf. *Grundriss*, 1905, 266 (Engl., 1907, 246).

[15] *Tonpsychol.*, ii., 1890, 283. Voluntary attention is "nichts Anderes als der Wille, sofern er auf ein Bemerken gerichtet ist." Involuntary attention may pass into voluntary: "sie ist nicht mehr davon verschieden, als der Wille überhaupt von Lusgefühlen verschieden ist. Fassen wir 'Gefühl' im weiteren Sinne, so kann der Wille ja selbst zu den Gefühlen, und zwar natürlich zu den positiven Gefühlen, gerechnet werden." The whole passage, 277 ff., is interesting, though there are parts that I do not find very clear.

[16] *Grundzüge*, i., 1905, 588, 607, 610 f. — On the other side, cf. A. Marty, *Vjs. f. wiss. Philos.*, xiii., 1889, 195 ff.

[17] *Op. cit.*, 603.

[18] *Physiol. Psychol.*, iii., 1903, 279; cf. *Grundriss*, 1905, 230 ff. (Engl., 1907, 213 ff.). The doctrine appears first

in the *Physiol. Psychol.* of 1880 (ii., 410), and is worked out in the essay on Die Entwicklung des Willens, *Essays*, 1885, 286 ff.

In *Essays*, 1906, 344, Wundt ascribes his "Bekehrung zu einem psychologischen Voluntarismus" to two influences: the positive indications of his own experiments on reactions, and the negative effect of J. Baumann's intellectualism. Now the reaction experiments were done ten years before the second edition of the *P. P.* appeared, whereas Baumann's *Handbuch der Moral* was published in 1879. Here, then, is another instance of the movement of Wundt's thought, as I have characterised it in Lecture IV.: the voluntaristic idea had been 'incubated' for a decade; it was gradually maturing in Wundt's mind; and Baumann furnished the external stimulus that brought it to clear expression.

[19] Art. Psychology, *Encyc. Brit.*, xx., 1886, 43.

[20] E. D. Cope, *The Origin of the Fittest*, 1887, 395, 413, 447. Cope's essays are the more interesting as he seems to have worked out his ideas independently, without knowledge of contemporary psychology; he makes at most only a casual reference to Carpenter or Bain.

[21] Cf. my paper in the *Pop. Sci. Monthly*, lx., 1902, 458 ff. I should now replace the Wundtian argument, 467 f., by pointing out that there does not appear to be any reflex movement — heart-beat, widening and narrowing of the pupil, etc. — that may not be brought, to a certain degree, under 'conscious control'; and I should urge that this state of affairs probably indicates a resumption, not an usurpation of sovereignty. Cf. G. H. Lewes, *The Physical Basis of Mind*, 1877, 367 ff.

I add only, to avoid possible misunderstanding, that my own position is that of parallelism, not of interactionism;

and that there is no reason to be scared by the bogey of 'the inheritance of acquired characters.' There are more ways than one of speculating oneself out of a biological difficulty!

[22] *Physiol. Psychol.*, iii., 1903, 348; cf. 116.

[23] *Grundriss*, 1905, 262 (Engl., 1907, 243).

[24] See Lecture VI., note 38, *sub fin.*

[25] I have avoided any detailed reference to the central conditions of attention. The most recent accounts are those of W. McDougall (*Mind*, N. S., xi., 1902, 316; xii., 1903, 289, 473; xv., 1906, 329; cf. *Physiol. Psychol.*, 1905, 90 ff.) and Ebbinghaus (*Grundzüge*, 1905, 628 ff.). Pillsbury gives a general review of theories in his *Attention*, 1908, chs. xiv. ff. As for the central conditions of affection, I do not see that we need travel beyond the *Körperfühlsphäre;* but this is mere guesswork.

[26] *Physiol. Psychol.*, i., 1893, 588, 590.

[27] *Ibid.*, ii., 1902, 357.

[28] *Grundriss*, 1905, 263 (Engl., 1907, 244). " Jeder Inhalt des Bewusstseins übt eine Wirkung auf die Aufmerksamkeit aus, infolge deren er sich teils durch seine eigene Gefühlsfärbung, teils durch die an die Funktion der Aufmerksamkeit gebundene Gefühle verrät. Die gesamte Rückwirkung dieser dunkel bewussten Inhalte auf die Aufmerksamkeit verschmilzt dann aber, gemäss den allgemeinen Gesetzen der Verbindung der Gefühlskomponenten, mit den an die klar bewussten Inhalte gebundenen Gefühlen zu einem einzigen Totalgefühl." Here it is the obscure contents that react upon the attention! We must surely conclude that the doctrine has not settled down to final form. Indeed, I am disposed to think that the section on 'Die Gefühle als psychophysische Vorgänge' is

intended to convey that idea (*Physiol. Psychol.*, ii., 1902, 358 ff., esp. 362).

Pillsbury, in his *Attention* (1908, 189 ff.), appears to refer to the Wundtian doctrine of 1893, and not to that of the current edition of the *Physiologische Psychologie*.

[29] *Physiol. Psychol.*, iii., 1903, 341, 342 ff.; Grundriss, 1905, 264 f. (Engl., 1907, 244 f.).

[30] See, *e.g.*, Orth, *Gefühl u. Bewusstseinslage*, 1903, 50.

[31] *Princ. of Psychol.*, i., 1890, 300.

[32] H. E. Kohn, *Zur Theorie der Aufmerksamkeit*, 1894, 48; cf. my *Exper. Psychol.*, I., ii., 1901, 210 f.

[33] Kohn says (*op. cit.*, 36): "wenn Wundt statt wir 'ich' gesagt hatte, so könnte man ihn den Satz [wir nehmen in uns in wechselnder Weise mehr oder weniger deutlich eine Thätigkeit wahr] nicht bestreiten. Ich muss jedoch dem gegenüber wiederholen, dass ich bei der sorgfältigsten Prüfung meiner Bewusstseinslage nur selten ein solches Gefühl gefunden habe."

[34] *Grundriss, loc. cit.*

[35] *Physiol. Psychol.*, iii., 1903, 342; *Grundriss*, 265 (Engl., 245).

[36] *Physiol. Psychol.*, 341.

[37] *Mind*, N. S., xi., 1902, 342 f. "The complexity of the upper levels [of the nervous system], their numerous interconnections, the extreme variability of the resistances presented by them, and the number of alternative paths that may be opened in turn to the excitation-process, are the physiological basis of the 'Lebhaftigkeit' of the presentation."

[38] *Grundzüge*, i., 1905, 628 ff. The effect of Ebbinghaus' cortical *Hemmungen* and *Bahnungen* is "die Herbeiführung diffuser und sich verlaufender Erregungen einerseits, konzentrierter und differenzierter Erregungen andererseits."

[39] *L'attention*, 1906, 194; *Attention*, 1908, 284.

[40] It is, of course, always possible to fall back upon blood-pressure and rate of pulse and respiratory changes, and so to save the motor character of the organism. I do not doubt that these internal reactions occur. But we are talking attention: and to make them available for the theory of attention, it must be shown, first, that a concomitant variation actually obtains, and then, secondly, that it is relevant, — that the two series of correlated phenomena are not referable to a common set of conditions. As things are, the observations upon the first point are comparatively rough, and the evidence available upon the second does not favour the motor hypothesis. See Pillsbury, *Attention*, 282f.

On 'motor' psychology in general, see I. M. Bentley, *Amer. Journ. Psychol.*, xvii., 1906, 293 ff., and the references there given; as well as my *Exp. Psychol.*, II., ii., 1905, 364 ff.

[41] *L'attention*, 1906, 280 f.; *Attention*, 1908, 311 ff.

[42] *Grundzüge*, i., 1905, 606 f. There are, Ebbinghaus declares, "gewisse reflektorisch ausgelöste Bewegungen," that we sense "als mannigfache Spannungen oder Betätigungen, ohne sie doch zumeist bestimmt zu lokalisieren, d. h.: man empfindet ganz allgemein *sich* als angespannt oder tätig, indem man aufmerksam ist."

[43] *Physiol. Psychol.*, iii., 1903, 254 ff., 342 ff.; *Grundriss*, 223 ff., 264 f., 266 (Engl., 207 ff., 244 f., 246 f.).

[44] We have mentioned this law above, p. 34 of the text. Wundt uses it, in connection with action, *Physiol. Psychol.*, iii., 1903, 277 ff., 471 ff.; *Grundriss*, 230 ff., 239 f. (Engl., 213 ff., 221 f.); and esp. *Die Sprache*, i., 1900, 31 ff.; i., 1904, 37 ff. It is also employed by G. H. Lewes, *passim;* see, *e.g.*, *Problems of Life and Mind*, i., 1874, 134 ff., 226 ff;

iii., 1879, 93 ff., 143 ff., 397 ff., 432 f.; *Physical Basis of Mind*, 1877, 322 ff., 367 ff.; *Study of Psychology*, 1879, 19 ff., etc.

[45] Cf. my *Primer of Psychol.*, 1902, 76 f.; *Outline*, 1902, 135 ff., 139 f.

[46] *Grundzüge*, 607, 610 f. "Bei der unwillkürlichen Aufmerksamkeit ist weiter nichts vorhanden als [ein energisch hervortretender interessierender Eindruck und Spannungs- oder Tätigkeitsempfindungen], bei der willkürlichen kommt noch hinzu eine unablässig den Eindruck als bevorstehend oder als fortdauernd vorwegnehmende Vorstellung. Sie verhalten sich also zueinander wie Trieb und Wille."

[47] Ebbinghaus writes (*op. cit.*, 611): "dass ich endlich sachlich die Beschreibung des Unterschiedes zwischen passiver und aktiver Apperception, als eines einfachen, nur durch *ein Motiv bestimmten* Wollens und eines zwischen mehreren Motiven *wählenden* Wollens, nicht zutreffend finden kann, geht aus der oben gegebenen abweichenden Darstellung dieses Unterschiedes hervor." This formulation is not quite fair to Wundt, since the *Wahlhandlung* is, for him, just as much 'bestimmt' as is the *Triebhandlung*. As for the 'nicht zutreffend,' I have shown in the text that Wundt's distinction includes that of Ebbinghaus, and simply adds a causal to the common descriptive account. The terminological issue, of the definition of 'will,' is, as Ebbinghaus says, a 'Zweckmässigkeitsfrage'; and here, again, I am obliged to side with Wundt. — The reader of Ebbinghaus' *Grundzüge* must, I think, feel that the author is not particularly interested in attention, and has not made the most of the available material. The chapter is, surely, far below the level of those on sensation and memory. I am sorry, nevertheless, to end these Notes with adverse criticism of a work which I greatly admire.

INDEX OF NAMES

References to the notes begin with page 321.

INDEX OF SUBJECTS

References to the notes begin with page 321.

397

2 D

CLASSICS IN PSYCHOLOGY

AN ARNO PRESS COLLECTION

Angell, James Rowland. **Psychology: On Introductory Study of the Structure and Function of Human Consciousness.** 4th edition. 1908

Bain, Alexander. **Mental Science.** 1868

Baldwin, James Mark. **Social and Ethical Interpretations in Mental Development.** 2nd edition. 1899

Bechterev, Vladimir Michailovitch. **General Principles of Human Reflexology.** [1932]

Binet, Alfred and Th[éodore] Simon. **The Development of Intelligence in Children.** 1916

Bogardus, Emory S. **Fundamentals of Social Psychology.** 1924

Buytendijk, F. J. J. **The Mind of the Dog.** 1936

Ebbinghaus, Hermann. **Psychology: An Elementary Text-Book.** 1908

Goddard, Henry Herbert. **The Kallikak Family.** 1931

Hobhouse, L[eonard] T. **Mind in Evolution.** 1915

Holt, Edwin B. **The Concept of Consciousness.** 1914

Külpe, Oswald. **Outlines of Psychology.** 1895

Ladd-Franklin, Christine. **Colour and Colour Theories.** 1929

Lectures Delivered at the 20th Anniversary Celebration of Clark University. (Reprinted from *The American Journal of Psychology,* Vol. 21, Nos. 2 and 3). 1910

Lipps, Theodor. **Psychological Studies.** 2nd edition. 1926

Loeb, Jacques. **Comparative Physiology of the Brain and Comparative Psychology.** 1900

Lotze, Hermann. **Outlines of Psychology.** [1885]

McDougall, William. **The Group Mind.** 2nd edition. 1920

Meier, Norman C., editor. **Studies in the Psychology of Art: Volume III.** 1939

Morgan, C. Lloyd. **Habit and Instinct.** 1896

Münsterberg, Hugo. **Psychology and Industrial Efficiency.** 1913

Murchison, Carl, editor. **Psychologies of 1930.** 1930

Piéron, Henri. **Thought and the Brain.** 1927

Pillsbury, W[alter] B[owers]. **Attention.** 1908

[Poffenberger, A. T., editor]. **James McKeen Cattell:** Man of Science. 1947

Preyer, W[illiam] **The Mind of the Child:** Parts I and II. 1890/1889

The Psychology of Skill: Three Studies. 1973

Reymert, Martin L., editor. **Feelings and Emotions:** The Wittenberg Symposium. 1928

Ribot, Th[éodule Armand]. **Essay on the Creative Imagination.** 1906

Roback, A[braham] A[aron]. **The Psychology of Character.** 1927

I. M. Sechenov: Biographical Sketch and Essays. (Reprinted from *Selected Works* by I. Sechenov). 1935

Sherrington, Charles. **The Integrative Action of the Nervous System.** 2nd edition. 1947

Spearman, C[harles]. **The Nature of 'Intelligence' and the Principles of Cognition.** 1923

Thorndike, Edward L. **Education:** A First Book. 1912

Thorndike, Edward L., E. O. Bregman, M. V. Cobb, et al. **The Measurement of Intelligence.** [1927]

Titchener, Edward Bradford. **Lectures on the Elementary Psychology of Feeling and Attention.** 1908

Titchener, Edward Bradford. **Lectures on the Experimental Psychology of the Thought-Processes.** 1909

Washburn, Margaret Floy. **Movement and Mental Imagery.** 1916

Whipple, Guy Montrose. **Manual of Mental and Physical Tests:** Parts I and II. 2nd edition. 1914/1915

Woodworth, Robert Sessions. **Dynamic Psychology.** 1918

Wundt, Wilhelm. **An Introduction to Psychology.** 1912

Yerkes, Robert M. **The Dancing Mouse** and **The Mind of a Gorilla.** 1907/1926

ence

be taken from this